The Seven Futures of American Education

Improving Learning and Teaching In a
Screen-Captured World

by

JOHN SENER

ISBN: 146797336X
ISBN 13: 9781467973366

Library of Congress Control Number: 2011961666
CreateSpace, North Charleston, SC

Contents

Part I. What Has Happened:
The How and Why of Cyberized Education

Part II. What Will Happen:
The Futures of Cyberizing Education

Part III. What Can Happen:
Cyberizing Education Strategically

Acknowledgements

This book is the product of many conversations with hundreds of colleagues, especially those in the Sloan Consortium, National University Technology Network, Quality Matters, and WCET communities. I wish to thank in particular those colleagues, friends, and others who helped me refine many of the specific ideas presented in this book or who have helped me share those ideas with others: Deb Adair, Lanny Arvan, Curt Bonk, John Bourne, Ed Bowen, Kelley Brandt, Judy Campf, Bruce Chaloux, Marti Cleveland-Innes, Jewell Dassance, Chuck Dziuban, Stephen Ehrmann, Candice Falger, Ajay Gupta, Lisa Gurwitch, Mark Halsey, Ghazala Hashmi, Patti Jennings, Kathy Kegley, Catherine Kelley, Mike Kolitsky, Ronald Legon, Robert Loser, Steve Lynch, Marian Macbeth, A. Frank Mayadas, Cynthia McCourt, Rodica Neamtu, Donald Norris, Dana Offerman, Marc Parry, Anthony Picciano, Alex Pickett, Janet Poley, Judy Redpath, Claudine SchWeber, Katie Fife Schuster, Eleanor Sontag, Judith Szerdahelyi, Lavina Velasco, Karen Vignare, Jeremy Wolf, and Marcie Zisow.

Special thanks to my colleagues who reviewed parts of the manuscript and provided helpful feedback: Kristen Betts, Cynthia Calongne, G.B. Cazes, Lisa Cheney-Steen, Ed Gehringer, Starr Roxanne Hiltz, Jennifer Kidd, Joan McMahon, Sharon Morgenthaler, Janet Moore, Casey O'Brien, Joy Ventura Riach, David Sachs, Reva Savkar, Jeff Seaman, David Shupe, Burck Smith, Brandon Thompson, and Murray Turoff. Also, special thanks to Barbara Hatheway for providing her deft editorial touch to the manuscript.

Extra special thanks goes to those colleagues who served as my core advisory group, reviewing chapters, offering encouragement, and giving me helpful guidance along the way: Gary Brown, Christine Geith, Susan Kannel, Jacquie Moloney, Gary Miller, Karen Swan, and Robert Ubell. Another extra special thanks goes to my son Chris for his understanding throughout the book writing process and for his insights which offered me another window for seeing the future.

Introduction

American education is entering the age of *cybersymbiosis* -- irretrievably dependent on digital technologies. This is not a fad, a niche, or even a trend; it is education's future. Over the past 15 years or so, online education in the United States has gone from zero to mainstream, integrating itself into higher education and positioning itself to do the same at the primary and secondary levels. In the process, online education has reached a certain maturity and is entering a new phase whose parameters are unclear and open to change. As someone who has watched this transformation and contributed to its progress, my original motivation for writing this book was to explore the question of what's next for online education. One possibility is clear, depending on how we respond to the opportunity at hand: if the first era in the history of online education was focused on providing access, the second era has the potential to be defined by improving quality -- not just for online education but for all education.

At the same time, the changes underway are much greater than the rise of online education. This book uses the term *cyberization*[1] and its variants to describe these changes and to highlight the current transformation as truly something new and different. The transformative effects of digital technologies on society and education may seem like old news to some, but these effects are much deeper and more important than is commonly recognized. Instead, most ideas about the cyberization of education focus on narrow, oversimplified outcomes. Many advocates promote the use of digital technologies to apply free market principles or "rigorous" standards to "fix" education, especially its inefficiencies and shortcomings in preparing people for employment. Some view digital technologies as the vehicle to make learning freely available at last for everyone. Others see cyberized education as a dystopia-in-waiting: social networking tools rotting our children's brains, the humanity of classroom interaction stripped away by soulless, isolating machines and their screens. Too many other educators seem to be oblivious to what's going on, or act as if they need only to hunker down once again and weather the latest storm.

Each of these viewpoints describes scenarios which collectively comprise five of the futures of cyberized education outlined in this book. These viewpoints also reflect powerful constituencies which will influence the future of cyberized education. However, education's key stakeholders -- faculty, teachers and administrators in higher and K-12 education, online education practitioners, policymakers, thought and opinion leaders, and anyone else who cares about education and its future -- need a broader, unifying perspective which integrates these viewpoints into a larger context by showing a sixth future: how to improve education by cyberizing it.

The book is divided into three parts. Part I provides a framework for understanding what has happened: the emerging cybersymbiosis resulting from the cyberization of society, the different levels on which cyberization is occurring, the foundational shifts which are transforming education, and the important role of online learning in cyberizing education. Part II describes the futures of cyberized education in terms of various scenarios, including their advocates, their downsides, and their potential influence on improving education. Part III describes key strategies for using cyberization to improve education, including the strategic role of online education, strategies for (re-)empowering learning and teaching in education, and strategies for revitalizing the educational enterprise on the institutional level. The final chapter describes a seventh possible, if distant future: one in which everyone's education truly matters.

The cyberization of education is happening within a larger context. Education is a fundamentally societal enterprise which is deeply cultural, highly political, inescapably moral, and intensely social. The prevailing tendency to define education in narrow and oversimplistic terms is counterproductive because education is a complex institution, and the cyberization of education raises the element of complexity to even greater importance. Seeking a better education for all students, coping with the high cost of education, and other current educational issues are challenging and important. However, this book also aims to remind the reader of the deeper forces which animate education but which are commonly ignored -- the perennial tensions between individual and society, equality and diversity, authority and freedom, nature and technology, stasis and change.

Americans tend to treat education with a peculiar mixture of deep disdain and an almost romanticized regard. The disdain comes from an enduring individualistic streak and a lingering anti-intellectualism in American culture which still distrusts "book learning." The source of the regard is harder to pinpoint -- maybe it's simply that distinctly American version of a "can-do" attitude -- but on some level Americans seem to believe that our educational system can do just about anything. Ironically, the sharper the criticism of education, the more this reflects an underlying belief in its power. The result for the past 40 years has been a growing gap between rapidly rising expectations and incremental improvements, along with a misplaced impatience with the progress made to date that belies the enormity of the task: building an education system which works for everyone in a large, heterogeneous society of 300+ million people -- a task which is unprecedented in human history. Leaders both inside and outside American education routinely bash it for its "failures" as if educational reform were little more than an elaborate repair project to "fix" something that's "broken," instead of seeing the current transformation of education for what it is: a historic, massive, formidable, and honorable undertaking which actually needs to be taken even more seriously.

Perhaps this seeming contradiction is inevitable given the clashing realities which coexist. American education has given us the "Dantesque wastes"[2] of a sinful, exploitative university system, Kozol's *Savage Inequalities*[3], and countless millions of hours of classroom boredom. It has also given us knowledge which has contributed to producing better lives and common wealth light years beyond the wildest imaginings of medieval monarchs, thanks to countless millions of hours of tireless dedication from an untold number of professors and teachers, some of whom Changed Our Lives. This combination is a recipe for a massive case of cognitive dissonance, but being able to hold these two realities side by side as accurately describing the same institution is the starting point for moving forward to make improvements.

It is against this backdrop that cyberization is irretrievably transforming education. The understandable tendency is to think of cyberization as a technology-driven change, but the interaction between humans and our technologies has always been more complex than that. The real drivers of change in education are *knowledge, access*, and *authority*. Education is society's chief way of transmitting, preserving, and generating knowledge, but the nature of knowledge itself is changing. The transformation of education in the past century from a nicety for a privileged few, to a necessity for the many, to an essential for nearly everyone, has changed society's expectations about its importance. These changes have both undermined and enhanced education's authority to define, deliver, and assess learning and to certify its attainment.

This book focuses on American education, particularly on higher education because that is where the cyberization of education has progressed the most so far in the U.S. The book spends little time on topics which have been well covered by others, such as pedagogical innovations or specific descriptions of new tools and technologies. Instead, it seeks to help shape the cyberization of education by highlighting some existing strategies and practices which would improve education if they were adopted more widely. These proposed improvements reflect particular assumptions, hopes, and biases, but they also aim to reflect our best aspirations for our educational system. There has long been a deep yearning for change in education among the many people who care about it. Practitioners who have worked in the field of online education have seen remarkable changes over a relatively short time; many have long recognized the potential for even greater improvement and have been working hard to realize that potential. The U.S. Department of Education's 2004 National Educational Technology Plan[4] envisioned the proliferation of digital technologies as moving American education "Toward a New Golden Age." The cyberization of education is, if not a new Golden Age, then certainly a golden opportunity, and we are just starting to learn how to make that happen.

Part I

What Has Happened:
The How and Why of Cyberized
Education

Redistributing
History-of-Online-Education
derappreciated Education-in-a-Cyber
Access
hift Online
Defining
Redefining
Knowledge

CHAPTER 1

Cyberized

Welcome to the age of iCrack...more than a third of [survey] respondents had received complaints they were using their iPhone way too much. Three-quarters reported that their iPhone actually made them happier people, and [almost 60 percent] agreed they actually felt a genuine love for their iPhones.

-- From a 2009 survey of 200 Stanford University undergraduates[1]

Around 5.6 million students were enrolled in at least one online course in fall 2009, a 21% growth rate from the previous year.

-- From Class Differences: Online Education in the United States, 2010[2]

"Look, mommy! That woman is texting with paper!"

-- A five-year-old kindergartener's comment upon seeing someone using a typewriter[3]

cyberize (*English; from cyber- [Used to form words relating to the Internet, or to computers more generally]+ -ize.*) *Verb: (transitive, intransitive)*

1. To adapt to digital technology or culture.

2. (science fiction, rare) To make into a cyborg; to fit with a cybernetic implant or prosthesis.

-- Adapted from Wikitionary[4]

Education has become cyberized.

More accurately, education has been, is being, and will continue to be cyberized. In the United States, cyberization has already mainstreamed into higher education and is poised to do the same in primary and secondary education (K-12) in just a few years. Its progress is unstoppable, and its culmination is inevitable. The matter is settled. It's a done deal. The only open questions are important ones, however: what forms will it take, and how will these forms shape us?

This is not news to most practitioners in online education, even though the speed and scope of its transformation over the past 15 years or so have been truly astonishing. Along the way, online education has run the customary course of innovations: from oddity to novelty to (perceived) inferiority to parity. Very soon, online education will attain full legitimacy and integration into mainstream education as its adoption reaches full scale.

Schools still routinely deliver a multitude of classroom lectures, but the diffusion of digital technologies into educational practice is reaching a critical mass. The numbers are growing; the trends are compelling. Classrooms, lectures, and blackboards are not going away any more than radio, horses, or candlelight have gone away, but the role of these and other staples of traditional education is going to be very different once digital technologies become fully integrated into mainstream education.

Perhaps you're skeptical that this is really happening, which is understandable. After all, this "cyberization" is really all about technology, isn't it? A long procession of highly hyped technologies has failed to transform education, including radio, television, and multimedia. Why should the current go-round of technological change be any different? Besides, education remains a resolutely durable social institution, legendary in its ability to resist rapid change and to evolve so slowly that most people don't even notice. Education will absorb this change as it has so many others and remain essentially the same as always -- won't it? In any case, saying that education is going to adapt to a digital technology or culture (to use the first Wikitionary definition of "cyberize") is pretty run-of-the-mill these days. Cyberization is a defining characteristic of our age; every institution is adapting to it. So saying that education has been "cyberized" is a no-brainer assertion; education has been cyberized because developed societies have been cyberized. In fact, the cyberization of society and education is already old news, at least in today's velocitized world where news ages very fast. So what's the big deal?

For starters, the cyberization of education is a very big deal because cyberspace is becoming central to our existence as a species. The informal use of the internet and other digital technologies to communicate, socialize, network, inform, and learn is widespread and growing rapidly; it has become an integral part of the culture in developed countries and increasingly in developing ones as well. Computer and Internet access is now widespread, although not (yet) ubiquitous. Our economy and our communication infrastructures have become dependent on the Internet; our physical infrastructures and even our social interactions are also in the process of becoming so, to a large extent. But it's much, much bigger than that.

Cyberspace itself is *huge* -- as large as all of the planet's lands, as voluminous as all of its oceans, as expansive as the skies, even as vast as space itself. Wild exaggeration? The United States military has a different view: in 2006, the Chairman of the Joint Chiefs of Staff declared cyberspace to be the fifth warfighting domain,[5] joining land, sea, air and space as a distinct and equal domain, and perhaps the most important one. As a U.S. Air Force briefing presentation described it, "cyber" is the "Nation's neural network," the "United States' Center of Gravity -- the hub of all power and movement, upon which everything else depends."[6] The U.S. military believes that its dependence on cyberspace will increase[7] just like the rest of society -- including education. As with all deeply profound transformations, it's taking us a while to grasp the implications of education in a cyber world, because this change is much bigger than we could have imagined.

Education in a Cyber World

Bossier City, Louisiana, may seem like a rather odd choice of places to experience firsthand the emergence of education in a cyber world. The first thing one notices about Bossier (rhymes with "closure") City and its sister city Shreveport is shaped by geography: its skyline of high-rise casinos built to attract a gambling clientele, especially those from nearby Texas and Arkansas where casinos are not (yet) legal. Located at the junction of the Texas Trail[8] (a path for wagons and horses used by Americans heading west because it followed the higher ground) and the once-unnavigable Red River, the cities also owe their existence to a prodigious feat of engineering and hard work: the removal of the Great Red River Raft,[9] a 180-mile-long natural log jam whose clearing enabled the city to become a center of river commerce.

Today, many of Shreveport's and Bossier City's citizens are preparing for a future shaped by forces beyond physical geography -- a cyber world. Why Bossier City, of all places? Why not? Cyberspace is everywhere, so it can be anywhere; gaining competitive advantage in cyberspace doesn't depend on the placement of navigable rivers or state lines. If anything, success in a cyber world depends first on recognizing that the world really has changed, and then figuring out how to take advantage of that opportunity. Shreveport/Bossier City's residents are taking strides to become an important place in this new cyber world, and are learning how to live in it in the process. The most obvious manifestation of this is Bossier City's Cyber Innovation Center (CIC),[10] a futuristic building located in a 3,000-acre National Cyber Research Park which was built to serve as a catalyst for expanding the region's knowledge-based workforce.

The CIC's activities related to cyber education are impressive in their own right, but you might have to visit the casino and racetrack to understand what's really going on. At least, that's how it worked for me in fall 2010 when I attended one of the CIC's monthly luncheon meetings at Harrah's Louisiana Downs. This meeting assembled a broad coalition of education, government, business and industry professionals working together to promote K-20 cyber education at all levels. Tables of middle and high school students received awards for their performances at various cyber summer camps: cyber forensics, robotics, animation and visual effects, computer science. A school principal shared the story about the student who told her mom about seeing someone "texting with paper." Eventually, it dawned on me: *these people are on to something*. Even after 16+ years of working in online education, I hadn't fully realized the magnitude of this change: something that is bigger than the Internet, bigger than digital technologies, bigger even than an entirely new warfighting domain. It is an entirely new place -- and our existing world is also a new place as a result. In fact, the Wikitionary definition of "cyberize" needs a little updating: cyberization is not just a digital technology or culture to which we must learn to adapt; it is also a place to live in. It is as if a whole new continent has been created, even if we don't have a consensus name for it yet. Some of us will effectively take up residence there. Some of us will visit frequently, others less so. All of us will have to live *with* it: cyberspace, like the land, sea, air, and space, is now a permanent feature of our lifescape. It's here to stay, as illustrated by that iconic sign of the times: the sight of someone staring into a screen.

Screen Captured

First there was the stone tablet. Then papyrus…then paper…then the book…then the blackboard. Now the screen.

Although this list makes it seem as if the technologies are driving things, in reality they are merely markers of change. The creation of new technologies is never solely an end in itself, but is driven by the desire for what a technology can do for us. The screen is simply the latest manifestation of this desire to expand our human capacities through our technologies.

In technospeak, "screen capture" is the process of copying or transferring an image of what is currently displayed on a computer or other screen to another source -- another application, file, printer, or computer clipboard -- to view, file, copy, or print it. Screen capture software records the activity on a computer screen and transfers it to a format where it can be re-viewed as a sort of online movie. Over the last ten years, we've gotten much better at capturing and reusing content that appears on computer screens.

In the meantime, the screens have made at least as much progress in capturing us, as they gobble up our time, attention, and energy in ever more numerous and compelling ways. Television screens have captured our leisure time and attention for several decades now, but computer screens are increasingly usurping this role both at play and work. Surfing the web at work has been described as being "as addictive as coffee,"[11] although studies disagree about its effect on productivity.[12] In education, computers have rapidly overtaken televisions as the screen of choice, with mobile phones, smartboards/whiteboards, e-books, and a host of other screen-based devices also vying for attention.

"Screen captured" is more than a metaphor for the capacity of digital technologies to absorb our attention; it is also a reflection of a deeper, more fundamental interdependency. In Katherine Hayles's words, we have become "symbionts,"[13] utterly dependent on a digital technology infrastructure for our lives. If digital technologies were to disappear tomorrow, the result would be a devastating economic and cultural catastrophe with millions or even billions of lives lost. As Hayles notes in *How We Became Posthuman*, human civilization has formed symbiotic relationships with its technologies for thousands of years. Our dependency on digital technologies is merely the latest iteration, and as society goes, so goes education, which will soon enter the realm of *cybersymbiosis*: as fundamentally dependent on online and other digital technologies as society is currently dependent on electricity. Education which does not utilize digital resources, tools, and delivery modes has already become as outdated as a traditional education would be without books, pencils, and blackboards. Except for the occasional boutique course or program, education without digital resources, tools, and delivery modes will soon become unthinkable: as unacceptable as segregated schools, as anachronistic as *Dick and Jane*, as irrelevant as mimeographs. The cyberization of education will be complete.

In Cloud We Trust:
Cybersymbiosis and the Futures of Cyberized Education

Digital technologies are transforming education because the foundations on which it has been built for centuries are shifting. The very nature of knowledge itself is changing: where it resides and how it's produced, categorized, transmitted, shared, and mediated. The redistribution of educational access from the privileged few to the ever-increasing many has been changing education in ways still not fully appreciated. Societal change is reorganizing the role structures of education from a model of imposed authority toward one in which authority is self-initiated, negotiated, and shared; this process is shifting authority toward students, market forces, and cyberized education itself. Online learning has been the leading wedge in cyberizing education by providing access for previously underserved learner populations. In the process, online education has became the main source of enrollment growth, pedagogical and technological innovation, and an important strategic element for higher education institutions.

What will the future of cyberized education look like? Some observers view the prospect of cybersymbiosis with alarm, as if we're all being assimilated into a Borg-like[14] "cyberdystopia" which will rob us of our humanity. Others see a standards-driven future in which cyberization transforms education into a model of consistency. Some see the dissolution of formal education as we know it through free market forces or "free learning." Still others see little or no change despite all the current fuss about digital technologies. Although these scenarios may seem mutually exclusive, the reality is that all of them will happen to some extent.

The most important future scenario, however, is the one in which we use cyberization to improve education. The new digital technologies are powerful, and formal education has a newfound cultural authority thanks to its growing role as essential to the well-being of individuals and society. This combination offers a spectacular opportunity: if we handle cyberization well (a big 'if,' to be sure), cyberized education will be vastly improved education.

Cyberization doesn't mean that in-person education is going away. Unless we truly become a species of cyborgs who are conquered by our digital creations, there will always be an important place for a human, physical presence in education. In fact, cyberization can **enhance** the value of in-person interaction and make us even more evolved social creatures. The value of instructors' time, *and* of students' time, can be better appreciated and utilized more effectively. Time spent interacting in person can be used much more often for better purposes. College faculty can spend more time contextualizing, modeling, facilitating, guiding, and coaching, and less time being transcription sources. K-12 teachers can spend more time being contextualizers, knowledge ambassadors, and role models rather than being reduced to disciplinarians, babysitters or test prep technicians. We can assess the entire teaching and learning enterprise more meaningfully and align it more closely with desired personal and societal outcomes.

All of these outcomes and more can happen if we work to make them so. Educators and other stakeholders can shape the use of digital technologies in education by embracing cybersymbiosis and taking a proactive role in *cyberizing* education. The capacities we need, and those which will be enhanced, are human ones. The challenges are considerable, and clearing away the related log jams will take a lot of hard, sustained work. A good place to start is to understand where these changes are happening and why.

The Six Levels of Change

Cyberization is happening on several distinctly important levels (Figure 1-1). On the three more basic levels, digital technologies serve as resources for our lives, learning, and education. On the three more advanced levels, digital technologies serve as the means to deliver formal education. These six levels can be briefly described as follows:

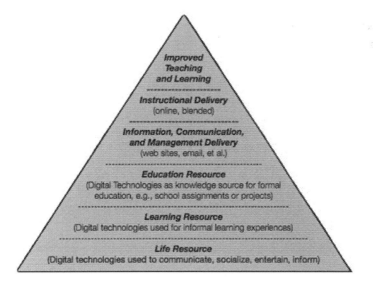

Figure 1-1: **Where Cyberization Is Happening: Six Levels of Change**

1. *Life Resource* refers to the informal use of digital technologies to communicate, socialize, entertain, network, and inform. The learning which happens on this level is incidental since the related activities are done primarily for other purposes. Surfing the web for fun, getting the latest news or sports results from one's favorite web sites, keeping in touch with friends through Facebook or My Space, booking a dinner reservation or doctor's appointment online, or making evening plans via email, are just a few of the ever-growing examples.

2. *Learning Resource* refers to the informal use of digital technologies with the intent to learn something, such as perusing web sites to research information about a particular medical condition, buying a new vehicle, or learning a new dance from watching an online video. Learning on this level is intentional but unconnected to any organized educational experience.

3. *Education Resource* refers to the use of digital technologies as information or knowledge sources for activities related to formal education, such as completion of individual homework assignments or collaborative work with fellow students on school projects. A digital resource can be explicitly designed to support academic learning or can simply be useful for that purpose. Learning on this level is intentionally applied to an educational experience.

4. *Information, Communication, and Management Delivery* refers to formal education's use of online technologies for information, communication, and management (ICM). Notable examples include school web sites, institutionally maintained email communication, learning and enterprise management systems which support the delivery of learning and the management of various institutional functions, and the use of online technologies to deliver student support services such as tutoring, advising, or library services.

5. *Instructional Delivery* refers to formal education's use of online technologies for teaching and learning. Online and most blended education happen at this level.

6. *Improved Teaching and Learning* refers to the use of digital technologies to support the evolution of education beyond current quality levels.

Why These Distinctions Are Important

The distinctions between these levels are important because they provide valuable clues about how cyberization is unfolding:

Life Resource vs. Learning Resource -- The main distinction between these two is one of intent. We are learning creatures; we learn through communicating, socializing, exchanging information, entertaining and being entertained. We learn many things informally or even inadvertently without thinking much about it, but sometimes we learn with intent. We learn from life resources incidentally; we use learning resources intentionally.

Learning Resource vs. Education Resource - Although learning and education overlap to some extent, the distinction between the two is also important. Education is society's means of transmitting, preserving, and renewing its core knowledge to its members. There is an individual dimension, but society created education to benefit the greater social good as well as to benefit its individual members. Learning is the means by which an individual makes sense of one's life, experience, society, and the universe. The individual dimension is more prominent, but all learning also has a social dimension since we are also social creatures. Although this distinction is clear in most cases, some see the rise in web-based informal learning as a revolution[15] which replaces or even eliminates the need for formal education as we know it.

Education Resource vs. ICM Delivery - This distinction is important because ICM delivery is where educational institutions become formally involved with digital technologies on an administrative level. Teachers and students tend to make the decisions about which education resources to use, but administrators and institutions decide which online technologies are used for ICM delivery. For example, teachers can assign or students can select web-based knowledge sources to use for assignments, and student groups can often decide which social networking tools to use (Wiki or blog to record our collaborative findings? Communicate through chat, Facebook, both?). By contrast, administrators use assigned committees, task groups, executive fiat, and other means to control the institutional selection of online technologies used for ICM such as learning management systems (LMSs), course management systems (CMSs), enterprise management systems, and web portal content.

This distinction is also important because the use of online technologies for formal ICM delivery is one of the main pathways to cyberizing education. Even institutions which have resisted offering online courses or programs have readily embraced the use of online technologies for formal ICM. Having an attractive portal web site has become a virtual necessity for most colleges and universities. Natural disasters and pandemic threats have knocked schools out of business for weeks, months and even entire semesters over the past 15 years, demonstrating the absolute necessity of having multiple ICM technologies in place[16] to respond effectively to future disruptions in service. The vast majority of college students (almost 90 percent according to one study[17]) have used at least one CMS or LMS.

At the K-12 level, school systems offer online services such as updated homework assignment postings or online grade books, enabling parents to keep closer tabs on their children's progress. Students can also use these tools for similar purposes. Remember not so long ago when the lack of telephones in classrooms was an issue?[18] Using email and other technologies has become commonplace instead, making it much easier for parents, teachers, and students to communicate with each other quickly and more frequently.

The use of online technologies for formal ICM also encourages their use for instructional purposes. Some college faculty use an LMS or other web portal to post syllabi, announcements, assignments, and other course information, while using classroom time for the "real" teaching and learning. From there, it's a small step to using the LMS's built-in features or web-based social networking tools to start doing some of the teaching and learning activities normally done in a classroom, such as online discussion, communication about group projects, or other student assignments. Then, post a short video or podcast here, a 'mini-lecture' slide presentation there, and soon online technologies become an integral part of the course.

The proliferation of LMSs is also gradually eroding away resistance to using online technologies at the K-12 level. Teachers see how online technologies offer certain affordances which can be used in the teaching and learning process. Administrators see how online technologies provide students with previously unavailable access for specific purposes such as credit recovery or Advanced Placement preparation. The use of these technologies helps mitigate the mismatch many students experience between the technologically abundant environment of their daily lives and the relatively technologically impoverished environment at school. Unions eventually see how these technologies can be used without threatening teachers' jobs.

ICM Delivery vs. Instructional Delivery -- This distinction is important because it's often the big dividing line which many teachers and faculty, and some administrators, do not want to cross. For example, many elite small liberal arts colleges and K-12 private schools have excellent web sites used for ICM delivery, but offering an online course for academic credit would still be unthinkable. A

March 2010 *San Diego Business Journal* article[19] described how the issue of perceived quality drives this distinction at local colleges and universities. At San Diego Community College District, "Online learning is the new normal -- and it's almost becoming a preference," according to Andrea Henne, SDCCD's Dean of Online and Distributed Learning. SDCCD has offered online general education courses since 2001 and offered over a dozen associate degrees online in 2010. By contrast, the University of California at San Diego had considered and rejected the adoption of online instructional delivery for undergraduate and graduate study several years ago. According to Scripps Professor of Oceanography William S. Hodgkiss, who chaired a UCSD academic task force on the issue, "The philosophical question that needs to be grappled with is, what does it mean to have a UC-quality course, and how do you preserve that notion of quality in the online course material?" Although online instructional delivery is "something we have not embraced," Hodgkiss noted that "financial pressures on the university have dictated" UCSD's renewed interest in its use. Concerns about the quality of online courses is also prevalent in K-12 education; one recent study found that almost half of the school districts which responded had concerns about it.[20]

Instructional Delivery vs. Improved Teaching and Learning - This distinction is important because too often digital technologies are touted for their ability to maintain current quality levels in education. In online education, for example, considerable effort is still wasted on trying to determine whether online education is as good as traditional classroom education, which is a sterile and largely useless comparison, as Chapter 4 explains. Besides, the cyberization of education offers a much greater opportunity than simply replicating more of the same quality; as more than one practitioner has noted during online learning's evolution into the mainstream of education, why aim low? Much of the rest of this book, including Chapters 8 through 12, focuses on the opportunity to use cyberization to improve education, which requires understanding how the foundations of education are shifting, how online learning has cyberized education, and how the futures of cyberized education will ensue from these developments.

CHAPTER 2

Shifting Foundations: The Changing Nature of Knowledge

Why It's Different This Time Around

Digital technologies have truly transformed our world in a breathtakingly short time: email, smartphones, social networks, the Internet; search engines which bring an unimaginable wealth of information to our fingertips; hyperlinks which connect it all. The technologies available today are ever more powerful, numerous, and amazing tools, and the cyberization of education is by definition a technology-enabled transformation. However, new technologies are not the source of change, even though they are helping to accelerate it. Things will be different this time around because of more fundamental shifts in the very foundations on which education has been built for centuries: knowledge, access, and authority.

The Smart Shift: Redefining Knowledge

Ve grow too soon olt und too late schmart.

– Pennsylvania Dutch proverb

...in ten years, our definition of intelligence will look very different. By then, we might agree on "smart" as something like a 'networked' or 'distributed' intelligence where knowledge is our ability to piece together various and disparate bits of information into coherent and novel forms.

– Christine Greenhow, educational researcher, University of Minnesota and Yale Information and Society Project[1]

The nature of knowledge has changed. In some ways we understand this change fairly well; in other ways, hardly at all. The notion that we are in the midst of an "information revolution" or "knowledge revolution" is familiar territory. The idea is often described in economic terms, linked with a fundamental transition from an industrial-based economy to a knowledge-based one.[2] Knowledge is a privately produced, "intangible public good" which is replacing land and machines as the primary factors of economic production.[3] Although the Information Revolution has been going on now for several decades, until recently it had simply routinized traditional practices, according to renowned management guru Peter Drucker. The advent of e-commerce created new distribution channels which changed consumer behavior (who they were, how and what they bought) and changed existing practices in the entire economy.[4]

A lot of thought has been given to the economic dimensions of this revolution, but not so much has been given to how it changes education, even though knowledge **is** the foundation of education. Trent Batson, executive director of the Association for Authentic, Experiential and Evidence-Based Learning, has described the "zeitgeist" of higher education "as the permanent cultural authority in every knowledge domain, the keeper of consensus knowledge, the generator of new knowledge."[5] Almost all the major functions of K-12 education, such as intellectual development, preparation for college and employment, preparation for citizenship, and development of human potential, use knowledge as their base, but this base is changing: cyberizing technologies are accelerating a historic shift in the very nature of knowledge itself (Table 2-1).

Change Factor	Old Smart	New Smart
Where it resides, where it's produced	Inside academia: campuses, libraries, professors	> Outside academia: Internet, workplace
How fast it's made	Knowable, manageable volume	Unknowable, unmanageable volume
The role of content	Content mastery	Content utilization
Size, timing, measure	Programs, courses; years/semesters seat time	All shapes and sizes; soon/now (e.g., "just-in-time"); outcomes, competencies
How new knowledge is created	Expert-authenticated	Collaboratively negotiated
How it's categorized	Discrete, siloed	Interdisciplinary; connected
How it's transmitted and shared	"Sage on the Stage;" Expertise	"Guide on the side;" networked, distributed, contextual
How it's mediated	Text/Lecture	Visual, Multimedia

Table 2-1: **Knowledge Is Undergoing a Historic Shift**

Where Knowledge Resides and Where It's Produced

Shift: from inside academia to outside it

Education's roles as society's designated creator, caretaker, and certifier of knowledge evolved over centuries. Universities were formed, and eventually campuses were built, as places to keep knowledge. Over time, campuses became defined by their exclusivity, as exemplified most notably by the metaphor of the Ivory Tower.[6] Academia also developed systems for producing knowledge, organizing it into fields or disciplines, and training select scholars who learn and profess (i.e., become profess-ors of) their discipline, who in turn apprentice other new scholars in that discipline. The generation of new knowledge has happened "in-house" for the most part.

Digital technologies have helped cause a major shift in this system. For the first time in centuries, academic institutions are no longer the primary locus of knowledge; it now resides both "in there" and "out here," outside campus boundaries.

Other factors such as the commercialization of university research and greater dependence on interdisciplinary and institutional collaboration for knowledge production[7] have also driven this shift. The mass adoption of the Web has accelerated this process, tipping the balance of where knowledge is located from on campus to online. This change in balance is also happening internally within higher education institutions themselves; for instance, the University of Maryland libraries provide online access to almost as many electronic journals (4,000) as campus-based print journals (~6,000).[8] A fall 2009 faculty survey found that academic research is also transitioning from print to digital media; more faculty are using electronic resources to start their research instead of using their campus's physical library facilities.[9]

Higher education is no longer the only important production source of knowledge either; companies, governmental agencies, and nonprofit organizations are also producing new knowledge in response to emerging needs. In some cases, these entities are creating entirely new fields which combine existing disciplines to deal with new problems, sometimes outstripping higher education's ability to keep up. Knowledge production is also increasingly a shared, distributed, and often collaborative activity which transcends campus boundaries.

This shift has also accelerated K-12 education's reliance on commercial or other outside sources such as media publishers to provide learning resources. The rise in online K-12 education has fed this trend; for instance, over one-third of school districts which offer fully online courses use outsourcing by independent vendors to provide these courses.[10]

The structure of education and its pedagogical practices at all levels are still largely based on the assumption that knowledge resides in specific places: libraries, faculty, people's heads. Educators at all levels are struggling to figure out what to do with this new proliferation of knowledge and knowledge production sources, as reflected for instance in the concern about enabling students to attain web research literacy. How will students know the difference between credible and dubious knowledge online? Is Wikipedia a credible and citable source? Are YouTube videos? How about podcasts on iTunesU? While disruptive, this shift in where knowledge resides and how it's produced is just one of the ways in which the nature of knowledge is changing.

The Acceleration of Knowledge Production

Shift: from a knowable to an unknowable volume of knowledge

Whether measured by patents, publications, or other criteria, knowledge production has accelerated in recent decades,[11] and it is now commonly recognized that the resulting volume of available knowledge has grown well beyond our capacity to know it all. We have been much slower to recognize how the acceleration of knowledge production changes the nature of knowledge itself. Knowledge has become more volatile; theories, concepts, even basic facts change ever more frequently as accelerated production yields new knowledge which changes what we think we know.

For example, consider this seemingly simple question: how many planets are there in our solar system? When I was in school, the correct answer was nine, but the answer is not that simple anymore. Blame it on Eris – a celestial object which was discovered orbiting beyond the planet Neptune in 2005 and which threw the existing definition of planets, which was based in part on size, into disarray.[12] Thought to be considerably bigger than Pluto and sporting its own moon, Eris was on its way to becoming the tenth planet in the solar system until the International Astronomical Union, realizing that many more Erises might be out there, decided to create a formal definition of the term *planet* for the first time. The resulting definition actually ended up reducing the number of planets; in 2006, the IAU's General Assembly voted to demote Pluto from the list of official planets because it does not have a clear orbital path, which is now the defining characteristic of a planet.[13] Pluto has become one of several "dwarf planets" even though it has a moon (Charon); or maybe Pluto is a double planet, since some scientists now say that Pluto and Charon revolve around each other.[14] So the actual number of planets in our solar system now depends in part on how you ask the question: there are now eight "official" planets, plus several dwarf planets, plus an unknown number of additional dwarf planets awaiting discovery. Will there be still more changes in how planets are defined and counted when some of these new dwarf planets are discovered? Now consider how a similar shift has occurred with thousands of other things we learned in school: new knowledge which has produced new theories, enhanced concepts, and changed facts, at an ever-growing rate.

Shift: from content mastery to content utilization

American education has increasingly focused on the notion that there is a core body of content which every student should know. However, the volatility and sheer volume of knowledge which result from its accelerated production raise several questions about how to define designated "core" knowledge:

- Does its size grow in proportion as knowledge grows, and if so, at what point does the core grow to an unmanageable size, too big for anyone to "master"?

- If core knowledge doesn't grow in size, what does it mean to have an ever-smaller core of knowledge relative to the total body of knowledge?

- If knowledge itself is changing more frequently, doesn't core knowledge also need to change more frequently in response? If so, who decides what remains core knowledge and what does not, and how do they decide it?

- How core can "core" knowledge be if its status is so provisional and subject to change?

- In a society which is fundamentally built on division of labor, what is the core body of knowledge which everyone *really* needs to master?

American education also tends to measure content mastery primarily in terms of the memorization and recall of facts, and popular culture reflects the view that these skills are the sign of being smart: think *Jeopardy!*, *Academic Challenge*, *Are You Smarter Than a 5th Grader?*, or your favorite trivia contests. Both fail to recognize the reality that mastering bodies of content has become less important, even pointless; there is simply too much to know.

More importantly, the acceleration of knowledge production is also increasing the potential value of knowledge itself because an abundance of knowledge increases its value. Knowledge wealth is like financial wealth; greater amounts can yield greater benefits from compounding its size and leveraging its power. However, this increase in value can only be realized by knowing how to *utilize content*, which goes well beyond the acquisition and recall of facts. Content utilization includes the ability to discern the interrelationships among facts by applying higher-level skills such as analysis, synthesis, and evaluation to understanding the underlying concepts and theories. For instance, knowing that there are now eight planets instead of nine is not nearly as useful as understanding *why* there are now eight planets; the latter involves understanding the role of size, shape, clear solar orbital paths, and official scientific deliberations in determining the prevailing definition of a planet.

The ability to utilize content effectively also requires developing the skills which enable learning when needed or desired, such as learning how to locate, differentiate, analyze, and use knowledge. Of course, most successful adults function quite well without knowing either how or why there are now eight planets in our solar system, which illustrates that knowing such individual facts and concepts is not what matters the most. What does matter is being able to utilize relevant content in the specialized contexts of work and other life spheres so that one has the *skills to learn* how planets are defined or to learn something else one wants or needs to learn.

The Explosion of Data

Shift: from a manageable volume of data to an unmanageable volume

A young marine biology student I knew in the mid-1970s had to change her career plans of becoming an oceanographer after suffering a severe bout of seasickness while collecting data on an ocean voyage. Things might be different if she were an aspiring marine biologist today, because instead of going out to the ocean to collect the data, now she could sit comfortably in an office hundreds of miles away and have the data come to her. Thanks to the Ocean Observatories Initiative (OOI) funded by the National Science Foundation, 1000 kilometers of fiber optic cable laid on the sea floor connects thousands of physical, chemical, and biological sensors into a massive data collection system, which is an amazing expansion in our capacity to generate data and produce knowledge at an accelerated rate.

The OOI also illustrates a new problem: we are now creating unmanageable volumes of data. As University of Washington computer science professor Ed Lazowska has observed, "There is simply too much [data] to look at." In his featured presentation at the 2009 WCET conference, Dr. Lazowska described the emergence of "eScience," the (semi-)automated extraction of knowledge through analysis of massive amounts of digitally generated data. Data-driven eScience is generating massive volumes of data at an unprecedented rate from a rapidly growing number of sources: telescopes generating 30 terabytes of data per *day*, a Hadron collider generating 700 megabytes of data per second (60 terabytes per day), genome analyzers processing 1 terabyte per day. The World Wide Web contains over 400 terabytes of data, an amount so huge that it would take a computer which can read 30-35 megabytes per second over four months to read all the information on the Web.[15] Those were the figures as of late 2009; they are only getting bigger, more impressive, and harder to manage. Computer scientists are developing an array of tools and techniques such as sensor networks, data mining, data visualization, and large-scale cluster computing to get a handle on this massive undertaking. More, better, and faster tools will be needed; in 2006, IBM projected that the world's information base would double every 11 *hours* by 2010.[16] The problem of coming up with *names* for quantities of data highlights just how big the issue has become: you've probably heard of megabyte, gigabyte, and terabyte, but how about petabyte, exabyte, zettabyte and yottabyte?

This unprecedented volume of data requires new skills[17] in accessing, managing, integrating, and evaluating it. This goes well beyond mastering or even utilizing content; there is also a greater need to produce *knowledge producers* – people who have the skills to process greater volumes of knowledge and can also learn to use the tools which convert data into knowledge. Current educational practices based on Old Smart concepts of knowledge are not well suited to address these new types of human performance.

The Size and Immediacy of Knowledge Needs

Shift: from larger, slower, broader to smaller, quicker, more focused

Some years ago, I met a student who was taking an introductory engineering course at a local college because that was the closest thing she could find relative to the knowledge she was seeking about specific engineering terms which related to her work at an import/export company. Unfortunately, this two-credit course was much larger than she needed, and the specific content did not match her immediate knowledge needs very well either.

Size matters and timing is everything when it comes to knowledge, but higher education's ability to provide right-sized and timely learning opportunities is limited. Higher education organizes its offerings into curricula (courses of study which need to be run) when learners' knowledge needs are increasingly smaller and quicker: no need for something that large, and no time to run through something that long. Courses typically run 12 to 16 weeks; degree programs typically take a minimum of two to five years. Completing a doctoral program can turn into a mini-career, sometimes taking eight to 10 years. Even a one-credit course often lasts four to 16 weeks with a substantial time commitment (typically about 15 hours total). A little downsizing has taken place in the past few decades; for instance, certificate programs are slightly smaller-sized program chunks which typically take nine to 24 months to complete. Nonetheless, higher education has been slow to adopt practices such as just-in-time learning, performance support systems, and various informal learning strategies which are commonly used in the corporate sector to provide needed knowledge in a right-sized and timely manner.[18] Even in the corporate sector, however, the ability to provide timely, right-sized knowledge has not kept up with need or demand.

The Creation of New Knowledge

Shift: from expert-authenticated to collaboratively negotiated creation

In traditional formal education, learners acquire factual knowledge produced and authenticated by credentialed experts. In this view, which is what Harvard professor Chris Dede calls the "classical" perspective, knowledge is a process where "unbiased research" produces "compelling evidence about systemic causes" which lead to singular, correct, and unambiguous interpretations of factual interrelationships.[19]

Dede contends that the current generation of digital technologies (commonly referred to as "Web 2.0" applications) is challenging this traditional paradigm of how knowledge is created. User-authored Web sites such as Wikipedia offer collaboratively negotiated knowledge creation as an alternative to expert-generated knowledge. For example, people commonly accept the accuracy of Encyclopedia Britannica articles based on its reputation as an authoritative source, but negotiation of accuracy is an explicit feature of the Wikipedia article creation process. As Chapter 10 describes, students using wikis to create textbook content employ a collaborative negotiation process between students and faculty to review, assess, and reconstruct content from various sources. The proliferation of content available on the Web through various social networking tools from Facebook to YouTube to Twitter also shifts the focus from expert authentication (i.e., the content is OK because the instructor says so) to collaborative negotiation (i.e., students and instructors need to negotiate criteria for figuring out the value of the knowledge source).

The Interconnectivity of Knowledge

Shift: from siloed knowledge to connected knowledge

Higher education's use of disciplines such as biology, psychology, and economics has both defined its knowledge and confined it in 'silos' which are largely disconnected from one another. In recent decades, a countertrend has emerged which emphasizes making connections across disciplines. More work on campus is becoming transdisciplinary,[20] interdisciplinary programs proliferate at prestigious institutions,[21] and the ability to conduct interdisciplinary research is seen as an essential activity which often becomes a competitive advantage.[22]

Interdisciplinary programs such as biochemistry, psychophysics, or geoeconomics still use the disciplines as their frame of reference, which assumes that emerging knowledge can be categorized into one or more disciplines. An alternate theory of learning developed by Athabasca University researcher George Siemens in 2004 takes a different approach. Connectivism is a "learning theory for the digital age" which aims to integrate principles derived from various theoretical sources including chaos, network, complexity and self-organization. Connectivism theory views knowledge as a social function residing in a "diversity of opinions" rather than as something which can be held completely in the mind of a single individual. Knowledge results from the interactions between individual learners and their personal and organizational networks.[23] Distributed cognition is another theory which illustrates the principle of connected knowledge as exemplified by the power of coordinated groups to connect their collective knowledge to accomplish tasks which would overwhelm an individual. This knowledge is both **distributed** across group members and **contextual,** as when a group forms to tackle a real-world problem and then disbands once the problem is solved.[24] Cyberizing technologies magnify the potential for creating distributed, contextual knowledge while also changing how knowledge is transmitted and shared through social cognition and social networks.

Transmission and Sharing of Knowledge

Shift: from 'sages on stages' to contextual sharing via distributed networks

New Smart is less about the knowledge in one's head and more about having a network and knowing how to use it. For example, while putting together a slide presentation, I realized that I didn't know how to do a screen capture on a Mac computer, so I sent an email to the staff of the client for whom the presentation was being prepared. Within five minutes, two responses arrived: a screen capture of the web page I needed from one staff person, and a set of instructions on how to make my own screen captures from "CarolJ." So my network not only includes people who are willing to help me learn at a moment's notice, but also people whom I don't even know, like "CarolJ." Although I've never met her and maybe never will, I am smarter for having her in my network.

The old way to be smart was to be an Expert, carrying vast knowledge around in one's head, able to produce facts on demand and project the image of knowing it all. Experts generally don't admit that they don't know something, and they even less often admit that they need help. The new way to be smart is to do just that: look for help in learning something one doesn't know. People networks are probably the best resource because they provide finer, deeper context.[25] Web-based content resources are also excellent, and web searching and other research skills are becoming more essential to being smarter.

In education, this knowledge shift is best described by the phrase "from 'sage on the stage' to 'guide on the side.'" The role of teachers and professors as transmitters of information or knowledge dates back to the days when lecturers actually read their lectures, and students wrote them down word for word.[26] This role has shown remarkable persistence for centuries; many professors still equate their course with its content, and they equate teaching with delivering a lecture on that content. The problem is that knowledge is no longer just an entity that is transmitted from someone who has it to someone who does not. Knowledge is now also something that is distributed rather than place-bound, constructed rather than transmitted, contextual and situational rather than fixed, and socially networked rather than isolated. This new concept of distributed knowledge has irrevocably altered how we think about, find, and communicate knowledge.

The Multimedia Revolution

Shifts: from text to multimedia; from low to high production values

My dad had told me it was big, but I hadn't realised he meant that big. It was the size of a small book... It took me three days to figure out that there was another side to the tape... I managed to create an impromptu shuffle feature simply by holding down 'rewind' and releasing it randomly... Did my dad...really ever think this was a credible piece of technology?

– 13-year-old web reviewer Scott Campbell, marking the 30th anniversary of the Walkman by using one for a week[27]

I wrote this section while on a train sitting next to a teenager who typifies the multimedia revolution: iPhone in hand, headphones on head, laptop on tray, music keyboard on lap. The visual on the computer screen looked as if it could be the control room of the train in which we were traveling. While not every teenager is surrounded by technology to this degree, today's students are thoroughly immersed in an increasingly visual, multimedia, high production value culture. By the time they reach college age, they have experienced and used a deluge of multimedia content delivered by technology that was barely imaginable 30 years ago.

More accurately, it only seems like a deluge to those of us who still remember the Walkman as a cool technological innovation rather than experiencing it as a discredited piece of technology, as teenager Scott Campbell did. Many older folks find the volume and pace of present-day media to be somewhat overwhelming and extreme – much like many of our parents found Elvis's gyrations or hordes of Beatle-induced screaming teenagers to be overwhelming and extreme. To younger people, however, it is simply what it is.

To measure how far the multimedia revolution has come, compare the visual blandness of a typical 1960s or 70s-era magazine with the visual richness of *Wired*. Find a 1950s or 1960s-era program on television and compare how slowly the images change[28] relative to today's programs. Movies, music, even radio are far more visually and/or aurally complex. Now project this trend 30 or 40 years into the future: ever more advanced technologies, more sophisticated experiences, more ubiquitous immersion.

We are still a text-based culture, but we are rapidly becoming a visually based one. To say that reading is dying, as many commentators have done,[29] is overstating the case, as there is some evidence that people are actually reading more than ever,[30] including young people. One 2007 article went so far as to declare a new "golden age of young adult literature."[31] However, there is also evidence that people are reading differently: much more digital content, shorter chunks, and less patience with large, dense bodies of text.[32]

Education has only begun to grapple with the implications of these changes, for instance by paying more attention to education in the "new literacies,"[33] but this misses the deeper point. The culture is moving away from its text base and toward a visual, multimedia, and digitized one, and knowledge itself is moving along with it, while education is in danger of being left behind. As society's chief knowledge institution, education has long been based in the printed and spoken word: journals, textbooks, lectures. There is a distinctly academic style of writing and speaking whose implicit message is "We are the knowledgeable keepers of knowledge. This is what knowledge is and how it's communicated." The common assertion that today's students are less well-prepared is partly based on a perceived decline in long-important, text-based academic skills. However, students are also far more capable of interacting with knowledge embodied in visual, multimedia, and digitized forms. Folk wisdom tells us that a picture is worth a thousand words, but no one has coined an aphorism yet which captures the relative value of multimedia. The new forms of media add power by themselves, but they add even more power in combination with text,[34] and the role of text itself changes when used with other media.

Proficiency with multimedia is also emerging as an important skill set, as illustrated by an assessment issue which an adjunct professor encountered in her graduate-level journalism class. The final class assignment included both a print and a multimedia component; she felt confident about assessing the student writing, but she was much less confident about assessing a multimedia project. She was struggling with how to assess one particular student who seemed to be relatively deficient in writing but excelled in the multimedia part. Journalism was once all about writing, but now there are plenty of journalists whose craft is based on other skills such as on-camera presence or multimedia creation. The problem is that journalism is being taught for the most part by teachers who excel at writing but not multimedia, so they have relatively little clue about how to assess it. The dilemma is understandable — writing is long-established, multimedia is relatively new — but it doesn't diminish the issue: multimedia is on the rise and requires new skills.

Another crucial but often overlooked aspect of the multimedia revolution is the gap in *production values*, the term used to describe the amount of effort, time, and resources expended to add value to a media production. Blockbuster Hollywood movies epitomize high production values with their exotic locations, spectacular special effects, and sophisticated computer-generated imagery. Behind each carefully crafted performer, dialogue, and scene on screen is a small army of professionals dedicated to making everything look and sound just so. High production values are common in other media as well; for instance, in some cases it can take the better part of a day and cost thousands of dollars to shoot a single-page ad for a magazine. High production values usually serve entertainment or marketing purposes to justify the high expense, but media creations with high production values often embody knowledge as well. Consider the new knowledge about animal behavior revealed in the astonishing cinematography of the 2010 Discovery Channel series "Life," which required 3,000 days of shooting over four years by 70 camera operators in 50 countries and a budget of $22 million.[35]

High production value educational programming and edutainment software[36] have been around for over 20 years, and their use has become commonplace.

Commercial sources provide an ever-increasing volume of educational materials with higher production values, and many classrooms use an array of technologies. For the most part, however, education remains mostly a low production value enterprise. Educational institutions at all levels usually lack the resources and expertise to create content with high production values, and most faculty and teachers are still relatively unskilled with using multimedia, especially when compared to their skills with using text. In the meantime, multimedia is becoming ever more deeply integrated into our culture. The more education fails to integrate multimedia, the greater the gap between education and society grows, and the more out of touch education becomes. Conversely, integrating multimedia into education is one of the many ways in which cyberized education is helping to redefine knowledge: learning in new ways from the power of new media, enhancing the power of text and changing the ways we use it. In the process, it may also be changing proverbial wisdom by offering us many new ways to get smart before we "grow too soon olt."

CHAPTER 3

Shifting Foundations: Access, Authority

The Underappreciated Shift: Redistributing Access

The redistribution of access to education in the U.S. and worldwide is one of its defining characteristics. This historic shift has been a long, gradual process which is well-known yet also curiously underappreciated, given that it represents one of the most far-reaching and ambitious societal initiatives humans have ever undertaken.

The idea of general educational opportunity for children did not even exist in America until the 19th century, and the idea of widespread access to higher education was a 20th century invention.[1] In 1910, fewer than 14 percent of Americans age 25 and over had graduated from high school, and fewer than three percent had graduated from college (Figure 3-1). High school diploma attainment rates started rising over the next 30 years as most states extended compulsory education[2] to the ages of 16 to 18. By 1960, the high school diploma attainment rate of adults age 25 and over exceeded 40 percent, and was 87 percent in 2009, although there is some evidence that the emphasis in recent years on compulsory exit examinations has reduced graduation rates.[3] In higher education, degree attainment rates rose more slowly. The post-World War II GI Bill stimulated educational attendance, but by 1960 college degree attainment had only risen to eight percent for adults age 25 and over. The Higher Education Act of 1965, the community college boom in the 1960s, the creation of permanent federal aid programs in 1972, and the rise in equal opportunity for women and minorities, all boosted participation rates. The number of college students more than doubled between 1970 and 2005, reflecting a sea change in attitudes toward higher education, including the now-widespread belief that nearly everyone should go to college. Degree attainment rates for American adults rose to 30 percent in 2009 (Figure 3-1).[4]

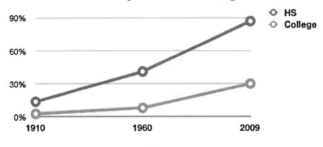

Figure 3-1: **U.S. HS/College Attainment, 1910-2009**

In the process, education has transformed from a privilege to something that is now widely considered to be a social right and an expectation. Redistributing access to education from the relative few to the 'as many as possible' is more than simple expansion because its intent is to reach new, previously neglected or underserved populations with different characteristics. Research universities, community colleges, and for-profit schools are relatively new types of institutions that were created to reach students which higher education had previously ignored.

Several factors are driving this redistribution: pivotal demographic shifts, the emphasis on higher education for almost everyone, the promotion of "education for all," the fruition of lifelong learning as human resource development, and the redefinition of access itself to focus more on results than on opportunity. Although many of these shifts have been underway for decades, traditional education has struggled to keep pace with them – but cyberized education is especially well-suited to address the challenges of providing greater access.

Higher Education for (Nearly) Everyone

Shift: from higher education as nicety for the few to necessity for the many

Not so long ago, a college degree was a nice thing to have, but not a necessary one. A majority of Americans were farmers until 1870,[5] and college graduates were relative rarities a century ago. The Industrial and Service Revolutions created millions of blue- and white-collar jobs that paid decent wages but did not require college degrees. Pursuing a prosperous business career without a college degree was also common during much of the past century.

Times have changed. Over the past several decades, the entirely new notion emerged that nearly all Americans should go to college, driven primarily by the economic argument that college graduates earn more money over their lifetimes. Having a college degree is "The Big Payoff" according to a July 2002 U.S. Census Bureau report. On average, college graduates with a bachelor's degree can expect to earn almost $1 million more than high school graduates during their lifetimes ($2.1 million vs. $1.2 million total), and those with a master's degree will earn more than twice as much as high school grads ($2.5 million total). As report co-author Jennifer Cheeseman Day notes, "At most ages, more education equates with higher earnings, and the payoff is most notable at the highest educational levels."[6]

A steady stream of reports has supported this notion since its inception, focusing on both increased earnings and projected shortfalls of college-educated workers. The 1991 report *America and the New Economy* described the need for a more highly skilled workforce to meet the "competitive realities of the new economy."[7] The report emphasized the need for improved academic skills, most notably to address changing workplace skill requirements which were becoming more abstract and conceptual. More recent research by the Georgetown University Center on Education and the Workforce indicates that a college education is becoming "the only path to middle-class earning power" in American society.[8] At the same time, the Georgetown center's 2010 report indicated that high-skill jobs are going begging in the U.S., with a projected shortage of three million workers with some postsecondary degree (associate or higher) and of 4.7 million workers with a postsecondary certificate.[9] Other data indicate that at least 70 percent of American jobs now require specialized skills and knowledge,[10] and that students need education that will help prepare them for jobs which haven't even been invented yet.

This notion of nearly universal college for Americans has also been criticized throughout its existence. Ivar Berg's 1970 study disputed the economic value of producing excessive numbers of college graduates,[11] while Caroline Bird's 1975 book *The Case Against College* argued that a college education was a dubious financial investment for individuals.[12] Similar arguments are being made today, for instance the assertion that many of the fastest-growing job categories do not require college degrees.[13] However, these criticisms simply illustrate that access to higher education has changed from a nicety for a privileged few to a perceived necessity for the many. The argument is now over how many: should nearly everyone attend college, or should there also be other alternative career paths for more people to follow?

Education for All

Shift: from education for the many to education as universal right

Beyond the notion of higher education for nearly everyone is a movement toward education at all levels for everyone, resulting in a similar redistribution of educational access at those levels. On a formal level, this is typified by the United Nations Educational Scientific and Cultural Organization (UNESCO)'s Education for All (EFA)[14] movement, launched in 1990 with an expanded vision of learning which included universalized primary education and massively reduced illiteracy. EFA's six current goals focus on satisfying learning needs for people of all ages worldwide by 2015. These lofty goals are unattainable within the targeted time frame, but they serve to direct efforts to provide redistributed educational access. In his book *High Noon: 20 Global Problems, 20 Years to Solve Them*, World Bank former Vice President for Europe J.F. Rischard identified EFA as an issue requiring a global commitment and a timely solution. As a "universal right," formal education has several indispensable major attributes:[15]

- Provides the "human capabilities" for having the "essential and individual power to reflect, make choices, and steer for a better life;"

- Enables building democratic societies and a "sense of global citizenship" which is required to solve global problems;

- Serves as an important tool for building a sense of shared global values;

- Links strongly to productivity growth and to improved human health;

- Is essential to participating in the world's new knowledge economy.

On an informal level, cyberizing technologies are opening the world to learning opportunities which are accessible "for students of any educational need, monetary status, background, or age level," as Indiana University professor Curt Bonk notes in his 2009 book, *The World Is Open*. By enabling us to "enhance, extend, transform, and share learning," cyberizing technologies are also making it possible to imagine a world where education is pervasive. Bonk's "WE-ALL-LEARN" model with its ten "openers for learning"[16] complements the vision of a world which redistributes educational access to everyone by viewing education as a universal right.

Demographic Changes

Shift: from traditional to nontraditional students as undergraduate majority

In U.S. higher education, the traditional undergraduate student has typically been defined as one between the ages of 18 and 22 who enters college directly out of high school, attends college full time, and graduates 'on time' in four years. Students who diverge from this profile, such as part-timers, ones who work full time while enrolled, or GED recipients, are considered nontraditional students. The expansion in U.S. nontraditional college student populations started more than 65 years ago with the post-World War II GI Bill program for returning veterans. However, most undergraduates were traditional students until the 1970s, when the majority shifted; by 1986, about 65 percent of undergraduate students were considered nontraditional.[17]

Even though this is now old news, mainstream higher education has been slow to adapt to this new reality. Much of U.S. higher education, including most policy issues and the related reportage of statistics, remains organized around the relatively fixed and narrow definition of what it means to be a traditional undergraduate student. Higher education is also still struggling to adapt to other major demographic changes such as gender, age, ethnic (Figures 3-2, 3-3, 3-4),[18] and geographic redistributions which have changed the landscape of American society.

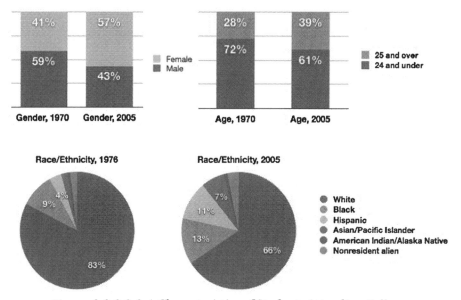

Figures 3-2, 3-3, 3-4. **Characteristics of Students Attending College, by Gender, Race and Ethnicity, and Age, 1970 (1976) and 2005.**

Redefining Access

Shift: from access as equal opportunity to access as more results-focused

As college attendance increased during the 20th century, a greater concern for equality of educational opportunity (or lack thereof) gradually developed and was eventually incorporated into policy.[19] For instance, public funding for some community colleges is based in part on the number of enrollments, which is a form of pro rata funding for providing equality of opportunity.

Recent government and foundation-funded initiatives are much more focused on results than on equality of educational opportunity. Higher education institutions face increasing pressure to improve graduation rates and produce more graduates; this pressure is reflected in initiatives which fund colleges based on course or degree completion[20] rather than on enrollments, as well as plans which call for providing federal financial aid based on such factors as job placements and post-graduation salary increases.[21] While such solutions might create more problems than they solve, they clearly illustrate a change in emphasis to a focus on producing results; simple opportunity is no longer enough. This shift helps redistribute access by drawing more attention to serving student populations which historically have had less success in college.

American K-12 public education has also become more focused on results, as reflected in the *No Child Left Behind Act of 2001*.[22] NCLB required states to implement a statewide accountability process for all public schools and systems, based on "challenging" standards in reading and mathematics and annual testing for all students in grades three through eight, with the goal that all groups of students would reach proficiency within 12 years. However, NCLB has arguably had a negative effect on redistributing access, based on research which links the use of high-stakes tests to higher dropout rates, including evidence that some schools have pushed out failing students to increase their overall test scores in order to meet NCLB's accountability provisions.[23]

The Fruition of Lifelong Learning

Shift: from sideshow to important player

Lifelong learning reframes education as a continual, lifelong process, extending access beyond the traditional school age population to learners of all ages. Although the notion of lifelong learning was introduced as early as the 1930s, it did not take hold during the mid-20th century when the lives of most Americans followed a stable, segmented progression of education, work, and retirement. The concept of lifelong learning which emerged in the 1970s focused on personal growth and human potential as a transformative force in schools and society, as expressed most notably by the 1972 UNESCO report *Learning to Be*. Interest in this concept of lifelong learning waned in the 1980s, but lifelong learning was revived in the 1990s through a more work-oriented focus on human resource development.[24] Lifelong learning is an increasingly important part of the American educational landscape, most notably as a competitive necessity for a workforce which now changes careers far more frequently. The ability to "learn, unlearn, and relearn" has been described as one of the new literacies for the 21st century,[25] and continuing education is now one of the fastest growing segments in higher education.

The Revolutionary Shift: Renegotiating Authority
Shift: from imposed authority to self-initiated, negotiated, shared authority

As Heidi and Alvin Toffler point out in *Revolutionary Wealth*, real revolutions break down and reorganize the role structure of society.[26] In that respect, education is also experiencing a revolutionary shift which is reorganizing its role structure: a movement away from imposed authority and toward self-initiated, negotiated, and shared authority. Youth and students have more power as consumers, education is becoming more dependent on business, and society is becoming more dependent on education.

How Redefining Knowledge and Redistributing Access Shifts Authority

When knowledge changes relatively slowly, and the means of knowledge production is held by a designated few, knowledge-based authority models can be built and sustained. When the nature of knowledge changes, it inevitably changes the nature of the authority relationships on which these models are built. Important knowledge no longer resides solely on campus or in people's heads and is no longer the exclusive province of adults. Kids realize that they know important things that their parents and teachers don't, in particular about how to use technology; students come to college having known important things for some time. Internalized knowledge confers less authority than it used to, because knowledge is increasingly 'out there:' distributed, social, constructed, contextual, complex and ever-changing. Computers dilute the authority of teachers and faculty by being an alternate source of legitimate knowledge and taking attention away from student-teacher interaction, usurping the teacher's traditional role of knowledge provider.[27] When knowledge changes quickly and the means of knowledge production is more distributed, knowledge-based authority models become less and less sustainable.

The redistribution of access to education also changes the nature of its authority relationships. Many traditional educational practices which are designed to sort and exclude, such as norm-referenced and letter grading, make ever less sense in a society aspiring to mass educational attainment. Education itself is gradually losing its mark of distinction and exclusivity as educational attainment becomes more commonplace.

Youth Power

Shift: youth as formidable economic, cultural, communications force

Remember when children were meant to be seen and not heard? Those days are long gone in today's society, especially now that children have become a formidable economic force through their role as big-time consumers. U.S. teenagers spend an estimated $160 billion per year (up from only $20 billion 30 years ago), and children influence a huge chunk of parental spending, estimated at $130-670 billion a year. Marketing to American children is itself an estimated $15-17 billion industry.[28] Over the past 50 years, this marketing clout has supported the emergence of a full-blown youth culture in American society – movies, fashion, books, entire television networks, and more – all of which youth experience as the natural order of things.

This economic and cultural power is now being augmented by communications power. Thanks to an increasingly sophisticated array of social networking tools, students of all ages have become or are becoming empowered communicators with access to a complete parallel communications infrastructure driven by online technologies. No more battles about tying up the house telephone (land lines are so 20th century anyway); many youth now have their own mobile phones, computers, and social networking sites. Youth culture is also being cyberized by new and powerful tools which enable them to become even more proficient at producing and sharing their own culture: new slang, fashion, and other cultural artifacts whose semiotics are far beyond adult awareness or comprehension for the most part (except perhaps for the marketers).

Student Power

Shift: students have more power as adults, customers, participants

Students have also gained more authority in their role as students. The rise of lifelong learning has populated higher education with millions of new adult learners in graduate and certificate programs with valuable knowledge and life experience. They are often as accomplished and knowledgeable as their instructors in many respects, and they do not require a socializing experience. Nontraditional undergraduates tend to have work, family, and other societal responsibilities, which diminishes the tendency to treat them as if they lack life experience and thus lack authority.

Changes in college life also give traditional students more authority in the educational process. Even students who use college as the place where they start learning how to grow up are far more economically, socially, and communicatively empowered than their counterparts of a generation or two ago. Administrative policies such as *in loco parentis* have faded away; the Family Educational Rights and Policy Act (commonly known by its acronym, FERPA) limits collegiate and parental control over student information and gives students more control over their financial responsibilities. Student power has also increased in the classroom, and cyberization accelerates this process in numerous ways, for instance by providing quick and easy access to an abundance of alternative educational resources through various mobile devices such as laptops, smartphones, and other portable media players. Formal student evaluations of professors are now commonplace and give students a greater de facto role in campus decision-making. Informal online rating systems such as ratemyprofessor.com[29] have been controversial but also somewhat influential, further tilting the balance of power toward students.

The related tendency to treat college students as customers also gives them more authority. Many colleges and universities have developed sophisticated customer relationship management (CRM) programs and models[30] to sustain mutually satisfying and beneficial transactions with student customers. CRM is particularly important for financially self-sustaining administrative entities such as continuing education units. Retaining students is more cost-efficient than finding new ones; graduating students produces satisfied customers and creates the potential to extend the relationship and increase revenue through alumni donations. Some observers cite various indicators of this 'student as customer' philosophy as a sign of pampering and decline, such as increased grade inflation, enhanced campus facilities, and reduced Friday class offerings.[31] Others view this trend as enabling students to be more responsible for their learning within an emerging paradigm of shared governance.[32] In either case, the net effect has been to empower students.

Business Power

Shift: educational institutions are more dependent on business

The business sector's increased influence in education can be traced to several sources:

- Education's evolution into being the preferred path to economic success has placed greater **emphasis on education as preparation for future employment**. Many students, parents, legislators, policymakers, and thought leaders consider this to be the most important function of higher education, and it provides an avenue for business to be more involved as an interested party in educational processes and outcomes at all levels.

- The 30-year **reign of a free market mythology,** during which a belief in the powers of privatization and free markets has dominated. Public funding support for higher education has eroded, and education at all levels has increasingly been viewed through this ideological prism.

- Business is also deeply interested in American education as a **huge and expanding market** – $43 billion in 2007 according to one set of estimates. The cyberization of education is providing abundant new opportunities for commercial vendors such as textbook publishers, educational materials providers, and testing services. For example, the rise of online education has created a greater reliance on commercial sector products and services such as computers, student information systems, learning management systems, information technology, and student support services. For-profit education providers have emerged as an influential market force in both higher and K-12 education.[33]

This trend has generated strong reactions which run the gamut: enthusiastic support, fierce criticism,[34] uneasy ambivalence. Some observers hail "market-driven" initiatives as suitable solutions to "fix" education's problems, while others decry the "corporatization" of education as a ruination of its once lofty aspirations. Education's current financial crisis makes it seem particularly vulnerable at present, which feeds the trend toward greater business involvement, but this vulnerability is a two-way street.

Education Power

Shift: society is more dependent on educational institutions

Given all these shifts in knowledge, access, and authority, it may appear that education is losing its influence in society. In reality, the exact opposite is happening: society is more dependent on education than ever, which shifts authority toward education. The shift of higher education from nicety to necessity, the aspiration of education as a universal right, the expansion of education to a lifelong activity, and the growing emphasis on greater student success, all increase the importance of education to society.

Education has also become an important economic sector at both the national and local levels. In 2008, educational services was the second largest industry in the U.S. economy, providing 13.5 million jobs.[35] At the higher education level, the local college or university is the largest employer in hundreds of communities throughout the country. K-12 education is often the biggest line item expense for local governments, but it is also commonly the largest or one of the largest local employers. The commercialization of university research has increased higher education's importance as a source of new knowledge which stimulates new economic activity.

* * *

Despite its increased importance, education has struggled mightily to keep pace with these foundational shifts in knowledge, access, and authority, and traditional education is not particularly well-suited to cope with them. Education is also commonly taken to task for being slow to adopt new technologies, with one notable exception: online education, which has become the leading wedge for the transition to cyberized education.

CHAPTER 4

From Zero to Mainstream in 16 Years: How Online Learning Cyberized Education

There is no longer any question that computers will increasingly pervade our everyday lives...the social invention of computer-mediated communication systems to support dispersed communities of active learners [makes me] feel optimistic about its future in offering a new option for lifelong learning.

– Starr Roxanne Hiltz, The Virtual Classroom, 1994.

Online learning is the new normal — and it's almost becoming a preference.

– Andrea Henne, Dean of Online and Distributed Learning, San Diego Community College District, 2010.

These two quotes aptly capture the trajectory of online higher education from the mid 1990s to the present. Pioneers like Roxanne Hiltz saw the potential of "computer-mediated communication systems" to provide new learning options, and American education is now realizing this potential. Online education has become a preferred learning option at many higher education institutions, and it is *the* preferred learning option at some of them. The cyberization of society has changed education, and online education has been the leading wedge of this change, so understanding its role in creating this change is essential to understanding education's present and its future.

Defining Online Education

The field of technology-enabled learning has long been characterized by a plethora of terms to describe it (Figure 4-1). Even the more basic terms such as "distance education" or "online education" have varying, and at times conflicting, definitions. For clarity's sake, the definition of online education used here is simply *the use of online technologies in formal education for teaching and learning* – the fifth level of change described in Chapter 1. This includes courses, programs, and other learning experiences which are delivered exclusively through online means, as well as those which combine online and classroom delivery modes, commonly referred to in K-12 and higher education as "blended learning"[1] or "hybrid learning."

Figure 4-1. **Common terms used in the field of technology-enabled learning**

The distinction between online and blended courses is somewhat arbitrary, and different definitions are used in practice.[2] This illustrates how online education delivery happens on a continuum which includes entirely online courses at one end, entirely 'face-to-face' courses at the other end, and a huge range of blended options in between which combine the two modes.

A Brief History of Online Education in the U.S.

Origins and the Early Visionaries

The rise of online education from zero to mainstream happened under the radar of many observers. It may seem as if online education emerged from nowhere, given that it did not exist until the 1980s and was not used to any appreciable extent in U.S. higher education until the mid 1990s. Its origins can be traced to three principal sources: distance education, network-based communication, and computer-assisted instruction.

The term *distance education* describes an educational process which involves some form of physical separation along with the use of one or more types of media to conduct learning. Distance education in the form of correspondence education can be traced as far back as the early 1700s,[3] although others trace its origins to the mid-19th century in Europe and the United States.[4] In the late 19th century, a few American public universities launched correspondence study programs to meet Industrial Age needs, which eventually became a national movement.[5] The main force driving distance education has always been the use of technologies such as print materials, audio visual devices, radio, telecourses and satellite broadcast to increase access to education and learning opportunities. Online technologies are the next step in that progression of delivery modes designed to increase access to education.

The development of *network-based communication* was inspired by the work of Norbert Wiener, who invented the field of cybernetics and whose 1948 book on the topic encouraged thinking about computer technology as a tool for extending humans' communications capabilities.[6] In 1962, Buckminister Fuller's book *Education Automation* envisioned a new global educational process facilitated by "the most comprehensive generalized computer setup with network connections."[7] Ivan Illich's 1971 book *Deschooling Society* proposed computer-based "learning webs" which would facilitate learning through a variety of features such as skill exchanges, a peer-matching communications network, and an educator reference service.[8]

The origins of *computer-assisted instruction (CAI)* can be found in the "teaching machines" first developed by psychologist Sidney J. Pressey in the 1920s and refined into "programmed instruction" devices by psychologist B.F. Skinner in the mid-1950s.[9] In 1963, Control Data Corporation and the University of Illinois developed PLATO, one of the first and best known computer-assisted instructional systems.[10] In the mid-1970s and early 1980s, CAI was more widely adopted in K-12 education, and to a lesser extent in higher education. Networked hardware and software packages with management and assessment capabilities called Integrated Learning Systems were developed and commonly used in U.S. K-12 education by the 1990s.[11]

Online Higher Education: Convergence and the Early Pioneers

I do believe that this form of human communication [computer conferencing] will become as widespread and as significant as the phone has been to our society.

— Murray Turoff, 1980.[12]

Online higher education in the U.S. essentially derives from a convergence of distance education and network-based communication. Distance education's emphasis on providing access was a critical component, and the development of network communication in the late 1960s and the invention of email and computer conferencing in the early 1970s added a key dimension: a primary focus on instructor-student and student-student interaction. This focus dovetailed with the instructor-facilitated, professor-centered learning environments which predominate in higher education.[13] Computer conferencing (the use of computer-based telecommunications to hold discussions among multiple people in separate locations) and email expanded the use of computer networks from content delivery vehicles to learning networks.[14] Over the past 20 years, these network technologies have evolved to support knowledge work in general and collaborative learning in particular, transforming education in the process.[15] The ventures of the earliest pioneers in online education share this convergence:

- The genesis of online learning in higher education can be traced to the use of computer conferencing starting in the early 1970s at the New Jersey Institute of Technology, where information technology professor Murray Turoff developed the Electronic Information Exchange System.[16] EIES used computers to facilitate the communication and exchange of written text and eventually was developed into the first learning management system. From the mid-1970s through the 1980s, Turoff, Starr Roxanne Hiltz, and other NJIT researchers offered the first instructor-facilitated college level online courses, developed the first "virtual classroom" by adding threaded discussion tools to EIES, and conducted the first quasi-experimental research which compared online and regular classroom courses.[17]

- In 1976, John Sperling founded the University of Phoenix (UoP) to serve working adults. From the beginning, UoP pursued the use of a highly interactive, collaborative learning model with relatively small class sizes. In the 1980s, UoP developed a prototype online education program and in 1989 launched the first online university-level degree programs.[18]

- In 1987, Glenn R. Jones launched the Mind Extension University cable television network to provide greater access to education; in 1993, Jones launched Jones International University as the first university to exist completely online, and JIU became the first fully accredited online university in 1999.[19]

Despite these ventures, very few educators in the early 1990s were seriously involved in creating and teaching online courses.[20] In the U.S., two major factors launched online education: the Alfred P. Sloan Foundation's Learning Outside the Classroom initiative, and a user-friendly World Wide Web.

ALNs: the Sloan Foundation's online learning initiative

The Learning Outside the Classroom initiative directed by Sloan Foundation program officer A. Frank Mayadas was based the concept of Asynchronous Learning Networks (ALNs), drawing from the work of Hiltz, Turoff, and Simon Fraser University professor Linda Harasim.[21] The ALN concept differed from previous distance education methods such as self-study or interactive television by emphasizing the importance of "asynchronous interactivity." The ALN concept encompassed both electronic computer networks and networks of people involved in the learning process, creating interactive communities which "provide learning to anyone who wishes to learn, at a time and place of the learner's choice" without the constraints of a classroom.[22]

When Mayadas traveled around the country in 1993 to ascertain faculty and administrator interest in his initiative, some told him that the idea was crazy: how could learning on a computer possibly compare to hearing an expert professor lecture in person? Eventually, Mayadas found a few others who embraced the concept, including professors at highly regarded colleges and universities such as New York University (Richard Vigilante), the University of Illinois (Burks Oakley II), Vanderbilt University (John Bourne, J. Olin Campbell), and Stanford University (Andy DiPaolo) among others. A few institutions were already involved with online education, such as Northern Virginia Community College, which through its Extended Learning Institute had been offering some courses which used online computer conferencing since 1990. These and several other institutions became grantees in the Sloan Foundation initiative and were among the first colleges and universities in the U.S. to develop online courses, degree, and certificate programs. Over the next ten years, much of the growth in online education was directly attributable to the Sloan Foundation initiative, which pumped over $40 million into development of online education programs.[23] More importantly, the Sloan

Foundation initiative helped establish the legitimacy of online education among mainstream institutions.

The World Wide Web and Mosaic

Originally designed as a way to make it easier to retrieve research documentation, the World Wide Web was conceptualized in 1989 by Tim Berners-Lee and scientists at the European Center for High Energy Physics (CERN) in Geneva, Switzerland. The World Wide Web was released to the public in 1991, but adoption was slow; there were only 50 web sites worldwide by the end of 1992, and no more than 150 web sites a year later.[24] That changed forever in November 1993 with the introduction of Mosaic, a graphical web browser developed by the National Center for Supercomputing Applications at the University of Illinois. Thanks to its user-friendly interface with features such as icons, bookmarks, and pictures, Mosaic made navigation easy and generated mass appeal. Mosaic and its offspring transformed education by providing a means for online learning to proliferate at relatively low cost.[25]

The Quiet Boom: Online Education Grows under the Radar

By the early 2000s, millions of students were learning online in the U.S. and around the world. Curiously, however, the rise of online education from zero to mainstream happened largely under the radar. Many researchers and thought leaders, as well as the entire mainstream media, missed what was happening for a long time because they were following the wrong trends, looking in the wrong places, or not paying attention at all.

Field of dreams: the dot.com boom/bust – For a variety of reasons, in the mid- and late 1990s the mainstream media largely equated the fortunes of online education with the dot.com boom. Well-known universities such as Temple University, New York University, and the University of Maryland launched for-profit virtual schools, and consortia of prestigious universities and other institutions started ventures such as Fathom and UNext, all with the hope of cashing in on the dot.com gold rush. Then the dot.com boom went bust, and these ventures rapidly perished, reportedly losing tens or even hundreds of millions of dollars in some cases.[26] Cause of death: call it "field of dreams" syndrome, in which a "if you build it, they will come" approach overrode usual business practices. For instance, Fathom failed because it lacked a workable business model; its high-end, high-production-cost courses didn't attract enough students.[27] However, although many people believed otherwise at the time, the "dot.com" boom and bust was not the real story of online higher education.

Falling short of the hype – Another common misconception at the time was that the innovative power of online learning would rapidly and thoroughly transform traditional education, which inevitably resulted in disappointing those who expected this to occur. This viewpoint was typified by the 2004 report *Thwarted Innovation,* which purported to explain why the e-learning boom went bust by piloting an experimental measurement method at six selected institutions which the authors identified as leaders in adoption of learning technology. The report concluded that e-learning was a case of "thwarted innovation"[28] because it fell short of its hype by not succeeding in totally transforming higher education over a ten-year period. However, the institutions selected for the report were not leaders in adopting online education, so the report's conclusion missed the more important point: online education was steadily growing at many other institutions for different reasons, even if it wasn't measuring up to an artificial, misplaced hype.

Looking in the wrong places – The mainstream media also missed the growth of online education because they were looking at familiar places instead of the ones where growth was actually happening. For example, although most of the early online growth happened at public institutions, the main campuses of universities largely ignored online education while their continuing or extension programs were deeply involved. Unfortunately, journalists and other opinion leaders often ignore extension programs, and even the institutions themselves sometimes overlook their own programs, as happened in August 2002 when the University of California at Berkeley reported offering its first entirely online course.[29] This was news indeed to Mary Beth Almeda, Director of the University of California Extension's statewide Center for Media and Independent Learning at Berkeley, which had been offering hundreds of online courses to thousands of students[30] for the previous six years. The mainstream media similarly missed the rebirth of New York University's online program, which thrived after its well-publicized for-profit venture failed, because it did not fit the prevailing narrative being reported at the time.

Much of the growth in online education also occurred at institutions which lacked brand name recognition, most notably community colleges. Many four-year institutions with large online programs were (and still are) simply less well-known than their counterparts. For instance, online courses were almost nonexistent at most University System of Maryland schools, while the University of Maryland University College (UMUC) became one of the largest online education providers in the U.S. and abroad, with over 87,000 online enrollments in 2002.[31] UMUC's extensive advertising campaigns reflected necessity as well as enterprise, as its brand recognition among the general public and the mainstream media paled in comparison to the University of Maryland's flagship campus in College Park, with its long-established reputation and the publicity generated by its nationally known athletic teams.

A sizable number of people weren't paying attention at all, including most of the faculty and many administrators at large research universities and small liberal arts colleges. Efforts to introduce online education at most of these institutions consisted mainly of individual faculty pioneers developing a few courses or the occasional online program, usually with little or no help from their fellow faculty, departments, or college administrations.

Some commentators at the time figured out what was actually happening, such as *Washington Post* columnist Christopher Shea, who observed in a September 2001 article that "community colleges and regional universities that have slowly, organically moved into the online arena – doing their old job in a new way – have succeeded where the flashy business types and big-time private schools have not...the nonprofit tortoises may have passed the dot-com hares."[32]

Since then, these patterns have continued with some new developments. An ever-larger group of "nonprofit tortoises" have left most of the "dot-com hares" in the dust; for example, UMUC's enrollments rose over 300 percent in nine years, reaching 196,000 online enrollments in 2009.[33] A number of for-profit institutions which focused on serving nontraditional or other underserved learners have also grown and prospered. Meanwhile, the mainstream media has gotten better at reporting trends, but is still not always looking in the right places. For example, the previously cited *San Diego Business Journal* article which described a lack of online programs at the University of California at San Diego's main campus overlooked UCSD-Extension's thriving online program, which in early 2011 offered 21 certificates in 13 areas of study.[34]

Why Online Learning Has Taken Hold in Higher Education

Online learning has gone from zero to mainstream in U.S. higher education because it provided new and improved ways for learners to gain access to educational opportunities. As a result, online education became the main source of enrollment growth, the leading wedge for pedagogical and technological innovation, and has achieved actual and perceptual parity thanks to an intentional focus on quality.

On the institutional level, online education has become an important means for enabling higher education institutions to achieve their strategic goals.

New and Improved Access

Online education improves access for all learners and provides new access for previously unserved learners. Providing convenient and flexible access is the main reason why online education has entered the mainstream of U.S. higher education within the past five years. Improved access is routinely cited as the most common and often most important benefit of online learning.[35] Students could watch telecourses on local cable television, and evening, weekend, and shortened-term courses increased flexibility, but "anywhere, anytime" online education gave learners options that they didn't have before. Online education improved access by:

- Reaching nontraditional learners whose life circumstances such as work, child care, or other obstacles precluded their pursuit of on-campus educational opportunities.

- Expanding lifelong educational opportunities through continuing education such as graduate certificate programs and community college programs for career-changers.

- Enabling higher education to reach students outside of its traditional service areas, including students located around the world.

- Extending off-campus access year-round through the use of summer online programs.

Online education succeeded by servicing learners which traditional education couldn't or wasn't interested in serving, in particular by serving lifelong and other nontraditional learners at institutions with a historical commitment to access and outreach. Conversely, it failed when it focused primarily on serving traditional learners or undefined audiences.

Main Source of Enrollment Growth

Online education is where the growth is happening. Between fall 2002 and fall 2009, the number of students in U.S. higher education grew by less than two percent per year, while the number of students taking online courses grew ten times as fast, at an annualized rate of almost 20 percent. The number of U.S. college students who take one or more online courses at degree-granting institutions during an academic year rose from an estimated 1.6 million in fall 2002 to 5.6 million college students in fall 2009. This represents an increase in 'market penetration' from about 10 percent in fall 2002 to 30 percent in fall 2009. Including students from all postsecondary institutions produces even more startling numbers: a report by the market research group Ambient Insight estimated that 12 million learners took online courses in 2010, and a projected 21 million will be taking online courses by 2015; the number of students taking all of their courses online is projected to triple in five years, from 1.37 million to 3.86 million.[36]

Although the Sloan Consortium (Sloan-C) issued a report on blended learning in 2007,[37] obtaining good estimates of blended learning adoption is extremely difficult. Faculty can easily add online discussions, assignments, or other components to classroom courses, but these additions are usually not tracked administratively. Nonetheless, there is some evidence that blended learning continues to grow. A few institutions that track both online and blended learning enrollments have found that blended learning has grown at their institutions. At the University of Central Florida, blended learning registrations increased over 40 percent from 16,781 to 23,397 between the 2005-2006 and 2009-2010 academic years and increased fivefold over a nine-year period; UCF's blended courses generated a 30 percent increase in student credit hours between fall 2009 and fall 2010.[38] At the University of Illinois at Springfield, blended learning rose from 29 percent to 34 percent of all enrollments between the 2005-2006 and 2009-2010 academic years;[39] the overall growth is even larger since UIS's total enrollments grew by about 15 percent during that period.[40]

The growth in U.S. online higher education has happened primarily at community and other two-year colleges, large public universities, private for-profit schools, and continuing education or extension units. The bulk of enrollment growth in online education has occurred at institutions that are fully engaged with large, established online programs.[41] Online education has especially taken hold at institutions where teaching and learning and/or career preparation and advancement are high priorities while research and scholarship are low or nonexistent ones. Community colleges have been very receptive to online education for several important reasons: they serve the students which traditional institutions struggle to serve or ignore; they focus on teaching and learning without the competing priorities of research and scholarship; online learning aligns closely with their central mission to provide educational access; and they tend to be more flexible institutions which are able to adapt to new delivery modes. For-profit institutions have also been receptive because they have operated from a growth imperative, and online education has fueled much of that growth. For example, in at least half of the 14 publicly traded for-profit institutions, which includes many of the largest ones, more than 50 percent of their students are in online courses.[42]

By contrast, online education has experienced relatively little growth at small liberal arts colleges or on the main campuses of large universities. The focus at these institutions is on granting bachelor's degrees in the traditional arts and sciences in the context of a 'classic' undergraduate experience, or on granting graduate degrees which relate to career paths in academic disciplines. Much of the governance at these schools is done by academic departments which often have little incentive to grow. Current funding patterns and competition pressures create disincentives against growth for the most selective colleges and universities.[43] Most elite small liberal arts colleges use their surplus of applicants to increase selectivity rather than expand enrollments; greater selectivity and promoting smallness also helps improve rankings and reputations. Less elite small liberal arts colleges also trade on the "personal attention" which their smallness enables. At the main campuses of large universities, teaching is often a lesser priority than research and scholarship, so taking on more students would divert faculty's valuable time and attention from their research and publication duties. Tenure and promotion policies at these large institutions have often provided disincentives for becoming too involved with teaching in general and with online education in particular.

Leading Wedge of Technological and Pedagogical Innovation

Because of its recent growth, online education has become the *leading wedge of technological* and *pedagogical innovation* in higher education. Online learning technologies such as LMSs, discussion and communication tools, online gradebooks and assessment tools have become the mainstays of online course delivery. As Penn State World Campus Executive Director Emeritus Gary Miller notes, these technologies address all the needs distance education has previously fulfilled: content delivery, access, interaction, and time flexibility. Web 2.0 technologies such as blogs, wikis, and social networks are also being adopted rapidly in online education; for instance, a 2008 Economist Intelligence Unit survey reported relatively high adoption rates (40 to 56 percent) for blogs, wikis, social networks, video podcasts, and mobile broadband.[44] By contrast, classroom adoption of innovative technologies tends to be irregular and instructor-specific rather than institution-wide, and it tends to lag behind adoption elsewhere.[45] Although classroom faculty may be catching up with using social media,[46] they still lag behind faculty who teach online.

As Miller also notes, online learning technologies support pedagogical innovation as well, in particular the capacity to "engage an active, collaborative, inquiry-based pedagogy at a scale that was unimaginable in the past."[47] Although technological innovation does not automatically produce pedagogical innovation,[48] the novelty of online education technologies gives some faculty a reason to try new teaching approaches, while it forces others to do so as they realize that their classroom approaches do not necessarily work well online. This has led faculty to discover that online and blended learning are well suited to support a wide variety of pedagogical innovations. The process of redesigning an online course provides ready-made opportunities to improve courses[49] by incorporating enhanced learning features and approaches such as critical thinking,[50] concept mapping,[51] and reflection.[52] Online education also offers innovations which traditional education delivery cannot match, for example giving greater access to guest experts for individual courses[53] or comprehensive programs such as Fairleigh Dickinson University's Global Virtual Faculty program.[54] The archival capabilities of online technologies greatly increase the permanence and utility of discussions, collaborative projects, and other student work by transforming them from evanescent, rarely shared products to ones which can be more easily accessed, shared, reused, and even repurposed. Online instructors have also developed other innovative techniques for facilitating discussions which are superior to those typically used in classroom discussions, for instance ensuring that everyone participates, providing clear guidelines for effective participation, assessing individual contributions in multiple ways, and assigning specific roles to students for facilitating the discussion process. As a result, many teachers report that online education generates more discussion among students, and students often report that they get the most effective learning from reading other students' posts or what other students have researched.[55]

The use of online courses to improve classroom courses[56] is also compelling evidence that online education has driven pedagogical innovation. Instructors often use online courses to try out new ideas which are then incorporated into classroom courses to improve them. This pattern has become commonplace, as Northern Virginia Community College chemistry professor Reva Savkar knows quite well; she's been using her distance learning chemistry courses for both science and non-science majors to improve her classroom courses for over 15 years. Savkar has incorporated numerous innovations from her online chemistry courses into her classroom courses, including lecture notes, animations, online gradebook, tutorials, and FAQs. Like many classroom instructors, she has also incorporated an online syllabus into her campus-based courses which use tried-and-tested features from her online courses.

Source of Faculty Development and Rejuvenation

Online education has also **become a major source of faculty development and rejuvenation** in U.S. higher education. College teaching is still largely based on the Old Smart model of knowledge: profess what one knows as the 'sage on the stage' whose authority to teach is based on knowledge of one's discipline. Most faculty learn how to teach by absorbing teaching skills and style informally from a mentor, or learn along the way through practice or trial and error. This model is commonly accepted reflexively without examination or question.

However, online education requires that faculty change their approach to teaching. For instance, faculty who might otherwise resist being told anything about how to teach are often willing to accept help with learning how to use new technologies to develop their online course. Faculty often receive institutional support in course design and development when they first start teaching online, and many online courses are developed by teams rather than by individuals. Getting involved in online education thus becomes an excellent opportunity for faculty to reflect on the teaching and learning experience and figure out ways to improve it. Many faculty who were initially highly skeptical but tried it anyway underwent a "conversion experience"[57] of sorts and became quite satisfied with teaching online. This transformation happens not because the medium or the related technologies are superior, but because the process of redesigning instruction changes teachers from reflexive to reflective; they examine long-held or previously unexamined assumptions about the craft of teaching and are able to act on that knowledge in the course development process.

Thus, it is not surprising that online education has also tended to attract faculty who are seeking the chance to innovate or to rejuvenate their teaching experience by trying new things.[58] This experience is not universal, particularly for faculty who begin online teaching without proper preparation, buy-in, or support; many faculty remain skeptical about online education, and most of these skeptics will never try it.[59] Nonetheless, teaching online has become an effective and valued professional development experience for hundreds of thousands of faculty.

Intentional Focus on Quality

People who innovate tend to focus on quality improvement, and online education has attracted numerous educators to explore the possibilities for improving quality through technological and pedagogical innovation.

Quality is inevitably defined in terms of both substance and perception, and a primary reason for online education's focus on quality was to gain acceptance. During its initial years, online education regularly encountered perceptions that it was inferior to traditional classroom instruction, and it was held to a much higher standard as a result.[60] For instance, the Institute for Higher Education Policy's 1999 report *What's the Difference?* called for an extremely high level of research verification before full-scale adoption of online learning would be considered acceptable.[61] The report's recommendations conveniently ignored the fact that classroom and other traditional educational practices have never been held to similar standards and thus do not meet them. This double standard reflects an unquestioning acceptance of the efficacy and superiority of classroom teaching. A colleague of mine at a large public university once described to me a discussion at a meeting to decide whether to allow a doctoral program to be offered entirely online or to require a residency period. My colleague argued for consideration of the completely online option but was told it was not feasible. He asked how they knew this. The response: "We just know."

This dynamic drove online education practitioners to pay closer attention to the quality of teaching and learning, including the creation of higher, more concrete standards and expectations for course quality, instructor involvement, and student engagement. One of the guiding principles of the Sloan Foundation's ALN initiative was that an "ALN" online course should have equivalent quality to the classroom courses on the campus where it originated; that is, a Stanford online course should have Stanford quality, a Northern Virginia Community College online course should have NVCC quality, and so on. Online education researchers began to amass evidence to establish the "equivalent" quality of online courses and programs relative to traditional ones. Probably the best known initiative was the No Significant Difference Phenomenon, a research project by North Carolina State University professor Thomas Russell, who compiled over 350 research reports and other papers which documented equivalent student outcomes between distance and face-to-face delivery modes.[62] Conceptual frameworks such as Penn State University professor Michael G. Moore's interaction types (learner-content; learner-instructor; learner-learner) also guided practitioners on how to provide quality instruction.[63]

Inevitably, practitioners began moving their focus from equivalence to superiority. On one level, this was simple to demonstrate, and research studies confirmed what online education practitioners had already learned: online courses were better because they served many students who otherwise had no alternative at all, and having something is infinitely better than nothing.[64] Beyond establishing online education as an option of last resort, practitioners soon began identifying ways which online learning equalled or surpassed face-to-face instruction: more student-centered, more writing-intensive, highly interactive discussions, enriched course materials, immediate feedback, and increased flexibility.[65]

A substantive body of research also emerged which demonstrated the effectiveness of online education. A 2002 review of available studies found overwhelming evidence that university-level online course delivery emphasizing instructor-student and student-student interaction was at least as effective as traditional classroom delivery.[66] A 2003 literature review documented the learning effectiveness of online education,[67] and a subsequent expansion of the No Significant Difference compilation included a number of studies which showed a significant difference in favor of technology-mediated instruction.[68] More recently, the National Survey of Student Engagement found that online learners reported more engagement, intellectual challenge, and deep learning, while interactive technologies were also "positively related to student engagement, self-reported learning outcomes, and deep approaches to learning."[69] Over the short span of about ten years, online education research moved from establishing legitimacy (online education belongs in the same conversation as traditional instruction) to parity (it's just as good) to a slight edge (it's better in some ways).

Online education also made huge strides in winning the perception battle as well. Filled with skepticism during the early years, mainstream media articles about online education soon featured stories of single mothers, career changers, and other motivated and grateful learners working away on their computers late at night after the kids were in bed, completing online courses and degrees at their own time and convenience, and changing their lives. Online education's reputation also received a huge boost from a 2009 U.S. Department of Education meta-analysis which found that "students in online learning conditions performed better vs. those receiving face-to-face instruction."[70] Despite this study's caveats and limitations, it has become widely cited[71] as evidence that online and blended learning are equal or superior to face-to-face instruction.

The USDE study findings also helped reinforce an already growing acceptance of blended learning as a quality alternative, often described as the "best of both worlds."[72] The quality of blended learning depends to a large extent on using each modality (online, classroom) for its maximum benefit. Despite some drawbacks such as required in-person or synchronous online meetings which can reduce learner access, flexibility, and convenience for geographically dispersed or time-stressed learners, the range of blended course design possibilities has vastly increased the potential for pedagogical innovation and quality improvement.[73]

Online Education is Strategic

The other main reason that online learning has taken hold in higher education is its role in enabling colleges and universities to achieve their strategic goals. For example, the 2007 Sloan-C *Online Nation* report asked academic leaders to rate the importance of fourteen strategic factors in their decision to provide online offerings. Although increasing student access was by far the most commonly cited reason for providing online education, most academic leaders considered a wide variety of factors to be strategically important reasons for providing online education (Table 4-1). The Sloan-C report data established the strategic importance of online learning in higher education by demonstrating that hundreds, and in some cases thousands, of institutions are actively using their online education offerings for such purposes as growing their professional and continuing education programs, increasing degree completion, enhancing the value of their institution's brand, improving student retention, and reducing or containing costs.[74]

A 2009 report which examined online learning at the nation's leading public and land-grant universities also found many examples of institutions that were using online learning to help achieve their strategic goals, and the report identified characteristics shared by successful strategic online learning initiatives.[75] Blended learning also enables higher education institutions to achieve their strategic goals by implementing learner-centered pedagogies, enabling initiatives on an institutional scale, and increasing classroom utilization efficiency.[76]

	Very Important (VI)	Important (I)	VI + I
Increase student access	62.8%	30.0%	92.8%
Attract students from outside traditional service area	53.0%	28.4%	81.4%
Grow continuing and/or professional education	40.1%	40.9%	81.0%
Increase rate of degree completion	33.2%	39.0%	72.2%
Provide pedagogic improvements	27.8%	42.8%	70.6%
Enhancing value of college/university brand	28.2%	41.4%	69.6%
Improve student retention	25.6%	40.0%	65.6%
Improve enrollment management responsiveness	20.9%	40.8%	61.7%
Increase the diversity of student body	23.7%	34.2%	57.9%
Optimize physical plant utilization	22.0%	32.6%	54.6%
Reduce or contain costs	18.2%	32.8%	51.0%
Increase strategic partnerships with other institutions	19.9%	29.6%	49.5%
Strengthen academic continuity in case of disaster	24.0%	24.1%	48.1%
Enhance alumni and donor outreach	11.8%	23.9%	35.7%

Table 4-1. 'Online Education Is Strategically Important for My Institution' –
Percentage Responding Very Important or Important – Fall 2006

Why Online Education Is Making Inroads into U.S. K-12 Education

The adoption of online learning in U.S. K-12 education is progressing more slowly and is lagging behind higher education[77] for several possible reasons:

- *(Relative) absence of an unserved audience* – U.S. online higher education got its foothold by serving previously neglected and underserved populations such as nontraditional and lifelong learners. However, since K-12 education is compulsory, there is no large unserved audience;[78] almost all the students who could be served by online education are already in school. The available opportunities are smaller in scope and will take a longer time to develop.

- *More caution* – K-12 education involves additional stakeholder groups such as principals, school boards, and especially parents who are also often more deeply involved in the process. This produces more negotiation among the interested parties; as a result, school districts have implemented online learning more cautiously than colleges and universities have.[79]

- *Greater scrutiny* — Another source of caution is that K-12 online education is unlikely to have the luxury of growing under the radar, given that the mainstream media and the general public pay much greater attention to K-12 education, and they have become much more aware of online learning thanks to its adoption in higher education. So the adoption of online K-12 education will be scrutinized by an even larger and often less knowledgeable audience.

- *Greater complexity* - Having to satisfy a larger number of more involved stakeholders also adds complexity to the process, as does having to align other important K-12 educational functions such as custodial care and socialization with the implementation of online learning.

- *More skepticism* — Even many advocates of K-12 online education believe that classroom education is better, but online education is adequate when a classroom option is not available. To some extent, K-12 online education is still somewhat stuck in the "option of last resort" phase of adoption. Evidence of effectiveness is "promising"[80] but still slim, at least in terms of defining effectiveness in comparison to the traditional classroom.

The adoption of blended learning has also been relatively slow to develop in K-12 education.[81] In short, online learning has not cyberized K-12 education — yet.

However, online learning is making inroads into K-12 education. The rate of adoption is low; only about two percent of U.S. schoolchildren took an online course in the 2007-2008 academic year. However, the absolute numbers are potentially large relative to higher education because there are so many more students in K-12 education (around 49 million public school students vs. around 18.5 million higher education students in 2007-2008). Approximately 700,000 K-12 students took online courses in 2005-2006, and slightly over one million students in 2007-2008. The growth rate is also high, slightly higher than that which higher education has experienced over the past eight years (47 percent between 2005-2006 and 2007-2008; 21.3 percent compound annual rate). A more recent estimate is that 1.5 million K-12 students were involved in online and blended learning during the 2009-2010 school year, which suggests that the high growth rate persists.[82]

Online education has gained a foothold in U.S. K-12 education by providing access in a variety of needed ways such as providing unavailable courses to rural students, credit recovery,[83] Advanced Placement, and alternative schools. The available evidence indicates that online learning is becoming an essential feature of the K-12 education landscape.[84]

How Online Learning Cyberized Education

Online learning has cyberized education by being the leading wedge for meeting the challenge of redistributing access in higher education, and increasingly in K-12 education as well. Online learning has also shown its potential for improving the quality of education, a journey whose destiny will be shaped by our responses to a confluence of unstoppable forces – the seven futures of cyberized education.

Part II

What Will Happen:
The Futures of Cyberizing
Education

CHAPTER 5

Six Scenarios for Thinking about the Future of Cyberized Education

The World Is Complex: Coping with Complexity

We live in a time of tumultuous change. Recent books have tried to make sense of this change by simplifying the world into a single defining characteristic: The World Is Flat…Spiky…Open…Curved.[1] These viewpoints offer many useful insights, but if the world can be defined in one simple characteristic, it would have to be – Complex. On the surface, complexity manifests itself in familiar ways: life is faster, busier, multiplicitous, and there are more things to do, be, buy, and know. Cyberization is feeding this "heyday of speed," and the world is still learning how to cope with being on Internet time.[2] In education, this complexity manifests itself through multiplicity, additive and transformative effects, the interplay of old and new fundamental tensions, and the emergence of a complex systems paradigm.

Multiplicity Is Complex

American education is complex because it serves a multitude of purposes besides learning. A college degree has become nearly indispensable for future employment prospects, and the traditional undergraduate collegiate experience retains its role as 'rite of passage' for millions of young adults. Higher education also provides numerous other important societal functions such as research, knowledge generation, entertainment, economic mainstay, business partner, human resource developer, global outreach agent, and social change agent. K-12 education remains society's chief mechanism for socializing its young, even though this role is now shared with popular culture (television et al.), economic participation (the mall), and now the Internet. The custodial function is arguably K-12 education's most essential one, as the rise in dual-income families has made the U.S. economy and workplace utterly dependent on these custodial services.[3] K-12 education also performs many of same functions as higher education such as entertainment, employment, and economic force, and it also performs a number of others such as recreational activities, health and social services provision, and community education.

American educational institutions are also complex because of their diversity. The American higher education system is renowned for its diversity of institutional types and distinctions among institutions of the same type. The source of diversity in K-12 education is local control; thousands of school districts do things in slightly but importantly different ways, as anyone who has tried to work with large numbers of school districts knows well.

Complexity is Additive and Transformative

The foundational shifts in knowledge, access, and authority have had additive, transformative, and transitional effects which increase complexity. New Smart may supersede Old Smart, but it will not entirely replace it anytime soon. Knowledge will still reside in academia, libraries, and people's minds; some bodies of knowledge will remain knowable, relatively stable, and deliverable in courses and programs. Academic disciplines will endure for the foreseeable future as the essential structure from which interdisciplinary studies are created. At the same time, New Smart is different and adds a new layer of complexity to what previously existed. New Smart is also transformative: multimedia-based knowledge is fundamentally different from text-based knowledge, collaboratively negotiated knowledge is different from expert-authenticated knowledge, and so on. Negotiating the transitions between the two paradigms, for instance synthesizing expert-authenticated and collaboratively negotiated approaches to knowledge creation,[4] is a lot more complex than simply following an Old Smart knowledge paradigm. The same holds true with access and authority. Figuring out how to provide meaningful educational access to the students who are hardest to reach is a lot more complex than providing it to students who already access education successfully. Learning how to negotiate, self-initiate, and share authority is more complicated than imposing it. Transitional states, transformed realities, and new layers are all shifts which increase complexity.

Complexity and the Perennial Tensions

The foundational shifts affecting education are not aligned forces moving in a single direction toward a unified outcome. Instead, they intensify perennial tensions and create new ones: authority vs. freedom, equality vs. diversity, inclusiveness vs. exclusiveness, stasis vs. change, 'business as ally' vs. 'business as threat,' proprietary vs. open knowledge, educational vs. external certification. The interplay within and between these tensions produces complex results. The cyberization of education aggravates these tensions by introducing a host of new, disruptive possibilities which will improve or simply change education depending on how they are realized.

Complex Systems: a New Paradigm

Emerging ways of thinking about complexity itself also offer a new paradigm for thinking about education. Complex systems theory describes the behavior of various real-life phenomena as complex systems which have the following basic characteristics:[5]

- They consist of large numbers of individual interacting components (agents, objects).

- They exist within an open system, i.e., they are affected by their environment.

- They can learn and evolve, i.e., they adapt their behavior through memory and feedback.

- There is a mix of orderly and disorderly behavior.

- They are self-organizing, i.e., they run on simple rules which lack central control or leadership.

- They produce emergent behavior which is hard to predict, often surprising, sometimes extreme.

- Non-trivial, self-organized, and unpredictable behavior makes them seem alive in some way.

Complex systems theory is itself (surprise) complex, and educators are just beginning to scratch the surface of its implications for transforming education. However, even a rudimentary consideration of its basic principles quickly leads to a very different conception of education relative to the prevailing scientific-rationalist paradigm which animates much of current educational practice. For instance, educational institutions tend to operate as relatively closed systems which shut out the "real world" environment, particularly at the K-12 level. Educational institutions learn and evolve fitfully at best, are distinctly not self-organizing, and generally strive toward maintaining orderly behavior and attaining predictable, consistent, verifiable, and repeatable outcomes. However, the basic principles of complex systems offer a much more useful paradigm in many ways for coping with the foundational shifts in education, which are characterized by many of the same principles: open systems affected by their environment, ability to learn and evolve, unpredictable and often surprising behavior.

Complexity and the Cyberization of Education

The human pursuit of new technologies is driven in large part by a desire to make life simpler, and it succeeds to some extent: push a button, tap a pedal, flip a switch, and once difficult feats become a lot easier. At the same time, new technologies are notorious for increasing complexity by expanding our capabilities and creating unanticipated consequences: the "paperless office" which uses more paper than ever, the labor-saving device which requires more labor to maintain, and so on. Cyberization has had the same effect on education. For instance, online technologies make it much easier to submit college applications; as a result, more students submit more application forms than ever, making the process more complicated overall.[6] The process of selecting social networking and other Web 2.0 tools is also more complicated since it is now far more discretionary (to Twitter or not to Twitter? Second Life or just stick with your first life?) because there are simply too many tools available to master them all.

The resulting complexity engenders a lot of conflict and confusion in education. For example, granting in-school access to social networking tools creates new issues which often defy simple responses because any changes have to account for multiple ancillary effects, even if one of those effects is improved learning. Ban college students from using mobile phones and laptops during class, or set clear expectations about acceptable use as learning resources? Block in-school access to social networking sites, or allow students to bypass the firewall? Fire a teacher for unflattering comments or photos on Facebook, or treat this behavior as an off-limits part of their private lives? Does social networking diminish or enhance the importance of school as a social venue? In other words, in-school access to social networking tools is more than a learning issue; it is also a resource, classroom management, information technology, school policy, custodial, and socialization issue. Who's going to be responsible for making sure that the school has enough bandwidth? What liability does the school have if a student is assaulted by an online bully while in school, or at home while accessing school-provided online resources for a required homework assignment? How do teachers deal with how social networking tools blur the line between studying and socializing? Such issues are resolvable, but they are numerous and definitely not simple. The element of complexity in education is an emerging foundational shift which also helps inform us about how to think about the future of cyberized education.

Thinking about the Future of Cyberized Education

Humans have experienced tumultuous change before, during the dawn of the Industrial Revolution, during World Wars, and numerous other times. With tumultuous change comes a high level of uncertainty. A guide for thinking about the future published by the Institute for Alternative Futures (IAF) notes that one response to high uncertainty is to conclude that thinking about the future is pointless or unnecessary, but another response is to see uncertainty as opportunity.[7] In times of great change when past experience is an unreliable guide to the future, thinking about the future increases the likelihood of long-term success.

Thinking about the future of cyberized education is not the same as trying to predict it. Forecasts are typically misconstrued as needing to be accurate (predict the future clearly and precisely), singular (predict one future out of many possible ones), and accountable (at some future date for the veracity of one's predictions). As a result, futurists tend to agree that the future cannot be predicted. As IAF notes, the word 'futures' in futures studies is plural because many different alternative futures are possible; the future is neither preordained nor singular.

The IAF guide outlines a specific two-part process for thinking about the future. The first part consists of two main steps for focusing on likely alternative futures: trend monitoring and scenario building. Trend monitoring involves detecting patterns in how important phenomena change over time. Uncertain trends require closer monitoring; trends become issues when they receive increased attention in the mass media and become the subject of action. The trend monitoring process includes scanning information sources to identify emerging developments, identifying and forecasting which trends and developments are likely to be key forces in shaping the future, and considering "wildcard" (low probability, high impact) events. These key forces, developments, and possible wildcards are then used to build scenarios, which are descriptions or stories designed to provide consistent frames about plausible alternative futures. Scenario building enables a systematic exploration of future challenges and opportunities which help its participants develop strategy by provoking imaginations, raising fundamental questions, surfacing tacit values, and expanding world views. Scenarios are not attempts to make precise predictions of the future or linear extrapolations from the present, but they encourage people to think about how to deal with different future circumstances by exposing possibilities which otherwise might have remained hidden. For instance, one common scenario planning technique is to imagine oneself at some point in the future (typically 5-20 years) and think about what that future might look like.[8] Scenario planning helps with looking at the big picture before looking at a smaller part of the picture such as the cyberization of education.

The other main part of this process is to imagine a preferred future, which consists of four elements: vision, mission, goals, and strategies. A vision is a coherent, actionable expression of a desired future which motivates people and aligns their efforts. A mission statement structures efforts to achieve the vision by defining the types of related activities to be undertaken. Goals establish success criteria and metrics aligned with vision and mission. Strategies are specific sets of actions which enable goal attainment, mission fulfillment, and vision realization.

This approach has its limitations. For instance, the mainstream media and most thought leaders missed the rise in online education because they were looking in the wrong places, which illustrates the drawbacks of using mass media to monitor trends instead of relying on information closer to the source. Some observers of online education had a preferred future in mind which precluded them from seeing what actually happened. Taken together, however, this two-pronged approach is far more productive, and freeing, than trying to prognosticate a singular future with accuracy. Thinking about the future, and scenario planning in particular, also becomes an opportunity to imagine and express what you'd like the future to look like.[9] Popular wisdom states that the best way to forecast the future is to create it, so scenario planning is also part of the process of doing what you can to create the future, or at least influence it.[10]

Scenario Planning Related to Cyberized Education

Scenario planning activities have frequently been used to think about the future of education.[11] In one large scale scenario planning exercise conducted in 2003-2004, a worldwide panel of thought leaders sought to create "challenging but plausible scenarios" related to the future of eLearning.[12] The discussions identified two critical uncertainties: whether related sources of power, influence, and new ideas are established or emergent, and whether technology's role in society empowers or frustrates. The four resulting possibilities formed a matrix which was named the Edinburgh Scenarios (Table 5-1).[13]

Virtually Vanilla: *Established power, empowering technology* => enhanced access to information and new learning opportunities. Centralized power means access and use is mostly governed by large corporations, governments and global universities.	**Web of Confidence: *Emergent power, empowering technology*** => an increasingly connected world where powerful technology advances enable individuals to learn together in new ways. Power shifts away from large organisations; new ideas come from elsewhere.
Back to the future: *Established power, frustrating technology* => a loss of trust in the integrity of on-line learning, return to "traditional" values, teaching and learning methods, seeking low-risk predictability in a turbulent world.	**U Choose: *Emergent power, frustrating technology*** => people find new ways to challenge authority, gain greater influence over learning, moving focus of attention away from big institutions and towards issues of local importance.

Table 5-1: **The Edinburgh Scenarios**

In 2001, the European-based Organization for Economic Co-Operation and Development (OECD) described six scenarios which were designed to enable thinking about probable and desired choices for schooling in society. Each scenario is described in terms of its effect on four main areas (learning and organization; management and governance; resources and infrastructure; teachers), and complex mixes of these possible futures are expected to emerge.[14] The OECD scenarios for the future of schooling are as follows:

1. ATTEMPTING TO MAINTAIN THE STATUS QUO:
    Scenario 1a: "Bureaucratic School Systems Continue"
    Scenario 1b: "Teacher Exodus - The 'Meltdown Scenario'"

2.   RE-SCHOOLING:
     Scenario 2a: "Schools as Core Social Centres"
     Scenario 2b: "Schools as Focused Learning Organisations"
3.   DE-SCHOOLING:
     Scenario 3a: "Learning Networks & the Network Society"
     Scenario 3b: "Extending the Market Model"

The Edinburgh Scenarios are a useful framework for considering some important issues related to the future of cyberized education, including the transfer of authority and the impact of technology. The OECD scenarios are good for thinking about the possible relative importance of formal education overall in the future. However, the Edinburgh Scenarios omit some of the other important trends to consider when thinking about the future of cyberized education, and the OECD scenarios are not focused specifically on the cyberization of education.

Six Scenarios for the Future of Cyberized Education

The next three chapters describe a new set of future scenarios focused on education (Table 5-2). Each scenario reflects a viewpoint whose advocates will determine cyberized education's future. Collectively, these scenarios are designed to be used as a tool for focusing on how to use cyberization to improve education. Most of these individual scenarios would be a disaster if they were fully realized, but the influences of each scenario can improve education.

Scenario	Description
Free Market Rules	Formal education as we know it dissolves via market forces
Free Learning Rules	Formal education as we know it dissolves via anarchic forces
Standards Rule	Formal education becomes driven by imposed standards
Cyberdystopia	Digital technologies degrade the humanity of education
Steady As She Goes	Incremental improvement; little changes
Education Improves	Digital technologies improve the educational experience

Table 5-2: **Six Scenarios for the Future of Cyberized Education**

Which scenarios will have the strongest effect on the future depends on how we deal with each of them, which requires a deeper understanding of each scenario.

CHAPTER 6

To Market, To Market?
The Driven Scenarios

Free Market Rules: Business, Efficiency Win

"Thirty years from now the big university campuses will be relics. Universities won't survive. It's as large a change as when we first got the printed book…Already we are beginning to deliver more lectures and classes off campus via satellite or two-way video at a fraction of the cost. The college won't survive as a residential institution. Today's buildings are hopelessly unsuited and totally unneeded."

– Peter Drucker, "Seeing things as they really are," Forbes, March 10, 1997.[1]

Colleges are caught in the same kind of debt-fueled price spiral that just blew up the real estate market. They're also in the information business in a time when technology is driving down the cost of selling information to record, destabilizing lows. In combination, these two trends threaten to shake the foundation of the modern university, in much the same way that other seemingly impregnable institutions have been torn apart….this transformation is…coming, and sooner than you think.

– Kevin Carey, "College for $99 a Month," Washington Monthly, September/October 2009[2]

Education is very much like, I've always thought, just like the real estate business…in education, [what matters] is: quality of teacher, quality of teacher, quality of teacher…[so to] double the class size with a better teacher is a good deal for the students.

– Mayor Michael Bloomberg, "Bloomberg: If I Had It My Way I'd Dump Half of NYC's Teachers," CBS New York, December 1, 2011.[3]

The Free Market Rules scenario can be summarized as "business wins; efficiency works." In this scenario, formal education is destined to dissolve under the pressure of market forces. U.S. colleges and universities are on the brink of demise, while primary and secondary education is poised to undergo a radical transformation driven by the twin forces of business and efficiency.

Many entrepreneurs, business-oriented policy makers, and thought leaders are Free Market Rules advocates who love the prospect of cyberized education. In fact, it can't arrive fast enough for them. They believe that the market is the main force of change for education. In their view, transmitting information is education's main commodity and its raison d'être. Higher education is currently riddled by high labor costs, redundant offerings, excessive overhead, and other inefficiencies. Fortunately, the Internet has made the cost of delivering education so cheap that institutions will have to change drastically or see other providers beat them in the marketplace. In the extreme version of this scenario, the drive to cut costs will come to rule higher education policy. The application of market principles will overwhelm the remaining structural barriers which maintain the current market-unfriendly system. Online education will drive out some of the systemic redundancies, resulting in the "structural disintegration" of higher education.[4]

The Free Market Rules scenario has made considerable inroads in U.S. K-12 education in recent decades. The guiding assumption is that the application of market principles to education would spur innovation, eliminate inefficiencies, and offer freedom from onerous government regulation, resulting in a radical transformation of K-12 education.[5] For instance, the 2009 book *Disrupting Class* attempts to apply co-author Clayton B. Christensen's theory of disruptive innovation, which is highly regarded in the business world, to K-12 education. In this case, computer-based online learning is the disruptive innovation that "will change the way the world learns," as the book's subtitle proclaims. The book argues that this will happen because computer-based online learning is a "student-centric technology" which will customize learning and produce more reliably standardized outcomes while circumventing existing roadblocks in the system, resulting in broader and more reliable quality. The predicted transformation will be breathtakingly fast and thorough: half of all high school courses in U.S. K-12 public education will be online by 2019, and 80 percent by 2024.[6] While *Disrupting Class*'s predictions may have been wildly optimistic, the Free Market Rules scenario has firmly established itself in U.S. K-12 education, unfortunately with increasingly perilous consequences.

The Dangers of the Free Market Rules Scenario

For Free Market Rules advocates, education is essentially just another market-driven business whose operation would be improved by the application of market principles. As noted in Chapter 3, education is a very important business, but it also much more than that. Applying a business model to education dangerously oversimplifies it, resulting in proposed "solutions" that are unrealistic, naive, and would be disastrous if implemented.

Free Market Rules advocates tend to oversimplify the societal roles of education. Business-oriented solutions tend to focus on learning as the core function of education, particularly at the K-12 level. More specifically, the focus is usually on learning as preparation for employment such as basic skills, job training, and functional skills related to job readiness. For example, Microsoft's "Future of Work" scenario-planning process conducted in 2006 explored "education through the lens of work" with a focus on how education might "contribute to the sustainability of global economies."[7] The resulting scenarios examined "educators, learners, and administrators in the context of creating, synthesizing, absorbing, sharing, and managing information." In the process, the other important and often competing societal purposes of education tend to get short shrift, as if doubling class sizes or other business and efficiency-oriented solutions could be implemented without considering any possible effect on other critical functions such as custodial care or provision of social services.[8]

Free Market Rules advocates also tend to oversimplify the teaching and learning process by equating it with content delivery or information transmission. Their mantra seems to be, "If you transmit it, they will learn," and since the Internet enables cheaper transmission of content, this should reduce the cost of teaching and learning to near zero. The corporate training world has long equated instruction with content delivery. The role of in-person "instructors" is typically limited to content delivery by standup trainers, and computer-based instruction is usually designed solely for learner-content interaction. Instructors are commonly seen as an added cost, which often makes sense since their role in corporate training is so limited. This also explains why the perennial mirage of improving educational quality by capturing the lectures of "top quality" professors and transmitting them cheaply en masse attracts many Free Market Rules advocates.[9]

In education, however, the teaching and learning process is a lot more complex than simply transmitting content. Imagine you were building a new home and could reduce the cost of the house's structure to zero. That would reduce building costs, but not nearly as much as you might think – maybe 10 to 20 percent or so. Course content and delivery contribute a similarly small proportion of the total cost of teaching and learning, as teachers fulfill many other essential or desirable roles such as classroom managers, caretakers, and many others.[10] Business-oriented solutions tend to ignore these functions as well; for example, Microsoft's "Future of Work" white paper does not mention these roles, and *Disrupting Class's* proposed solution for transforming K-12 education says nothing about the importance of building citizenship, nurturing understanding of differences among people, and maximizing human potential – "common" and "high" hopes for schools which the book itself identifies.[11]

Free Market Rules advocates also tend to oversimplify the role of students, who are viewed either as customers or as raw materials which can be converted into employable individuals or other useful finished products with the right interventions. In reality, students fulfill multiple roles; higher education's students are "customers" and products but also performers, producers, future benefactors, and tribal members. Even with its greater emphasis on employability preparation, the college experience remains far more than a seller-customer transaction. K-12 students are not customers at all, although they are also products and performers. While business-oriented solutions tend to recognize the power of students as customers, they usually ignore their status as producers or as unique contributors to the learning transaction.

Curiously, some Free Market Rules advocates also oversimplify the free market itself when they assume that student and other stakeholder behavior will be driven primarily by cost. The high cost of higher education is a serious concern, but what drives consumer decision-making for essential, high-ticket items like education is not cost but perceived *value*. Highly competitive colleges charge high tuition and aim for greater selectivity for the same reasons that automobiles in certain market segments and homes in certain neighborhoods cost more: value is determined by a complex interaction of multiple factors, of which cost is only one. "College for $99 a month" will definitely appeal to many prospective customers – and repel others. At the K-12 level, Free Market Rules advocates (along with almost everyone else) routinely ignore the economic value of K-12 education's various other societal functions, most notably the custodial function which enables the productive and purchasing power of dual income families.

If the more extreme Free Market Rules advocates are correct that colleges will be "torn apart"[12] by the Internet and driven out of business by low cost content providers, then the resulting dissolution of current institutions would not be good for formal education or for society, which would have to figure out how to replace many important functions which educational institutions currently fulfill. So it seems highly unlikely that this will happen in higher education. Anyone who believes the notion that cheap online content delivery spells the end of education as we know it might consider chilling out at a tailgate party[13] during college football season. While munching on your hot dog or drinking your beer along with millions of other tailgaters, ask yourself what could suddenly cause all these tailgate parties to disappear in less than 20 years. Low-cost content available on the Internet? A sudden collective urge to stay home and do lawn care instead? Or is it more likely that fulfilling the other valued purposes of higher education will keep universities from becoming "relics?" The same goes for K-12 education: its other vital functions are just too important for a purely business-driven K-12 education system to emerge.

At the same time, the three-decade reign of free market mythology in American society has produced a parallel degradation of public-oriented values. According to former University of Michigan president James J. Duderstadt, higher education is becoming more "revenue-driven" and "market-responsive," and market forces "are rapidly overwhelming public policy and public investment in determining the future course of higher education."[14] The potentially destructive effects of market forces in K-12 education have also prompted serious concern,[15] which reflects an ongoing tension resulting from the interdependence between business and education.

The Tension between 'Business as Ally' and 'Business as Threat'

This tension occurs because education and business are fundamentally different cultures with deeply conflicting value systems. The main purpose of business is relatively simple: profit.[16] Higher education values such as academic freedom, pure research, and intellectual risk-taking,[17] or K-12 education values such as providing a public good, building character, or maximizing human potential,[18] are often incompatible with the profit motive.

So the threat part is not hard to understand. Supported by stakeholders' increased interest in education as preparation for employment, pro-business forces exert considerable pressure on education to be run like businesses and become de facto vocational training grounds at the expense of their other important societal functions. Taxpayers, parents and students complain about the rising cost of education, while policymakers worry about the reduced affordability of higher education and the perceived lack of improvement in K-12 education. Free Market Rules advocates extrapolate from these concerns that market principles will eventually dominate formal education.

At the same time, many emerging "edupreneurs" recognize that the success of their business depends on the continued well-being of formal education as their target market. Business does not have core expertise in all of education's key functions and is not all that interested in developing it. Education and business are key allies that have forged relationships for mutual benefit in numerous ways, ranging from research initiatives to internship programs to low-cost training to athletic sponsorships. The adoption of technology has long been another important entree for these relationships, from computers to student information systems to Integrated Learning Systems. The rapid growth in online education[19] has spawned an emerging industry with products and services that support online education delivery such as course management systems and assessment software; management information, CRM, information technology, and business continuity ICM technologies; and instructional design and course management services.

The tension between 'business as ally' and 'business as threat' is illustrated in the ongoing furor about for-profit colleges and universities, which operate right at the intersection between education and business values. For-profit colleges seek profitability by limiting their offerings and eliminating the 'frills' which make mainstream colleges and universities more expensive, such as dormitories, dining halls, social facilities, athletic programs, research facilities, and study abroad programs. Ironically, many of the largest for-profit colleges are utterly reliant on government money for their profitability and existence. The University of Phoenix derived 88 percent of its revenues from federal government student aid programs during its 2010 fiscal year, while Kaplan Education obtained over 90 percent of its revenues from the same source.[20] However, an August 2010 Nexus Research report argues that for-profit institutions actually "cost the taxpayer nothing" because the amount of tax and interest revenue which the federal government receives from for-profit institutions offsets the amount of student aid funds provided to them, and that they are thus more cost-effective than public institutions.[21] They also claim to have comparable learning outcomes based on comparative test scores and postgraduate average earnings, and that they are more successful than traditional institutions at serving students who are most in need and at risk.[22] Other observers characterize the offerings of for-profit colleges and universities as a "subprime opportunity:"

high-cost degree programs with little prospect of leading to high-paying careers while burdening lower-income students with debt.[23]

Free Market Influences: Invasion or Coevolution?

At times, market forces appear to interact with education as if they were an invasive species requiring vigilant management to ensure that they don't entirely overrun their host environment. At other times, market forces appear to have learned how to coexist and even coevolve with education. The cyberization of education will intensify this interdependency, so the key question becomes how business and education can work together for mutual benefit while respecting each other's very different values and culture. For example, will free market influences help reopen the American dream of affordable college education for all, or will they degrade education by simply profiting from it? The easy answer, of course, is that they will do both; the more difficult answer is to figure out how to use these influences to improve education.

Standards Rule: Consistency Wins

Every state and every school must establish meaningful standards for what students should master in the core subjects…Every 4th grader should be able to read independently; every 8th grader should know algebra…every state should test every student in the 4th and 8th grades to make sure these standards are met…all our students must master the basics.

– National Standards of Academic Excellence, U.S. Department of Education, 1997.[24]

The Standards Rule scenario can be summarized as "consistency wins." Standards Rule advocacy comes in several different varieties: a belief in a core curriculum with "rigorous" standards; assessment of learning through standardized tests; the use of experimental and quasi-experimental design approaches to assess program efficacy; and a belief in the power of widely distributed, high quality content to improve learning. The common element is an emphasis on establishing accountability by imposing standards which apply a uniform measure to students, teachers, and institutions. Excellence is defined as the collective attainment of a single set of standards, and the ultimate aim is to attain consistent results.

Standards Rule advocates also love the prospect of cyberized education because they see technology as a game-changer which will enable consistency. In this view, established practices and entrenched special interests have stymied fundamental reform, and recent educational innovations have also gone too far afield, so there is also a need to return to "basics."[25] At the K-12 level, this is typically characterized by a strong emphasis on standards-based measures such as subject proficiency standards, high-stakes testing, and systemic curriculum revision, along with various market-based reforms such as merit pay for "successful" teachers, data-driven decision making, and greater school choice for parents. The onus of accountability is placed on teachers, principals, schools, and districts. In higher education, it is placed mostly on the institutions themselves and is most commonly manifested through calls for cross-institutional comparisons of effectiveness. Another guiding assumption is that great content embodies high standards, so creating great content and "great courses" is a solution to education's problems.

The Standards Rule scenario has held sway in U.S. K-12 education since the implementation of the No Child Left Behind Act of 2001. NCLB has placed a heavy emphasis on standardized test performance, particularly in math and reading. This has also supported other standards-driven initiatives such as the use of "scripted curriculum," commercially prepared instructional materials which require a teacher to deliver lessons by reading from a script, often word for word.[26] The presumption is that such methods promote greater accountability.

This pressure to demonstrate accountability and articulate higher standards has reached American higher education as well. The best-known initiatives such as the Voluntary System of Accountability (VSA) and Collegiate Learning Assessment (CLA) rely on standardized measures of cross-institutional comparisons to attain this aim. The use of standardized tests is more focused on enabling cross-institutional comparisons than on measuring student performance.

Standards Rule advocates also tend to favor free market "solutions" to "fix" educational "problems," so there is some overlap with the Free Market Rules scenario. However, not all Free Market Rules approaches rely on implementing standards, and not all standards-based approaches rely on the free market for implementation. For instance, the federal government's increased emphasis on using experimental and quasi-experimental assessment approaches in its grant programs funded through the Education and Labor departments is not free-market driven, nor are standards-based initiatives such as the VSA or CLA.

A Foolish Consistency: the Downsides of Standards Rule

In its extreme, the Standards Rule scenario is a social engineering disaster in the making, particularly in K-12 education. Many Standards Rule advocates are perhaps the worst offenders when it comes to oversimplifying education, often with destructive results. The "value-added" analysis (also known as "value-added assessment") methodology used to assess Los Angeles Unified School District teachers illustrates this oversimplification in action:

> "Value-added" analysis is a statistical method that estimates the effectiveness of a teacher or school by looking at the standardized test scores…in this instance, math and English scores on the California Standards Tests. Past scores are used to project each student's future performance. The difference between the child's actual and projected results is the estimated "value" that the teacher or school added (or subtracted) during the year.[27]

Despite numerous studies which warned against the failings of this approach,[28] the LAUSD methodology reduces the measurement of teacher quality (at least in terms of public perception) not just to their students' standardized reading and math test scores, but essentially to a single *equation* based on those scores.[29] Even though "value-added" assessment is only a portion of a teacher's total evaluation,[30] the *Los Angeles Times* decided to publish a list of the "Top 100 value-added teachers" based largely on the results of that single equation.[31] From there, it's an inevitable short step to making thoughtless judgments about the quality of teachers based on these rankings.[32] Other voices have taken a more sensible view, such as education historian Diane Ravitch's reminder that "our schools will not improve if we value only what tests measure…not everything that matters can be quantified."[33] One of LAUSD's "top 100" teachers was less than impressed with the value-added assessment process, noting that

> …[even highly educated people] are often led astray by 'statistics' [which] do not include the human element. The Times has managed to demoralize outstanding teachers by branding them…Children are not statistics. Children are our living, breathing future…Think about some of our great men and women in history…Their teachers probably would not have passed the value-added test, but they inspired these people and encouraged them to move forward on their ideas.…[34]

Unfortunately, the voices of Standards Rule advocates are much louder, and so the "test scores = teacher quality" meme continues to wreak havoc on the K-12 public education system.[35]

Using a narrow definition of "evidence-based practices" in educational research is another standards-driven approach of highly dubious value. For example, the 2009 U.S. Department of Education study *Evaluation of Evidence-Based Practices in Online Learning* enhanced the perception of online learning as a viable delivery mode, but it was not very useful from a research perspective. By focusing primarily on comparison of delivery modes and including only "rigorous" studies which used "experimental or quasi-experimental design and objectively measured student learning outcomes,"[36] the study excluded most of the really good research in the field. The more savvy researchers in online education moved beyond sterile comparisons of delivery modes[37] a long time ago; instead, they use a broader definition of evidence and focus on more productive issues such as learning effectiveness, which has produced a substantial body of research that is far more useful to practitioners in the field, as described in Chapter 4.

Missing the boat on redefined knowledge

Many standards-driven initiatives also fail to account for how the nature of knowledge is changing. Initiatives such as No Child Left Behind are based on the notion that a certain and fairly large body of content needs to be installed in every student and demonstrated through a particular type of high-stakes performance (standardized tests). As Chapter 2 described, the notion of a unified core curriculum which manifests core knowledge is highly problematic: consensus on core knowledge is unattainable in an age of exploding knowledge production. The use of siloed knowledge to determine content standards, as if each student will become a professional in that field, aggravates the problem. The collective result is a huge conglomeration of uncoordinated content and skills which is impossible for most students to master in the time available.[38] High-stakes standardized tests designed to document student mastery of various subsets of siloed content tend to lead students to find right answers; they ignore assessment of skills such as creativity, curiosity, synthesis, or making new connections. Reliance on content generated from siloed knowledge also discourages classroom teaching designed to elicit deeper understandings and performances.[39] As a result, standards-driven approaches based on siloed knowledge and simplistic assessment encourage instruction which is inadequate for preparing today's children for the world they will experience and the skills they will need as adults.[40]

Content-driven initiatives that equate great content with great education also fail to accommodate the changing nature of knowledge. For example, the notion that at least "one great course"[41] can effectively replace many existing mediocre courses ignores the fact that content and delivery are only two of many possible elements in making a course great, not least of which are the participants themselves. Extreme content-driven approaches assume that absorption of great content alone is enough, which overlooks the collaborative, user-produced, networked, and contextual nature of redefined knowledge.

More access or less? A false equity

With its emphasis on applying standards more consistently, rigorously, and accountably, the Standards Rule scenario appears to focus on increasing educational access by expanding educational success. Unfortunately, some standards-driven initiatives are having the opposite effect of reducing access in K-12 education. Implementation of NCLB has narrowed the curriculum by reducing time spent on non-tested subjects such as science, social studies, music, and art, while damaging teacher morale in the process.[42] The reduction of curriculum to test preparation falls disproportionately on students in minority and low-income schools, thus having the perverse effect of reducing access and increasing inequity.[43] The impending implementation of the Common Core Standards has raised concerns that it will degrade the curriculum even more.[44] The degradation doesn't happen with the standards themselves, which in most cases are seemingly more rigorous than the ones they replaced. It happens through what the standards leave out: all the other important activities and processes which are difficult to quantify but where students really learn and value is added, such as science, art, music, recess, physical education – not to mention love of learning, the value of discovery, or the appreciation of a poem for its beauty rather than as an opportunity to demonstrate explication or word derivation skills. Likewise, common core standards are likely to encourage a national standardized test; alternative forms of assessment will frequently be abandoned due to time and resource constraints. The resulting drive toward educational monoculture will jeopardize or extinguish other effective varieties of learning and assessment.

Standards Rule = imposed authority

In their extreme, standards-driven approaches impose authority on students, teachers, and institutions. Standardized tests, value-added assessment, experimental research designs, core curricula, and content-driven initiatives all treat students as if they were inert inputs, merely needing treatment from "effective" teachers to produce the desired standardized performance outputs on cue. Responsibility for improving results is not directly placed on students at any level. At the K-12 level, scripted curriculum and other increasingly standardized instructional inputs treat teachers as technicians or as system components to be 'idiot-proofed.' For young students, core standards overemphasize cognitive skills despite emerging research which shows that cognitive development is inseparable from physical, social, and emotional development.[45] Assessment of skills mastery requires extensive, time-consuming testing which increases stress and may impede rather than promote learning. One Milwaukee teacher reported having to give over 150 assessments during the 2008-09 school year – to her *kindergarten* students.[46]

Collectively, such efforts are more about sorting and indoctrination than about improving learning. Despite the constant assertions that comparison of international test scores show how American children are falling behind the rest of the world and that our economic competitiveness hangs in the balance, no one has demonstrated how these standards or test results directly relate to success in the workplace. The fact that America led the world economically without having such national standards in place is conveniently forgotten. Even though the credibility of international test scores is highly questionable,[47] the results of these and other standardized tests are routinely misused to make misleading assertions about the quality of American education. The defects in the underlying assumptions behind these assertions are blithely ignored, even though the same assumptions can be used to reach similarly defective conclusions: that I am a better basketball player than Michael Jordan,[48] for example. Imagine if every American adult's job depended on demonstrating content mastery by passing a high school or college level standardized test – tomorrow. Now *that* would be an economic catastrophe. Fortunately, most Americans seem to be able to do their work quite well enough without being able to pass a typical standardized assessment on demand.

The problem is not with standards, testing, educational research, or great content per se, but with how they are being misused in this giant, unprecedented experiment in progress. How has the pursuit of standards produced such distorted and grotesque results? Part of the reason can be explained by the two perennial tensions which animate the Standards Rule scenario: authority vs. freedom, and equality vs. diversity.

The Tension between Authority and Freedom

The shift in authority from an imposed agency to a shared, self-initiated and negotiated one is a microcosm of one of the most important long-term revolutions in American and world culture: the transition away from authoritarianism. Americans are accustomed to taking their individual freedoms for granted, so it is worth remembering that this condition is still relatively new in human history. Several hundred years ago, the concept of individual freedom did not exist for most humans; instead, a person's role was defined by religious or cultural orthodoxies within authoritarian societies. Erich Fromm's classic 1941 book *Escape From Freedom* describes the trajectory of this transition in Western society from its origins in the Protestant Reformation, noting that "modern European and American history is centered around the effort to gain freedom from the political, economic, and spiritual shackles that have bound [people]."[49] Fromm describes how the process of individuation – the creation of identity by individuals rather than by cultural tradition and authority – has been a centuries' long, challenging process. Humans' "longing for freedom"[50] found expression in the social structures and principles which were developed in the past few hundred years: economic liberalism, political democracy, religious autonomy, scientific rationalism, the very concept of a personal life. The process of gaining independence through individuation came at a price: isolation from a social structure which bound but which also gave ready-made meaning.[51] The responsibility of making one's own meaning drives some individuals to flee from this burden and seek solace by re-creating societal sources of certainty such as fundamentalism and totalitarianism. The result is an abiding tension between authority and freedom as both an individual and a societal conflict.[52]

The Authoritarian Strain in Education and Its Consequences

Our schools teach you by pushing you around, by stealing your will and your sense of power, by making timid square apathetic slaves out of you – authority addicts.

– Jerry Farber, The Student and Society: An Annotated Manifesto, 1969.[53]

In the earliest public schools, teachers taught, and students listened. Teachers commanded, and students obeyed. Teachers did not rely solely on the power of ideas to persuade; they relied on discipline to maintain order….to meet their educational objectives, schools required absolute obedience…

– Justice Clarence Thomas, Morse vs. Frederick (Concurring Opinion), 2007.[54]

The evolution of American education reflects the struggle between authority and freedom. The American system is considerably less regimented than most of its counterparts throughout the world, but it is hardly a model of freedom. Justice Thomas's opinion crystallizes the authoritarian strain in education quite succinctly: teachers taught and commanded; students listened and obeyed; schools demanded authoritarian control.[55] The factory model of education extended the authoritarian approach through design which reflected a desire to socialize the poor inexpensively through mass schooling.[56] Many traditional elements of education such as rows of desks, age-segregated classes, and undifferentiated whole-class instruction impede learning but persist because they continue to be convenient, inexpensive, or functional means of control.

The authoritarian strain in K-12 education has lessened somewhat in recent years, but it remains alive and well. For instance, corporal punishment in schools remains legal in 20 U.S. states,[57] scripted curriculum increases both student and teacher dependency, and Justice Thomas's opinion in *Morse v. Frederick* invokes the historical precedent of authoritarian education to justify the restriction of student speech in schools. In higher education, the students are more mature, the custodial function is largely absent, developing independence is a higher priority, and authority is based more on knowledge and intellect. Nonetheless, the authoritarian strain is still present and often produces dependent students, "authority addicts" who rely on school authorities to tell them their role. This dependency manifests itself in the remarkable persistence of lecture transcription. Instructor anecdotes abound concerning how many students seem incapable of thinking or how many of them express actual resentment at being asked to think about problems instead of depending on having the right answers supplied to them.

However, the tension between authority and freedom is also about managing their competing demands. Many educational purposes, most notably its custodial function, demand a certain degree of authority and control. Classroom management has little to do with teaching and learning per se, but it is an essential skill for fulfilling the custodial function of schooling and for creating an environment where students have the chance to learn. The term "classroom management" encompasses a huge variety of approaches from the highly open to the highly regimented, reflecting the abiding tension between authority and freedom.

The Tension between Equality and Diversity

Standards-driven initiatives also aggravate the tension between equality and diversity, mainly because our society hasn't yet figured out how to handle the issue of egalitarianism. For instance, standardized tests are commonly justified because they express results in standard forms which allow for "fair" comparison.[58] There is significant value in having standards which are outside the vagaries of local curricula, personality conflicts, variable instructional quality, and many other subjective factors.

Unfortunately, the notion of a singular set of standards which define universal academic success is an unattainable illusion. As educator Alfie Kohn has argued, getting a great education is different from getting the *same* education as everyone else.[59] Uniformity enforced by common standards creates illusions of both excellence and equity. Making everyone learn the same things is a reliable recipe for inequity, as it creates needless and often insurmountable obstacles which prevent learners from discovering their own unique paths to success. Trying to reduce variation by imposing a standardized regime of core common standards on everyone will only reduce learning, skill diversity, curiosity, and many other attributes which make education valuable.

There are basically two ways to achieve egalitarianism. The easy but bad way is to provide a common standard which cuts everyone down to size. The hard but good way is to try to achieve equity through diversity by providing multiple paths to success.

Standards Influence: a More Sensible Consistency

The cyberization of education can help with using standards to exert a positive influence. In higher education, it is well-accepted that different colleges and universities produce differing types of excellent outcomes. Supporting customized outcomes increases access by allowing for multiple paths to success. In principle, a set of "lean" standards[60] can be used to customize learning within a broad framework of commonly agreed-upon outcomes using a variety of assessments which ensure sufficient accountability. Standards can also encompass a broader range of evidence-based practices, help with integrating great content into great learning experiences, and support self-initiated and negotiated authority, as Chapters 10 and 11 will discuss.

CHAPTER 7

Dream or Nightmare?
The Dramatic Scenarios

Free Learning Rules: Openness Wins

"Your institution[s] will be irrelevant by 2020."

– David Wiley, quoted in The Deseret News, April 20, 2009.[1]

The Free Learning Rules scenario can be summarized as "openness wins," and the extreme form of this scenario also envisions the dissolution of formal education. Its advocates believe passionately in the vast potential of digital resources to revolutionize learning and education. Many of them believe that openness is itself the key quality which will lead to radical transformation; for instance, Brigham Young University professor David Wiley has described openness as the "cornerstone" which "underpins everything interesting happening online."[2]

In this context, openness has two important dimensions: open content and open interaction. Open content, most commonly referred to as open education resources (or OERs), means many different things to different people. For example:

- Creating free or low-cost content as an antidote to the spiraling (and to some, out of control) costs of textbooks and other commercial education resources.

- Offering access to educational opportunities for aspiring students in poor countries by making courses and other learning resources more available.

- Providing convenient and flexible access to online video lectures by distinguished professors at prestigious universities such as MIT, Harvard, and Yale.

- Improving instruction by building courses which use various tools and techniques which foster improved learning, as is the focus of Carnegie Mellon's Open Learning Initiative.[3]

The term "open educational resources" was first adopted at a 2002 UNESCO Forum on the impact of open courseware.[4] OERs can include learning content such as courses, course materials, content modules, and learning objects; tools such as software which supports open learning content, open learning management systems, open content development tools, and online learning communities; and implementation resources such as intellectual property licenses which promote open publishing. Inspired by the UNESCO Forum, the 2007 Cape Town Open Education Declaration described OERs as "openly licensed course materials, lesson plans, textbooks, games, software and other materials that support teaching and learning" which are "licensed to facilitate use, revision, translation, improvement and sharing by anyone."[5] The OER Commons web site describes its content as having the similar purpose of enabling teachers and learners to share what they know.[6]

Sharing open content is also one form of open interaction. Indiana University professor Curt Bonk believes that this "sudden trend toward sharing educational resources" is a potent new force for educational change.[7] At the higher education level, long-established web sites such as MERLOT (Multimedia Educational Resource for Learning and Online Teaching) have thousands of educational resources available for faculty to use,[8] while many other web sites such as the OER Commons offer resources at both the K-12 and higher education levels. Another form of sharing is learner participation in open information communities, which is one of Bonk's ten "openers for learning."[9] Learner participation can take many forms, such as discussing topics of interest on global message boards such as Chinswing, sharing homemade videos on YouTube, or compiling and sharing world news using tools such as Current TV. Sharing, learning participation, and other forms of open interaction are supported by a huge variety of social media tools, as Overdrive Interactive's Social Media Map for Social Media Marketing so graphically illustrates.[10]

Various initiatives are attempting to create "free" education by using open content and open interaction. In early 2009, the University of the People (UotP) was launched as a nonprofit venture with the goal of revolutionizing higher education by providing universal access to college studies worldwide, even to the poorest students. UotP's web site states that its students learn through a combination of peer-to-peer teaching and instructor support. Students are divided into classes of 15-20 students and all participate in the same online course, and they use online study communities to discuss weekly topics and share resources, supported by "respected scholars" who participate in class discussions and oversee student assessment.[11] UotP's intent to reach millions of students eventually.[12]

Another model based on peer learning and free sharing of resources is Peer2Peer University (P2PU), which aims for a different target audience: learners and facilitators who want to participate in open, online study groups for short-term, university-level courses. P2PU helps participants find available open education materials, create small learner groups, and design and facilitate courses. As P2PU advisor Steve Carson puts it, "Making educational content open is just the first step in making educational opportunity more widely available. P2PU takes the next leap, making interactive communities freely available to anyone with the motivation to learn."[13]

As with the Free Market Rules scenario, there are two strains to the Free Learning Rules scenario. One strain focuses on coexistence; for instance, P2PU "creates a model for lifelong learning alongside traditional formal higher education."[14] The more extreme strain is more intent on dissolving formal education as we know it.[15] For example, David Wiley sees open content as the first step in a process which "transforms everything we know about higher education,"[16] while Curt Bonk noted that "perhaps society is finally being deschooled as Ivan Illich wished decades earlier."[17] One key element of this vision is the notion that practically everyone will become a teacher, so they will be numerous and available for anyone at any time.[18]

The Downsides of the Free Learning Rules Scenario

It may seem insensitive or worse to find fault with the notion of free learning. How could anyone criticize such a noble cause as University of the People's goal of providing tuition-free universal access to education? What could possibly be wrong with a world where "anyone can now learn anything from anyone at anytime"?[19] Speaking specifically about OERs, George Siemens described this viewpoint as a "cute kitten syndrome" which periodically afflicts educators: an idea or concept evokes "perceived universal favor" which seems inhuman to oppose.[20] Unfortunately, free learning is not entirely cute, cuddly, and beyond reproach, as there are several downsides to this scenario.

No free lunch: In theory, anyone can use OERs freely and openly and can also remix, improve and redistribute them under some licenses. In practice, free learning is not as free as it appears to be. In many instances such as the Open Learning Initiative, courseware is free to use for informal learning but not for formal education. Some web sites require paid memberships, subscriptions or other fees to access content.

OERs are also not as easy to use "off the shelf" as they may appear. In U.S. K-12 education, for example, an OER typically requires modifications to meet a particular state's set of standards or even a local school system's specific curriculum. In higher education, college faculty are often reluctant to use learning resources which they didn't create or at least personalize. Most OERs are currently written in only one language (English),[21] and many OERs include other cultural barriers such as difficult-to-translate idioms, references to country or region-specific historical events or cultural figures, and embedded pedagogical approaches that may cause culture clash, although some observers feel that these obstacles can be readily overcome.[22] Many OERs also require additional components before they can be used such as related lessons, assignments, or assessments, and some OERs work only on a particular LMS platform[23] or operating system (for example, Windows but not Mac). Open source LMSs such as Moodle or Sakai offer low startup costs, but total operational costs are often comparable to commercial LMSs, and at times are even higher.[24]

As a result, "free" learning resources and tools often require their users to invest a certain amount of sweat equity to find, learn, and use them. Using "free" learning resources also often means incurring a number of hidden and not-so-hidden costs. For example, use of the "free" social networking tool Facebook raises concerns about loss of privacy and grants content ownership rights to a company which seeks its long-term business survival by vigorously exploring options to monetize that content. The summer 2010 conversion of the Ning social networking platform from a free to a pay-only use forced members to choose between exerting extra effort to try to preserve their content or abandoning their sites and losing that content.[25]

Education ≠ learning: Most so-called open education resources are really open *content* resources. Carnegie Mellon's highly touted Open Learning Initiative (OLI) illustrates the distinction. OLI Open & Free Courses include self-guiding materials and activities which independent learners can use, but students who want the additional services which enable an educational experience, such as access to an instructor, graded exams, tracking of student learning, verification of course completion, and course credit, need to arrange this on their own somehow unless they happen to be enrolled at an institution and can register in an "academic" course where an instructor is using OLI resources.[26] OLI and many other open courseware initiatives maintain this clear distinction between using open courseware for formal education and using them as learning resources, even if they use the same course content for both purposes.

The support for ventures such as the University of the People also reflects this common tendency to conflate learning and education. The limitations of the peer learning model and the lack of creditable accreditation are glaring shortcomings.[27] Peer learning has many benefits as a learning strategy, but it is not a particularly effective education model for learning complex subjects. Although some advocates think that UotP's model represents a "new reality" for education,[28] it is hard to see how UotP will become an accredited institution with its current model.

Free Learning Rules advocates too often oversimplify education by equating it with enabling individual learners to learn what they want. Education is more of a two-way street, because it's also about what society wants its learners to know.

Openness is also relative, so the emphasis on openness poses some problems when taken at face value, since the real-world implications of total openness are unrealistic and even dangerous. Can I really learn how to become a billionaire from Donald Trump at any time? Do we really want knowledge on how to make a dirty bomb or launch an urban chemical attack offered freely and openly for anyone to use? The spirit of openness can also be problematic when it fails to inform us how to deal with real-world implementation issues which cross the boundaries between open and closed. For instance, OLI and similar resources set clear boundaries between the use of content for learning versus educational purposes, so it is arguably misleading to tout them as educational resources when their use for that purpose is so limited.

Uneven quality: Another aspect of the "cute kitten" syndrome is a common tendency to accept the quality of OERs uncritically, particularly when the courseware is produced by prestigious colleges and universities. In reality, evaluating the quality of OERs is a major challenge since quality assurance is complicated, contextual, and in part a perceptual issue.[29] The quality of available resources is variable or unknown in some cases because the vetting process can be resource-intensive. For instance, only a tiny fraction of the resources in the MERLOT collection include published peer reviews, due primarily to the amount of faculty time required.[30]

Free Learning Rules advocates also tend to equate the quality of free resources for learning and their quality for education. For example, consider one of the crown jewels in MIT's OpenCourseWare offerings: physics professor Walter Lewin, extolled in a 2007 *New York Times* article as an "international Internet guru" and one of the most popular professors on iTunesU.[31] Professor Lewin's online video lectures reflect decent production values, varied activities including some audience participation, considerable attention to design and choreography detail, and extraordinary dedication. It would be hard to find a better lecturer than Professor Lewin, and it is easy to see the appeal of his lectures. However, MIT offers something quite different to its own undergraduate physics students. TEAL (Technology-Enabled Active Learning) is a pedagogical approach modeled in part on the "studio physics" model instituted in the mid-1990s by Rensselaer Polytechnic Institute professor Jack Wilson. MIT's description of its Electromagnetism I course (8.02) explains why:

> ...even with an outstandingly effective and charismatic lecturer like Professor Walter Lewin, lecture attendance at the end of the term in MIT introductory courses hovers around 50%...no matter how strongly one feels about the intrinsic worth of the lecture format, it is hard to argue that it is broadly effective when half of the students do not attend the lecture.

Even the best lecture courses are mostly passive learning experiences: listening to the professor, reading blackboard notes, watching demonstrations. As the MIT 8.02 course description notes,

> ...this lack of student engagement is arguably one of the major reasons for the failure rates (typically 15%) in these introductory courses. More importantly, this lack of engagement is the reason many students leave our introductory courses (usually their last courses in physics) feeling that physics is dry and boring.

By contrast, the TEAL method emphasizes teacher-student and student-student interaction, active learning, problem solving, collaborative work, and "hands-on experience with the phenomena under study." The intended result is a course that "engages the students more deeply, so that they come away from these introductory courses with more of an appreciation for the beauty of physics, both conceptually and analytically."[32] MIT's actions speak loudly: they give their paying students a learning experience which reaches beyond the limitations of the lecture approach. While MIT OpenCourseWare materials have their obvious advantages, they are hand-me-downs, and it is hard to get too excited about even high quality hand-me-downs.

Some of the OERs which have been produced are of much poorer quality than MIT's offerings. For example, in the Open Yale video lectures I viewed a few years ago, there were no blackboard notes, so slides, no student faces, no student questions – only an unremitting focus on the lecturer's image and speech. In one video lecture, the lecturer looked up at least six times within the first minute to refer to a blackboard with notes that the viewer doesn't get to see. The implicit message: a lecturer's image and speech are really all that is needed for a learning experience – lecturer as "magical sage."[33] When they were first released in 2007, the Open Yale Courses were characterized as having the potential to "redefine expectations for online learning."[34] In reality, the production values of these courses were several decades behind the state of practice embodied in a typical community college telecourse. MIT's TEAL program has it right: a quality educational experience needs more than a magical sage.

Unimpressive track record and prospects: It appears unlikely at present that free learning initiatives will radically transform education. The more successful ventures such as Western Governors University limit themselves to a narrow range of offerings. The University of the People venture started slowly;[35] despite attracting much favorable attention and forming some promising alliances,[36] UotP's long-term prospects of delivering on its stated aspirations appear doubtful at best. OERs have yet to attain sustainability and critical mass, and even many of their supporters believe that progress has been slow.[37] Ventures such as Virginia Virtual University and United States Open University failed to launch because their target audience of highly self-directed learners is still relatively small and has taken longer to emerge than some anticipated. Academic autodidacts (i.e., students who are capable of acquiring an education on their own) who are likely to use OERs independently are an even rarer species.[38]

Free Learning Influences: The Upsides of Openness

Despite its many drawbacks, the Free Learning Rules scenario can positively influence the cyberization of education in many ways. Open resources can be valuable[39] for many audiences:

- College students who are taking a similar course at other institutions and are seeking additional insight or another perspective on the subject;

- Faculty who seek other ideas or alternative approaches to teaching a comparable course;

- High school students who are studying the related subject;

- Learners who are pursuing a documentable experience to gain formal credit for prior learning;

- Adult learners looking for noncredit enrichment or self-improvement learning experiences.

The main value of open resources for improving education is in *increasing access to learning and education resources to support teaching and learning*. In many cases, OERs provide access to previously inaccessible resources such as lectures by distinguished professors. Digital media also increase access to open interaction by enabling peer-to-peer learning and other forms of learning through collective participation.[40] Using OERs can also *increase student readiness for formal education*, including online education. OERs can provide an opportunity for informal remediation, and using them appears to help some prospective students believe in their ability to pursue an education. Using OERs is a way to practice for the real thing; although getting an education is more than just watching lectures and doing assignments, being able to handle the lectures can provide confidence in one's ability to handle the rest of the collegiate academic experience. As the Open Yale Courses web site notes, well-designed OER lectures go beyond content acquisition and toward cultivating "skills and habits of rigorous, independent thought: the ability to analyze, to ask the next question, and to begin the search for an answer."[41]

Open content also helps *reduce the costs of education* by providing an alternative to textbooks and other commercially produced educational materials which have become a substantial expense, particularly for community college students. For example, Flat World Knowledge, a publisher of free and open college textbooks, projected that it saved 150,000 college students an estimated $12 million in college textbook costs during the 2010-2011 academic year.[42] Another encouraging trend is the federal government's increased emphasis on OERs as exemplified by a joint grant program by the U.S. Departments of Education and Labor that will provide $2 billion over four years to create a library of web-based learning materials which will be made freely accessible for public use.[43] As Creative Commons Director of Global Learning Cable Green commented, "Taxpayer-funded educational resources should be open educational resources…[and] accessible to the public that paid for it – without artificial restrictions and/or limits."[44] Some observers believe that this federal support of OERs will hasten their adoption.[45]

Free Learning influences on foundational shifts in knowledge are less clear. At present, most OERs are not notably more visual or multimedia than other resources, likely because media-rich educational resources are expensive to produce. Open interaction resources are more likely to exhibit New Smart characteristics such as being networked, distributed, sometimes collaboratively negotiated, and occurring in various shapes and sizes. Many free learning initiatives renegotiate authority by shifting it to students and by broadening the concept of who is a teacher. New initiatives such as UofP and P2PU are clearly exploring the use of new relationships which emphasize self-initiated and shared authority. How much actual influence these initiatives will have on improving education, however, remains to be seen.

Free Learning Rules advocates risk becoming irrelevant if they insist on imagining a future where formal education institutions will soon disappear, and an Aquarian dawn of free learning will rise to take their place. At the same time, free learning initiatives clearly get many people excited about the possibilities of using cyberization to improve education. Perhaps the most valuable function of free learning influences is to provide an effective foil for formal education by being a *resource*, *innovation source*, and *recourse* which counterbalances formal education's tendencies toward inertia and helps support its improvement.

Cyberdystopia: The Dark Side of Cyberized Education

"Visionaries see a future of…interactive libraries and multimedia classrooms…Who needs teachers when you've got computer-aided education? Bah…What's missing from this electronic wonderland? Human contact. Discount the fawning techno-burble about virtual communities. Computers and networks isolate us from one another…A poor substitute it is, this virtual reality…where–in the holy names of Education and Progress–important aspects of human interactions are relentlessly devalued."

- Clifford Stoll, "The Internet?" Bah! Newsweek, February 27, 1995[46]

Cyberdystopia can be summarized as "nobody wins; humanity loses." Unlike Free Market, Standards, and Free Learning Rules advocates, Cyberdystopians see the cyberization of education as an impending disaster. These scenarios are Cyberdystopian nightmares: business completes a hostile takeover of education, turning schools into glorified vocational training centers; the efficiency of standardized education engineers the humanity out of us; key human interactions are "relentlessly devalued" by computers and networks, turning us into isolated robots. Twitter lowers our intelligence,[47] while social networking sites harm children's brains.[48] Online and distance education are even worse: in this view, they lead to a business-oriented, efficiency-driven, inhuman, spirit-crushing dystopia. An essay in the Chronicle of Higher Education's Brainstorm blog entitled "The Dystopia of Distance Learning" captured all of these:

> … [If] higher ed is heading toward a world where higher ed is mostly distance learning – what are its advocates waiting for? Why not cut to the chase and work to turn on-site secondary education into distance learning, or even abolish grammar schools in favor of computers in the home? If we want our kids to end up sitting alone in isolated little rooms when they're 18 and 20, staring at computer screens instead of facing other real human beings, thinking in a way that turns thought into nothing but bits of information, why not start training them earlier? We could insert them into comfortable little cocoons in their homes from the age of, oh, say seven.
>
> Those who embrace distance learning as a reasonable substitute for students going to college argue their case in the name of efficiency and productivity.…I say to hell with efficiency and productivity if it means any more distance learning than we already have. What's the point of living if we all turn into robots?[49]

Many articles on online or distance education often elicit similar responses from commenters. Online education is isolating and can't compare to being there in person. It's a plot to eliminate faculty, reduce labor costs, and diminish education in the name of efficiency and productivity. It's a plot by the administration to enable business to complete a total takeover of academia. There's something inhuman about sitting in front of a computer all day. It threatens Civilization As We Know It.

Such criticisms about cyberized education, and online education in particular, tend to be full of straw men and false dichotomies. No one has seriously proposed abolishing elementary schools in favor of computers, and "staring at computer screens instead of facing other real human beings" is not an either-or choice. Online education is much more than staring at a computer screen, and the classroom is hardly the optimal venue for interacting with other human beings. Ironically, many iconic features of classroom instruction as we commonly know it were designed to promote efficiency[50] rather than human interaction. Numerous education critics over the past 50 years have argued that classroom instruction is itself dystopian. Considering the legacy of its design and the ever-increasing emphasis on standards-driven, rote ritualized performances, it is an open question as to which education method turns students into robots.

Countering the relentlessly gloomy pessimism of the Cyberdystopian viewpoint is an ever-increasing accumulation of substantial evidence which indicates that online education is an effective, interactive, engaging experience, often more so than traditional classroom education. Beyond the substantial body of supporting research evidence is a host of anecdotes known and routinely shared by practitioners. One of my favorites involved a cohort of students in an online graduate education program some years ago who met for the first time in person at their graduation. The ceremony was a reunion of long-lost friends; graduates in other campus-based programs looked around and wondered what all the noise was about, since most of them didn't have such close relationships with their fellow students.

Beyond the obvious shortcomings of the extremist Cyberdystopian viewpoint, however, there is a deeper concern which is not so easily dismissed: what are we truly giving up when we embrace cyberized education? As we use digital technologies to extend our capabilities in once-unimaginable ways, have we thought deeply enough about what we value and wish to preserve about the human elements of education to ensure that we don't lose something important? What physical, mental, and other dangers will accompany the ubiquitous presence of cyberized education? These questions are not excuses to turn away from cyberized education, which is no longer an option in any event. Human society and culture are inextricably linked with our technology, and refusing to embrace a potent technology also goes against human nature itself. Our technologies do not define us, but our relationship with them certainly does.

These considerations are often lost in the hype and enthusiasm of adopting new technologies, which are often described in what MIT professor Sherry Turkle calls "a heroic, triumphalist narrative:" an uncritical, celebratory acceptance of new technologies, often accompanied by disparagement of the previous technologies.[51] For example, traditional reading is too linear, disconnected, and exclusionary, while hypertext is freeing, connecting, and democratic. As Turkle notes, there is another side to this story: books invite readers to linger and look inside themselves through daydreams and personal associations, while hypertext and web pages constantly beckon readers to look elsewhere, interrupting and fragmenting their attention.

Human history teaches us that adoption of new technologies always involves a tradeoff; something is gained, something else is lost. When humans gain by extending our capacities, we also tend to lose something of our prior capacities. Let's face it, as a species our skills have slipped when it comes to pyramid building, cooperage, catapult fabrication, and many other human capabilities. From the legend of John Henry,[52] to computers beating grandmasters at chess, to schoolchildren losing the capacity to do simple math in their heads in an age of ubiquitous calculators, there is usually something lost and a concomitant sense of ambivalence when we adopt a new technology. In most cases, the adoption of a technology has usually resulted in a net gain; the losses are real, but losses by themselves are not an argument against change.

There are also always dangers associated with adopting a new technology. Some of the cave dwellers who first used fire surely burned their hands, set themselves aflame, or died of smoke inhalation. We marvel at the wonders of Rome, but the slaves who built them experienced more misery than marvel. The horrors of working in factories during the Industrial Revolution are well-documented. Cyberized education is no different; there is a real danger of giving up human capacities in favor of digital ones. This happens with low-production online video recordings of classroom lectures that reduce interaction to watching an image and listening to a voice; online courses that try to "replicate" the classroom experience in an online setting are another common example.[53]

A more persistent concern is the loss of important capabilities as the result of becoming dependent on newly adopted technologies. For instance, a high school chemistry teacher told me a story about giving his students some paper flip charts to prepare presentations. They were lost; they only knew how to make PowerPoint presentations and had no clue about how to use a flip chart for the same purpose. How concerning is the decline in penmanship resulting from the use of keyboards for most written communication? With so many devices and resources to do this work for us, to what extent do we need to be great spellers? Navigators? Fact recallers?

These examples illustrate the central issue with adopting technology: preserving the human capacity to do a function without the aid of technology versus becoming dependent on a technology by offloading our capacities onto it. Adopting a new technology involves making tradeoffs in terms of capacities gained and lost, but too often this happens without enough regard for the possible consequences. We need to get better at making these tradeoffs intelligently by reflecting on our existing capacities and deciding what is worth keeping and what is not.

Another concern is the creation of new dangers caused by the implementation of these technologies. These include physical dangers such as the potential long-term health effects of using mobile phones, putting an unshielded laptop on one's lap, or simply sitting at a desk staring at computer screens for long periods. Widespread implementation also creates new problems and can magnify previously existing ones. For instance, online education has made it easier for diploma mills and other educational scams to proliferate. The use of online education for credit recovery has been a boon for many high school students, but it has also been misused in many cases.[54] References in online documents become plagued over time with broken links as web pages are removed or readdressed.[55]

It is helpful to remember that some of today's problems were also solutions to previous problems. For example, automobiles solved a horse manure hygiene problem, while the factory model enabled education for the masses. Mastering new technologies also places new demands on us and at times reveals previously hidden deficiencies. According to ophthalmologists, for instance, it is a myth that excessive reading causes eyestrain; in reality, the huge increase in reading over the past century has exposed previously hidden vision problems. This is important because the most potentially pernicious danger of digital technologies is also their greatest asset: their ability to capture our attention, keeping us engaged, absorbed – and away from the rest of life. Cyberdystopians have a point in warning us about this quality; digital technologies aggravate the perennial tension between technology and nature, as do all important technologies.

There are dangers to being screen captured, but the issue is more complex than simply finding a balance. For instance, social networking technologies isolate us from each other *and* enhance our abilities to socialize by providing new ways to manage transactional distance and enhance interpersonal communication. Using Twitter can discourage detailed thought *and* encourage succinct communication akin to the art of writing captions, while also increasing student engagement and improving their grades.[56] The task is to figure out how to create new solutions to the problems which digital technologies have generated and how to increase our capacities to overcome exposed deficiencies. In her book *Alone Together*, Sherry Turkle uses the term *realtechnik* to describe a process by which we critically examine our technologies and confront their true effects on us.[57] As Turkle notes, we get into trouble when we believe that our inventions will solve all our problems, and when we become so enamored with their affordances that we overlook their consequences.[58] Engaging in *realtechnik* reminds us to acknowledge the costs of adopting new technologies and to recognize those things we seek to preserve and protect from the transformations which new technologies bring.

Cyberdystopia Influences: a Healthy Caution

The concerns of Cyberdystopians are useful for reminding us not to simply adopt new technologies reflexively and uncritically, but to ask questions about the possible consequences. Cyberdystopians fit into a long-standing tradition of predicting catastrophe as the result of major, far-reaching change. One could argue that this trait represents the current state of our species' ability to protect itself while adapting to change. Still, the extreme Cyberdystopian response is overwrought and overcautious. Getting better at anticipating the possible ramifications of cyberized education and figuring out workable responses is far more useful, even while knowing that it is impossible to anticipate all the consequences of the changes which await us.

CHAPTER 8

Change or Not?
The Decisive Scenarios

Steady As She Goes: Education Endures

For more than 100 years much complaint has been made of the unmethodical way in which schools are conducted, but it is only within the last 30 that any serious attempt has been made to find a remedy for this state of things. And with what result? Schools remain exactly as they were.

— John Amos Comenius, The Great Didactic, 1632

This Too Shall Pass

It seems as if just about everyone wants to fix education and has their own pet ideas about how to go about it. Free Market Rules advocates want more business-driven solutions; Standards Rule makers want standards-driven solutions; Free Learning Rules proponents want more learner-centered solutions; Cyberdystopians want to halt the march of technology and restore more "human"-centered approaches. These voices have joined the chorus of those who have been seeking to "find a remedy for this state of things" in education for centuries.

Calls to fix education tend to have this in common: the crisis is perpetually dire, the need for change is ever urgent, and the magnitude of the needed change is always great. Very few voices these days talk about education's capacity for slow and steady evolution – who wants to hear about boring, incremental change? Yet based on past history, the Steady As She Goes scenario would be the smartest bet to describe education's future. In this scenario, education will continue to evolve slowly but steadily; any substantive change will be gradual and often barely noticeable. This scenario may be the most difficult for some to imagine in this time of tumultuous change, but it is the one which best describes education most of the time. Ideas for change come and go, but education endures. Calls for radical change remain strong, but this too shall pass.

The Steady as She Goes scenario frustrates advocates of reform: how can there be so little change when so much change is needed (especially to fix education the way they want it fixed)? The strength of this scenario is reflected in the fact that calls to fix, reform, or improve education usually take pains to explain why things will be different this time around, this book included. But what if we're wrong (again)? And how does education remain so seemingly impervious to major change? Asking who wins in this scenario leads to some revealing answers, which helps explain one of education's most defining characteristics: durability.

Education Is Durable

Education's durability reflects an emphasis on stability rather than change, which is what differentiates the Steady As She Goes scenario from the other ones. Boston College professor Philip Altbach has described the university in modern society as a durable institution because of its capacity to serve society's needs by evolving during periods of massive social change while also maintaining key structural elements of the models which have historically shaped it.[1] Johns Hopkins University research scientist Robert Balfanz has described the American high school as a "much maligned but durable institution" which has helped shape the nation since its mid-19th-century inception.[2] Education is durable mostly because it fulfills many valuable societal functions, as described previously. Like other social institutions, education also tends toward preserving and perpetuating itself. Educators have a strong stake in durability since their livelihoods and professional identity depend on it.

Education's durability is a double-edged sword which provides protection from destructive changes but also impedes constructive change. This durability manifests itself in several varieties, including resistance, stasis, and incremental change.

Resistance

Education's function of transmitting preserved knowledge is an inherently conservative one which promotes resistance to change. Both the foundational shifts in knowledge and the cyberization of education challenge this function, which increases the tendency to resist. Sometimes, apparent resistance is simply the result of having to deal with complexity. For example, administrators who appear to be resisting the adoption of social networking tools in schools may simply be struggling to avoid making changes which would make things even worse. Usually, however, the resistance is very real, for instance the continued resistance which online learning has encountered in certain sectors of education. To an extent, this resistance also reflects resistance in the larger culture; for example, employer resistance to accepting applicants with online degrees is still a factor, although a diminishing one.[3]

Stasis

Stasis is perhaps the best way to understand the Steady as She Goes scenario. While resistance involves trying to block something from happening, stasis is the result of many forces neutralizing each other. Things stay the way they are because the sum of the vectors adds up to little. Educational institutions must balance a host of competing pressures:[4] political, parental, social, organizational, administrative, and financial, among others. Educators in charge often struggle with the complexity of making changes in this environment, so change is often thwarted; the status quo wins out, attesting to its durability.

An even more powerful reason for stasis is because of who advocates for keeping things the way they are: just about everybody, including you and me. As cartoonist Walt Kelly's iconic character Pogo noted several decades ago, "We have met the enemy, and he is us."[5] This is not what many "reformers" would have you believe, or want to believe. Surely the problem is with the entrenched elements of the system: teachers, administrators, accrediting agencies, unions, commercial vendors, lifetime-tenured faculty, the National Education Association, consultants, and all the other elements with a stake in the status quo. If only we could eliminate or bypass or co-opt or otherwise break their stranglehold, then change would occur – or so the fantasy goes. In reality, stasis is such a powerful force precisely because practically everyone has a stake in the way education is constituted right now. Most would-be reformers want to change the system to their particular liking while keeping the elements which currently benefit them.

Not coincidentally, those who advocate the strongest change are often the ones who have the least to lose. Futurist Alvin Toffler has the luxury of recommending that we "blow up" the current system[6] because he has relatively little stake in it. Homeschoolers have successfully disengaged from the current system, even though the learning part of education is important to them, because they derive the least benefit from its custodial and socializing functions, which they want to do themselves in their own particular ways.[7] The more extreme Free Market and Free Learning Rules advocates seem to have given up on the present system, but most advocates of change also have a stake in stasis. Free Market moderates want to make the existing system a more business-friendly market. Standards Rule advocates want to preserve formal education's role as certifier of attainment by making it even more uniform and consistent. The emphasis which Free Learning moderates place on education as learning requires leaving many other system elements intact. Cyberdystopians want to limit the adoption of educational technology. In each case, stasis is an essential element in their vision of what education should be.

Incremental Change

Education's capacity for incremental change may be its most effective strategy for remaining durable. Over the past century, education has evolved from an institution which served a relatively small proportion of the population to one which serves everyone by offering a myriad of important functions. K-12 education has evolved to provide universal custodial care[8] and education for almost every child, help keep America competitive, and help eliminate poverty.[9]

There have been numerous periods of rapid change in American education. For instance, the Morrill Land Grant Act of 1862 transformed higher education by establishing numerous land grant universities and colleges which focused on more democratic admissions and practical curriculum.[10] The establishment of the comprehensive public high school in the early 20th century revolutionized U.S. education by dramatically increasing attendance and completion rates.[11] The GI Bill in the late 1940s nearly doubled college enrollments in one decade, and the establishment of community colleges in the 1960s rapidly expanded enrollments.[12]

However, most change in education happens gradually, and incremental change can be deceptively powerful due to its cumulative effect. For instance, enrollment in American degree-granting institutions increased at an annual rate of 1.4 percent between 1987 and 1997; that rate almost doubled between 1997 and 2007 (2.6 percent per year).[13] As a result, American higher education added one million new enrollments every six years or so between 1980 and 2000; since then, it has added one million new enrollments about every two and a half years. The higher education system of today is now the size of two higher education systems in 1970, and these millions of new students have distinctly different characteristics: they are older, more interested in career preparation, more ethnically, culturally, and linguistically diverse, and there are more females in previously male-dominated areas of study. Many of these changes also characterize the K-12 student population, even though it has fluctuated in size. The result of these incremental changes is a very different student population from the one which education served several decades ago.

Incremental growth is not the only powerful form of incremental change; the shifts in knowledge, access, and authority quickly become apparent when one observes just about any classroom carefully enough and compares it with the classrooms of 30 or 40 years ago. The problem is that incremental change is no longer enough; many observers believe that the changes which are currently happening are an actual threat to education's long-term durability.

Threats to Durability

Failing to keep up with increasing expectations and accelerated need

During a conference in 2008, my colleague Gary Miller and I listened to a presentation which included commonly cited statistics to demonstrate the perceived crisis in U.S. educational attainment: out of 100 ninth-grade students, only about 67 will graduate on time; 38 of them will go on to college; 26 of them will still be enrolled by their sophomore year; and only 18 of them will graduate from college within six years.[14] At that point Miller turned to me and commented, "That's exactly what the current system was designed to do." And he's right. American education in its current form was designed to give access to a certain proportion of the population and to enable a certain subset of that population to succeed, primarily by judging and sorting students based on various standards of merit. What has changed the most are the *expectations* placed on education now that it has evolved from a necessity for the many to an essential for nearly everyone, and we are struggling to catch up with increased expectations and accelerated need. Even though the dual expectations of near-universal success in K-12 education and near-universal access to higher education are now several decades old, building a system to meet these expectations has been a work in progress, and much work remains to be done. Which makes sense if you think about it: why should a society suddenly be able to educate all its citizens simply because it decided to do so? The reality is that no large heterogeneous society in the history of humankind had ever before even tried to provide higher education for all its interested citizens, nor has one succeeded yet in providing basic education for all its citizens.

Incremental change has produced considerable progress. Although "on-time" diploma attainment rates have remained relatively flat over the past several decades, educational attainment among adults has continued to rise steadily. High school attainment among adults age 25 and over rose over 30 percentage points (from 55 percent to 87 percent, or about 0.8 percentage points per year), and bachelor's degree attainment almost tripled (from 11 percent to 30 percent, or about 0.5 percentage points per year) between 1970 and 2009.[15] However, the rise in degree attainment due to incremental change has clearly not been fast enough to satisfy most commentators, critics, or consumers who claim diminishing returns for education at all levels. In particular, critics juxtapose rising costs with relatively static graduation rates and conclude that things are going downhill. The increases in quality, amenities, facilities, additional services, number of students, and diversity of students served somehow escape notice.

The bigger issue is figuring out how to accommodate increased expectations and accelerated need. Higher education has not yet learned how to scale in response to the demands society has placed upon it. The traditional core of higher education is not well-suited for scalability since it is hamstrung by long-standing practices which prevent rapid expansion. K-12 education hasn't yet figured out how to reach all of its students effectively, and American society remains fixated on processing almost all its ever-more diverse youth through one funnel with a singular aim: a high school diploma attained on time at age 18.

This is why education is so often described as "failing," even though in reality it is simply falling short of accelerated expectations. Education has improved overall, but it hasn't improved quickly enough. Substantive progress resulting from cumulative incremental change is no longer sufficient; society is asking for more, and at a time where there is an even bigger threat to education's durability.

Financial crisis and collapse

The financial crisis which sent the world's economies into recession in 2008 came at a particularly bad time for education, which has been experiencing its own long-brewing financial crisis. College tuition has been rising faster than the overall cost of living for many years,[16] and college has steadily become less affordable for growing numbers of families.[17] State appropriations per student to public higher education have been steadily dropping;[18] for example, state funding for the University of Missouri declined even while enrollment increased 26 percent over the past decade.[19] Spending per pupil has also steadily risen in K-12 education[20] while expectations of commensurately higher performance haven't been realized.

The Obama Administration's economic stimulus program helped forestall some of the disastrous effects in 2010 by infusing considerable funds into education budgets, but the crisis has continued. Ray Schroeder's blog "Recession Realities in Higher Education" has chronicled how the global recession has changed "realities for students, institutions, and faculty members engaged in higher education," as these sample headlines illustrate: "Utah Higher Ed budget cuts coming"; "Shortchanging higher education" (Texas); Missouri colleges to cut 116 degree programs"; "N.C. Universities on the block for the budget ax" (North Carolina).[21] No state is immune, and 43 states cut higher education funding between 2008 and 2010.[22] Customary cost-cutting measures may not be enough this time around; major restructuring may be necessary.[23]

The situation in K-12 education is not any rosier. K-12 education budgets are even more dependent on public funding through property taxes; since the current economic downturn has reduced housing values and thus property tax valuations, it has been especially hard on schools.[24] Federal stimulus money also temporarily averted deep cuts in public school funding,[25] but two-thirds of the states cut K-12 education funding between 2008 and 2010, and the budget crunch got worse when the stimulus funding ended.[26]

Steady as She Goes: Who Wins?

The answer: everyone and no one. Education has fulfilled its functions well enough to satisfy nearly every stakeholder to some extent, but almost no one expresses the idea that things are going just fine. These days, American education seems to be in perpetual crisis mode. Crises, whether perceived or real, produce competing reactions. One response is to hunker down and do as little as possible until the danger passes, while another response is to insist on incremental change because times are too difficult or dangerous for big changes. Still, foundational shifts, expectation gaps, and imminent tough times raise the question of whether even incremental change will suffice this time. Many observers believe that a breaking point is approaching and that eventually something will have to give. From this perspective, any version of Steady As She Goes in the extreme would also be a disaster for formal education.

The Chinese proverb "a crisis is an opportunity riding the dangerous wind" suggests a different tack: treat the crisis as an opportunity to question and improve current practices. Another option is to recognize that this opportunity exists whether or not there is a crisis. Whether the current situation is a "dangerous wind" or simply the winds of change, we need to learn how to ride these winds by learning how to use cyberization to improve education.

Making the Most of Cyberization: The Potential for Improvement

Incremental Change vs. Improvement

Distinguishing incremental change from substantial change, or change from improvement, poses some difficulties such as determining the boundaries, threshold values, size, and speed of change. The rise of online education illustrates the issue, as reflected in David Wiley's claim that online learning is essentially just a different channel[27] which has left philosophy and pedagogy largely unchanged, even though online education has served tens of millions of learners and created numerous positive benefits. The Sloan ALN initiative focused on providing superior access and equivalent quality, and early online education research also focused primarily on establishing equivalence among delivery modes. Efforts to use online learning to improve all of education are still relatively rare in higher education and nearly nonexistent in K-12 education, except insofar as providing access is itself a form of improvement. Relative to these expectations, online education has arguably been a form of incremental change rather than vast improvement.

The distinction is important because continued incremental change will only increase the gap between rising expectations and unmet need. Instead, we need to close this gap by stepping up the pace of improvement, and cyberized education can help with this process. How much improvement can happen depends on how willing we are to embrace its possibilities.

Education Improves: The Sixth Future

There are many important ways to use cyberization to improve education (Table 8-1). Collectively, these suggestions comprise the sixth future: Education Improves. This scenario involves working actively and consciously to implement specific improvements instead of just letting current initiatives take their course. Unlike the other scenarios, the extreme version of this future is a best-case scenario, and any version of realizing this future is desirable.

• **Moves beyond trying to equal classroom quality** and toward the improvement of learning and teaching (the sixth level of change described in Chapter 1)
• **Applies to all formal education**, not just online education
• **Incorporates the influences of the other future scenarios** for positive change: - Enables business/market forces and education to coevolve for mutual benefit; - Uses open content and open interaction to complement formal education; - Applies standards in a broad framework that offers flexible paths to attainment; - Discovers the potential dangers of cyberized education & minimizes their ill effects; - Conserves current educational practices which are worth keeping.
• **Enables formal education to deal effectively with the foundational shifts:**
Realigning Education with Redefined Knowledge: • Connects higher/K-12 education with knowledge generated or residing outside of it • Makes knowledge more attainable in various shapes, sizes, and in a timely manner • Makes knowledge attainment more measurable in meaningful ways • Helps learners develop the metacognitive skills required to learn new knowledge as needed • Helps learners learn to use new tools for handling the ever-increasing explosion of data • Connects knowledge across disciplines; connections enable generation of new knowledge • Enables knowledge sharing via distributed networks • Enables knowledge to be understood in more relevant, meaningful contexts • Utilizes knowledge in visual, multimedia, and digitized forms
Realizing Redistributed Access: • Expands educational access to previously neglected or underserved populations • Expands educational access universally while preserving individual autonomy, dignity • Helps more learners develop knowledge and skills required to live better lives[28] • Reaches nontraditional students more effectively • Accommodates more lifelong learners in an ever-greater variety of ways • Provides quality access which increases chances of broadly defined student success
Managing Renegotiated Authority: • Shifts authority relationships between teachers and students from an imposed, authoritarian model to a self-initiated, negotiated, and shared model of authority • Enhances teacher value, student value, and how they work together • Creates a more transparent, accessible, and detailed certification system • Strengthens the connection between credentials & expertise by aligning them more closely

Table 8-1: **Using Cyberization to Improve Education**[28]

For example, consider how the cyberization of education can help shift relationships between teachers and students from an imposed, authoritarian model to a self-initiated, negotiated, and shared model of authority to improve teaching and learning.

Recalibrating authority relationships between teachers and students

The perennial tensions between authority and freedom tend to elicit bipolar, reactive, and often extreme responses to this issue. Some educators cling to the authoritarian approach to education, even pushing for regression to a harder-line authoritarianism if they can succeed in imposing it. Other approaches are clearly a reaction to educational and societal authoritarianism, such as John Holt's argument for giving children full adult societal privileges,[29] which has spawned the present-day "unschooling" movement.[30] The cyberization of education has aggravated this tension and produced similar calls for reactive solutions at both extremes. For example, author Andrew Keen views the Internet as a threat to professorial authority because lowering the cost of content devalues education. Keen also believes that educators' authority is conferred by their hard-won wisdom, and this existing relationship must be maintained since children or young adults don't know anything of value.[31] Some Standards Rule advocates seem intent on imposing authority by using rigorous and inflexible standards and standardized test scores to define educational progress. At the other extreme, some Free Learning Rules advocates envision cyberization as the vehicle for a new age of free learning which will replace the authority of formal education.

Shifting from an imposed, authoritarian model to a self-initiated, negotiated, and shared model of authority is an integrative, dialectic approach, not a reactive one. It does not mean ceding all the power to students. Children and young adults are still developing creatures who fundamentally need the guidance and wisdom of their elders to help them find their way in the world and a place in society. A better approach is to recalibrate existing authority relationships in a way which increases the value of education by enhancing the value of both teachers and students.

Enhancing teacher value

In the phrase "from sage on the stage to guide on the side," the implicit shift in authority is obvious: teachers give up both the "stage" (being the center of attention) and the role of "sage" (content expert and information transmitter). Many synonyms are commonly used to describe this new set of roles, such as facilitator, coach, mentor, and of course, guide. These roles enhance teacher value by enabling them to help more actively with the learning process.

Several other teacher roles also enhance their value. Educational content and delivery are often criticized for being too decontextualized.[32] To redress this imbalance, teachers at all levels often serve as **contextualizers**, helping learners make sense out of content by providing context – information, anecdotes, assignments, stories, and other ways to relate content to other knowledge domains, to the world of work, and to the rest of life. In fact, nearly every story about teachers who Changed Our Lives involves their role as contextualizers – how what they taught was valuable to students later in their lives. Teachers at all levels are also *role models* who are worthy of emulation as people who also know something about a subject. Teachers can serve more broadly as role models particularly in the middle and early high school years. In higher education, teachers are role models for their academic discipline; more importantly, they model what it is like to be an adult with an intellectual life. In many cases (first generation college students, for example), a college professor or high school teacher may be the first person a student has ever seen or met for whom intellectual concerns matter. Teachers at all levels, particularly K-12, also serve as *knowledge ambassadors*[33] who represent the academic subjects they teach. This role includes being a contextualizer and role model, but it also involves demonstrating why a particular subject is worth knowing by introducing students to its particular characteristics and by serving as a personal representative with various degrees of inside connections to the discipline itself. Even insofar as authority is projected by force of personality, the value of these roles derives more from an increased emphasis on negotiated or self-initiated authority rather than on imposed authority.

Another way to enhance teacher value is simply to appreciate this diversity of roles which teachers fulfill. Canada National Research Council senior researcher Stephen Downes identified 23 different roles for educators and pointed out the ease of identifying many additional roles as well.[34] Focusing on this role diversity discourages seeing teachers in narrow terms (as if their main role was to raise standardized test scores, for example) and encourages finding ways to use these various roles to add value to the teaching and learning process. For example, teachers who function as action researchers improve their teaching in response to what they learn from conducting action research.[35]

The cyberization of education can be used to enhance teacher value in many ways. Many online teachers have figured out how to fulfill many of these roles effectively in online settings by mastering the nuances of creating "instructor presence"[36] and "social presence,"[37] which support effective online instructor-student and student-student interaction respectively. Digital technologies can also enable teachers to unbundle and outsource certain roles. Automated grading programs, well-constructed test banks, and well-designed rubrics can save time, so teachers can spend time doing higher value tasks such as guiding, coaching, or mentoring, instead of composing test questions or grading exams. Teachers can 'outsource' roles such as discussion leader, task assigner, or content developer to students through strategies such as peer review, peer assessment, or cooperative learning techniques. Even when the importance of in-person contact is crucial, digital content and technologies provide a vast array of educational resources to enhance the teaching and learning process, and will do more so in the future.

Enhancing student value

The cyberization of education enhances student value in a number of important ways. The flexibility and convenience of online education is commonly viewed as improving access, but it also confers greater *learner control*. For example, it is widely believed that online learners need to be more "self-disciplined" to succeed in online courses. While this is true to some extent, the corollary to this principle is usually overlooked: online education enables learners to *exercise more self-discipline*. Cuesta Community College professor David Diaz noted in a study on dropout rates in online courses that many online students drop classes "because it is the *right thing to do*" for them, i.e., as a "mature, well-informed decision that is consistent with a learner with significant academic and life experience."[38] They do so not just because of the maturity that comes with age, but also because they have greater control over the process.

Ever more powerful technology tools for learning enhance student value by increasing access to a vast amount of information and content and by providing students with increased access to the means of production. Students can spend their time more effectively engaging in purposeful activities,[39] interacting dynamically with peers and tools,[40] generating meaningful content and products,[41] and attaining higher-level learning outcomes in ways that value their time in the process. Specific strategies for doing this will be covered in detail in Chapter 10.

Enhancing teacher and student value can also be accomplished by enhancing how they work together. This means moving beyond a teacher-centered approach and taking a "*learning-centered*" approach instead – not "learner-centered," because education is not just about the students. The term "learning-centered" captures the inherent dialectical nature of education and puts the emphasis on learning as a product of both teacher and learner participation in the process. This dynamic is captured well by the Community of Inquiry (CoI) model developed by University of Calgary professor D. Randy Garrison and several of his online education colleagues. The CoI model focuses on creating deep and meaningful learning experiences by developing the three interdependent elements of social, cognitive and teaching presence.[42] This model guides many online education practitioners in implementing more learning-centered approaches to improving education.

The Education Improves scenario provides a framework for understanding key strategies for using cyberization to improve education, including the strategic role of online education, strategies for (re-)empowering learning and teaching, and strategies for revitalizing the educational enterprise. It also offers a possible path to a seventh possible, if distant future: one in which everyone's education truly matters.

Part III

What Can Happen:
Cyberizing Education
Strategically

CHAPTER 9

The Strategic Role of Online Education

Developing in our students the ability to create knowledge, to become good citizens, and to be able to solve problems…takes the active involvement of students through inquiry, collaborative problem solving, and evaluation of the results — things online learning can do at a scale we've never had before.

– Gary Miller, Executive Director Emeritus, Penn State World Campus[1]

Online learning has been the leading wedge in the cyberization of education, and it can become the leading wedge for cyberizing education strategically to improve not just online education, but all education. If the first era in the history of online education was focused on providing access, the second era could be defined by improving quality – the sixth level of change. In higher education, this is possible because the use of online technologies for teaching and learning will soon be a routine, commonplace, and integral part of formal education.

Online Higher Education Attains Full Scale

Online education will achieve full scale[2] in U.S. higher education within the next four to eight years. "Full scale" online education will have the following characteristics:

- Practically all higher education students will experience online education in some form during their collegiate career. The experience will become as commonplace for them as owning a telephone in the U.S. (95 percent availability in 1990; around 98 percent from 2003-2008[3]).

- A majority of students will take at least one online course during a given academic year.

- A large majority of students (70-80 percent) will take at least one online course during their collegiate careers.

- Online courses will comprise a sizable proportion (20 percent or more) of the total credit hours.

- Blended courses will comprise much of the remainder of the total credit hours.

- College students will be able to take a full complement of online or online/blended degree programs and certificates in almost any subject of their choosing at the associate, bachelor's, master's, and postgraduate certificate levels.

The collegiate careers of practically all higher education students will soon be a blended learning experience. Most students will take a mixture of online, classroom and blended courses to complete their degree programs. Many classroom courses will blend online lessons, assignments, group projects, and other online learning experiences into the teaching and learning process. Online technologies will be used for independent study, specialty courses, research projects, and other assignments even in places where purely online degree and certificate programs do not become widespread, such as doctoral degree programs and elite liberal arts institutions. Students who do not take at least one online course will become the exception, and courses which do not use online technologies will be seen as quaint, outdated, or worse. Online learning will even perform a magic trick of sorts: becoming more popular by disappearing.

How and Why Full Scale Online Education Will Happen

Full scale online education will happen for several compelling reasons:

1. ***The compounding effect: growth breeds growth.*** U.S. online higher education grew at an annualized rate of almost 20 percent from fall 2002 to fall 2009. If this pace continues, a majority of higher education students will take at least one online course by the 2013-2014 academic year. Even if the growth rate is cut in half to 9.7 percent per year (the lowest annual rate of increase reported by the annual Sloan Surveys from 2002 through 2009), this benchmark will be reached by the 2017-2018 academic year.

   This scenario is highly plausible because of several factors conducive to continued growth. There are numerous short- and long-term pressures on higher education to grow, and online education remains higher education's chief engine of growth. Online education enables higher education to scale rapidly while maintaining its broad array of offerings, and to scale relatively cheaply compared to other available options. The effects of compounding growth can already be seen in mature online programs which have reached full scale. For instance, annual online course registrations at the University of Central Florida grew from fewer than 6,000 enrollments to 66,000 enrollments from 1999-2000 to 2009-2010. Over the first five years of that period, UCF's online enrollment grew by about 23,500 students; over the last five years, by over 37,300 students.[4] This pattern is being repeated at many other mature, larger scale online programs; they experience larger numerical increases even when their internal growth rates slow, and these large increases contribute disproportionately to the total increase in online learners nationwide. In addition, a majority of higher education students do not take an online course within a given academic year, so there is still plenty of room for online education to grow, even within larger scale online programs.

2. ***The mainstreaming effect: familiarity breeds attempt.*** The rise in online enrollments means greater familiarity with online education. More students are currently taking online courses, have current and previous experience with taking online courses, know other students who have taken or are taking online courses, and know other graduates who have completed online courses or programs. Growing familiarity also affects faculty attitudes toward online education. Once faculty have actual experience with developing or teaching an online course, their concerns about online education tend to diminish, and online learning gains their acceptance.[5] As more faculty accept online education, more of their peers may be more likely to try it themselves.

3. ***The acceptance effect: a worthy alternative.*** Now that almost one third of college students are taking at least one online course each academic year, online education has become an accepted part of the landscape[6] in most sectors of higher education. Most students are aware of it even if they are not directly involved, just as most liberal arts majors are aware of the engineering building on their campus even if they never set foot there. Another major indicator of acceptance is that most institutional transcripts do not differentiate between degrees earned online and those earned from taking classroom courses.

4. ***The diversity effect: different ways of attaining scale.*** Online learning programs have attained or are in the process of attaining full scale in a variety of ways, for example:

- For-profit mega-campuses (e.g., University of Phoenix, American Public University System);

- Public mega-campuses (e.g., University of Maryland University College);

- Statewide networks (e.g., Illinois Online Network, Colorado Community Colleges Online);

- Systemwide implementations (e.g., San Diego Community College District);

- Individual institutional models (e.g., University of Central Florida's Distributed Learning Initiative, Thomas Edison State College's entirely online, multi-modal independent study programs, and University of Illinois at Springfield's "mirror campus");

- Regional and national collaborations (e.g., Western Governors University).

Although a number of common factors have contributed to their success,[7] the variety of these models for attaining scale strongly suggests that higher education is successfully applying the strength of its institutional diversity to the online education arena.

5. ***The wildcard effect: growth from unpredictable sources.*** A recent example is the surge in online enrollments at many institutions during the oil price shock of 2007-2008. As University of Illinois at Springfield professor Ray Schroeder's "Fueling Online Learning" blog reported, many students cited high gas prices as a major reason for enrolling in online courses.[8] Unpredictable sources such as

current government and foundation initiatives to improve retention and graduation rates, or institutional responses to severe disruptions of service caused by
natural disasters or other crises (also see "Bricks and Clicks" below), may similarly
spur future growth in online education.

Online K-12 Education Enters the Mainstream

Online learning will go mainstream in K-12 education within the next five to
ten years. Exactly how mainstream it will go is more difficult to predict since
the total number of students involved in K-12 education is much higher and
the current penetration rate of online education is much smaller (about three
percent vs. 30 percent in higher education). Opinions also differ about the likely
reasons that online learning will enter the K-12 mainstream, including the need
for quality improvement to raise educational attainment, an impending funding
crisis, a looming teacher shortage, and the potential for customized learning.[9]
Still, K-12 online education has also experienced sustained, compounding growth;
extrapolating reported growth rates and current enrollment estimates into the
future yields about four million K-12 online learners by 2014-2015 and over 10
million K-12 online learners by the 2019-2020 school year.

Strategies for Using Online Learning to Improve Education

As Chapter 4 described, online education has become an important means for
enabling higher education institutions to achieve various strategic goals: increasing
student access, growing professional and continuing education programs, improving student retention, and many others. There are also several emerging strategies
for using online learning to improve education.

"Bricks and Clicks": Building a Robust System

In 2005, the twin disasters of Hurricanes Katrina and Rita provided an example of how natural disasters could devastate educational delivery. The hurricanes
caused over one billion dollars in physical damage and over two billion dollars in
total economic losses to higher education institutions alone.[10] The Sloan Semester
was one initiative which helped mitigate the effect by providing free online courses
to students impacted by the storm, but the experience demonstrated the need for
higher education institutions to prepare for future disasters.[11] Many larger colleges
and universities have one or more staff assigned to maintaining *business continuity*,

an institution's ability to maintain or restore its business-related services when a disaster, crisis situation, or other circumstances disrupt or threaten normal operations.[12] However, even though learning is the core mission of educational institutions, very few of them are focused on the issue of *academic continuity*, the process of continuing to provide students with the opportunity to learn when circumstances disrupt or threaten academic operations.[13]

Since the massive disruptions caused by Hurricanes Katrina and Rita, several relatively isolated episodes have required individual institutions to respond to a disruptive disaster, but there has been nothing on a comparable scale – yet. The H1N1 "swine flu" virus scare of 2009 turned out to be a false alarm which had little effect on education. Still, relatively few schools, colleges or universities are prepared to maintain academic continuity when (not if) the next disaster strikes.[14]

A proactive response to this prospect would be to adopt a *"bricks and clicks"* strategy for educational delivery, in which every course and program offering is available through multiple delivery modalities (online, blended, classroom) which complement and reinforce each other when needed. One advocate of the "bricks and clicks" approach is Mike Abbiatti, Executive Director of the Arkansas Research and Education Optical Network. Abbiatti chaired a Higher Education Standards Committee for the American Society of Mechanical Engineers Innovative Technologies Institute which codified a risk assessment methodology for higher education that was approved as an American National Standard in July 2010.[15] This intersection of emergency management planning and academic continuity is crucial because colleges and universities play important roles as economic engines and disaster recovery facilities, especially in the hundreds of U.S. communities where a local college or university is the largest employer. As Abbiatti notes, maintaining academic continuity in response to a disaster or other crisis "is vital to protecting the economic health of the community as well as the institution."[16] Unfortunately, it is most likely that educational institutions will adopt a "bricks and clicks" strategy reactively rather than proactively, perhaps after seeing one or more institutions cease to exist as the result of failing to recover from a devastating disaster.

As a 2006 "Map of Future Forces Affecting Education" notes, education is also becoming a health issue.[17] Soon, we may be reading headlines such as these:

Students learn online to avoid disease
Flu epidemic drives students to online learning

Public health is already a key function of education, which provides health care and helps protect public health, in particular by ensuring that schools are not incubators or carriers of epidemics. The 'bricks and clicks' solution becomes important as a strategy for maintaining academic continuity during long-term public health crises, an especially important issue in K-12 education. During the H1N1 virus scare of spring 2009, for example, Rockville High School in Montgomery County, Maryland, was closed as the result of a single "probable" case of H1N1 virus. Authorities were prepared to keep the school closed for as long as 14 days, which would have halted instruction for over a thousand students, resulting in hundreds of thousands of lost instructional hours. Fortunately, the outbreak was not as bad as anticipated, and Rockville High was closed for only three days. According to a radio report, a small private elementary school in nearby northwest DC was closed during the same time for an entire week due to a single probable H1N1 case, but the school coped with the crisis by using email and other online technologies to continue learning without interruption.[18]

Online education also has the capacity to provide continuity of instruction through short-term interruptions. For example, after the historic snowfalls in Maryland during winter 2009-2010, the state Board of Education granted permission for public schools not to make up lost snow days, resulting in millions of hours of lost instructional time for students.[19] Schools, colleges and universities routinely lose instructional time due to snow days and other minor emergencies such as fires, instructor illness, special events, or other occurrences. Students who are taking online courses, however, can continue their instruction without interruption in most cases. Online learning can be used to provide short-term academic continuity with online and classroom-based courses with appropriate planning and preparation. For instance, school systems in Maryland have used online course resources to provide instruction to students at home because of extended illness, pregnancy, or other reasons. As a result of the H1N1 crisis, the U.S. Department of Education issued recommendations for ensuring continuity of learning during extended school dismissals, including the use of online learning technologies and delivery methods.[20] In practice, several different "bricks and clicks" models currently exist,[21] and many more will be developed in the future, not simply as a "just in case" strategy to protect against interruptions in service, but also as a strategy for improving quality by providing more delivery options for everyday use.

Online Education as Professional Development

Teaching online has been an effective professional development experience for hundreds of thousands of faculty in U.S. higher education. Large-scale online education programs such as the Illinois Online Network (ION), SUNY Learning Network, and the University of Central Florida, and nationwide initiatives such as Quality Matters, have routinely reported high levels of faculty satisfaction with online higher education as a professional development experience. As online education grows, learning to teach online will become a more important professional development activity. For instance, ION's Making the Virtual Classroom a Reality (MVCR) faculty development program reached 1,000 enrollments in 2010, and MVCR has impacted an estimated one million learners since 1999.[22] Learning to teach online as professional development can also be an effective strategy for making improvements. For example, Quality Matters (QM) is a faculty-centered peer review process which promotes continuous improvement in online and blended courses. QM works because its peer review process and course assessment rubric provide an effective structure for improving quality; faculty reflect on their teaching and course design practices, identify useful changes, and create an action plan to implement those changes. QM has helped foster a culture of pedagogical improvement among its participants, with over 500 institutional members and over 1,500 course reviews conducted since its inception in 2004.[23]

The tradition of professional development related to teaching and learning is stronger in K-12 education, and there are signs that this emphasis on professional development is spreading into online teaching as well. A 2007 North American Council for Online Learning (iNACOL) report asserts the importance of professional development for virtual schooling for teachers, site facilitators, instructional designers, and other staff involved in complementary roles of online delivery and support.[24] A more recent iNACOL survey of K-12 online teachers found that 87 percent of all respondents, and three-quarters of brand new online teachers, reported receiving professional development specifically for K-12 online instruction.[25] The Southern Regional Education Board is another source of professional development resources for online teachers.[26]

From the Unthinkable to the Indispensable: Summer Online Programs

Students who take summer college courses usually do so away from their home institutions, which lose out in several ways as a result: lost revenue, loss of connection with their students, and decreased retention rates. Many colleges and universities with substantial online education programs have expanded them into the summer, but the idea of online courses and programs at any time of the year remains unthinkable at some schools, especially many small liberal arts colleges. However, starting a summer online program provides an avenue for institutions which otherwise might resist online education to try it out, and some small colleges have discovered its value. For example, Emmanuel College's summer online program started in 2007 with seven courses and 155 students; three years later, it had expanded to almost 400 students and two online degree programs which were subsequently offered year-round.[27] Emmanuel's summer online programs also help students maintain the connection with their college community over the summer while allowing the college to retain tuition revenue. Summer offerings have also been an important part of Notre Dame College of Ohio (NDC)'s online programs since their inception. NDC's fully online programs all include a summer session, which has generated crucially important enrollments while also helping NDC reach its valued target audiences.[28]

Along with generating increased enrollments, summer online programs help reduce students' time to degree, improve faculty development opportunities, and revamp the quality of on-campus summer programs while providing greater convenience and flexibility for students and instructors. Summer online programs also help online and blended education gain acceptance throughout the school year at many institutions, becoming an indispensable part of their program offerings in the process. Thus, summer online programs are an excellent strategy for using online learning to improve education.

A Disappearing Act: Integrating Online Learning into Education

Although distinctly online courses and programs will continue to grow, the integration of online learning into mainstream education will become an even bigger source of growth. So another strategy for using online learning to improve education is by having it disappear into the background – fully integrated and thus essentially indistinguishable from mainstream education.

Blended learning courses and programs blur the distinction between online and classroom education by utilizing a wide range of course designs which integrate the two delivery modes into one. This will continue because emerging online technologies are getting ever easier to integrate with classroom-based learning and because these technologies are increasingly known and used for what they can do rather than by how they are delivered. For example, students work online or in person using an online technology (wikis) to create content for wiki textbooks in classroom courses; other online technologies such as specialized software for writing wiki textbooks facilitate other aspects of the process such as assessment and peer review.[29] Podcasting enables students to listen to recorded lectures or other content and to (co-)create content for course assignments, review sessions, or other purposes.[30] The practice of adapting online learning resources for class-room use is now well-established, and learning resources are now being intentionally developed for use in multiple modalities, as the OER Commons web site illustrates.

Mobility also helps online education disappear. Users can listen to podcasts online by using a desktop computer or mobile device with wireless access, or they can download the podcasts onto a mobile device and listen to it anywhere. The California State University, Monterey Bay's Wireless Education and Technology Center web site describes a variety of diverse mobile learning projects where local K-12 and college classrooms and teachers use wireless interactive web conferences to share images and data, conduct field archaeology with Internet connectivity to a classroom via a satellite dish, and do field geology using GPS & GIS (Geographic Information Systems)-equipped Tablet PCs as digital field notebooks.[31]

Online education is also going offline. Emerging "portable cloud computing" initiatives such as Thomas Edison State College's FlashTrack project make it much easier for students and instructors to work offline. This initiative enables students to keep up with their online studies on-the-go using a variety of mobile devices, including laptops, Netbooks, gaming devices, and mobile phones. Entire courses can be stored on an inexpensive USB flash drive which contains content, productivity applications, and even a basic course management system. The course is essentially self-contained and requires no installation onto a computer. Students can work offline, going online only to send assignments or receive updates.[32] Given the continuing trend toward ever greater storage capacity in ever smaller devices as exemplified by currently available USB flash drives and wrist bands with considerable storage capacities (2-16GB) at low cost ($15-40), it may be time to start talking about "offline education."

Courses which enable students to choose the delivery mode are becoming more readily available. Early examples included Ohio State University's "buffet" style calculus course, which allowed students to select a delivery mode at the beginning of the course,[33] and Virginia Tech's Math Emporium, where students can choose whether to do assignments online in a computer lab, access the course materials from their dorm computers, receive one-on-one tutoring, or attend a small group tutoring session.[34] San Francisco State University's "HyFlex" course design enables students to choose between online and in-class participation modes.[35] In effect, each student creates his or her own individualized mix of delivery modes in such courses; as a result, "online," "blended," or "classroom" increasingly describe choices rather than courses.

Cyberizing the Core of Formal Education

The cyberization of education will continue to happen at all levels of change. Digital technologies will become an ever-more important life resource, increasing the pressure on education to keep up with the rest of society. A cornucopia of learning and education resources which provide "openers for learning" will continue to proliferate, as will the use of digital tools and technologies for information, communication, and management delivery.

Beyond access to educational resources, content, or interaction, the core of formal education consists of two things: the teaching and learning relationship, and the institutional enterprise which supports that relationship and the many other vital societal functions which education is called upon to fulfill. The next two chapters describe some potentially transformative but currently underutilized strategies for using cyberization to improve education by re-empowering and revitalizing these two core functions.

CHAPTER 10

Strategies for (Re-) Empowering Learning and Teaching in Education

Learning-Centered Engagement

One of the best ways to re-empower something is to make it more engaging: the more participants engage themselves, the more rewarding their participation becomes. Increasing engagement re-empowers learning and teaching almost by definition, and the term *student engagement* has become one indicator of educational quality in U.S. higher education. Results from the annual National Survey of Student Engagement (NSSE) indicate that relatively low levels of student engagement are still commonplace in post-secondary education. For example, the 2010 NSSE results from over 362,000 students at about 600 higher education institutions in the U.S. and Canada reported that only about one-third of college freshmen and fewer than two-thirds of college seniors reported that they made class presentations "often" or "very often," while almost 40 percent of college freshmen and almost 30 percent of college seniors reported that they asked questions in class or contributed to class discussions "sometimes" or "never."[1] These results reflect an ongoing need for learning strategies that promote student engagement.

Increasing student engagement is also a major issue in K-12 education, as the 2006 Gates Foundation-funded study *The Silent Epidemic* indicates. Interviews of 467 dropouts indicated that most of these respondents felt disengaged from school – bored, unmotivated, unchallenged, and disconnected from the school environment. This lack of engagement applies to many capable students; over half of the study's respondents with high grade point averages cited uninteresting classes as a major factor in their decision to drop out of school.[2]

Current education practices contribute to this lack of engagement by treating teachers and students as instruments that can be manipulated and reliably controlled with sufficiently effective design, great content, or other "high-quality" inputs. By contrast, the common thread in strategies for re-empowering learning and teaching in education is *learning-centered engagement*, and the cyberization of education can be used to increase engagement in a wide variety of ways. As previous chapters have described, online education has been a rewarding professional development opportunity because it increases teacher engagement. Learning-centered engagement can be promoted in a variety of ways; some of these are new, some have been around a long time, and all of them would improve education if implemented more broadly.

Learner-Generated Content and Knowledge

I had never seen such creative presentations and pride of accomplishment.

– Malcolm Knowles, The Adult Learner: A Neglected Species[3]

One way to promote learning-centered engagement is to change the learners' role from passive recipients to active producers of content and knowledge. Learner-generated content has long been an integral part of American education: term papers, lab reports, science fair projects, oral presentations, and of course the elementary school art work which graces millions of American refrigerators. In practice, however, the role of learner-generated content is highly marginalized in American education. Students at all education levels are generally treated as content consumers who demonstrate that they have "learned the material" developed by academics or other expert professionals. Learner-generated content is most commonly used for this limited purpose in the form of work products which help students complete assignments, prepare for tests, or otherwise demonstrate comprehension or knowledge attainment. Student work products are usually not valued as primary content sources. The purest learner-generated content such as original artwork is generally the least academically valued, and its role in promoting intellectual development is still greatly underappreciated.

Anyone who has ever witnessed the excitement of learners who have created their own content knows its power to increase learner engagement. Although Malcolm Knowles' comment referred to his experience with adult learners, students of all ages can engage in generating content, knowledge, and work products in developmentally appropriate ways. Learner-developed primary content sources can produce more effective learning of content and contribute to intellectual development. Learner-developed work products can also have lasting value beyond the educational experience itself. Students can create learning resources for future students to use, work products which have actual benefit to society, and knowledge which will benefit the students themselves in their future studies, career, or other life pursuits.

Learner-generated content can result in effective learning. For instance, research has found that students involved with wiki textbook creation were more engaged with their text, interacted with it more frequently, and achieved academically at a comparable level to students who used instructor or publisher-created materials. In one study, students regarded their wiki textbook to be just as credible and useful as the traditional textbook they were using. Another study found that student wiki textbook creation increased collaboration, improved the accuracy of student writing, and increased students' sense of empowerment.[4]

Learner-generated content is a particularly powerful strategy for sharing knowledge and making it more accessible when needed. For example, podcasts are commonly used to record lectures for later playback, but University of Connecticut psychology professor David Miller moved beyond "coursecasting" lectures a long time ago. Since 2005, Miller and his students have created a series of weekly discussions about the course content which answer student questions that are asked in person or submitted in advance by email. The length of each podcast is open-ended and student-driven, depending on student questions. Student feedback indicated that the process of making podcasts for other students enabled in-person attendees to "gain more learning skills by discussing" in a way which was not possible in large lectures. Students also reported that the podcasts were valuable throughout the semester by answering common questions, and the interactive, unrehearsed conversation format with repetition of lecture material was seen as an engaging combination which enhanced perceived learning for most students.[5]

Learner-generated content also enables learners to be partners in the knowledge creation process. For the past several years, computer science professor

Edward Gehringer and his colleagues at North Carolina State University have used a custom-designed software tool called Expertiza to facilitate electronic peer review for a variety of purposes such as writing research papers, making up homework problems, and creating student wiki textbooks. Students select tasks, submit individually designed work products, and peer review their work. Performing tasks which resemble real world responsibilities enhances the learning experience, and Gehringer's research found that learner-generated exercises were as useful for learning as instructor-created ones.[6]

In higher education, learners can also create content to help others learn and to generate new knowledge which advances the field. At present, this level of knowledge development is generally reserved for the relative few. One blended learning approach which expands the opportunity to create useful knowledge is the Real-Time Case Method (RTCM) pioneered by Jim Theroux at the University of Massachusetts. In an RCTM course, students from multiple institutions study an actual company in depth based on case study materials developed in real time. Students use this material to generate valuable recommendations which the host company can implement to address real-life problems. Multiple studies indicate that RCTM has been highly effective in generating student engagement and satisfaction.[7]

Moving students from consumers of expert-authenticated content[8] to producers of content within a collaboratively negotiated process changes how knowledge is produced and gives students more power over their learning. Learner-generated content also enhances the teacher role by enabling instructors to focus on using higher order skills such as evaluating content or coaching and facilitating students through the creation process, while still maintaining a role as content expert.

Learner-generated content in K-12 education tends to focus more on activities that promote effective learning of content or intellectual development. Blogs are an increasingly popular online tool for enabling learners to generate and share content.[9] Allowing learners to generate their own content is deceptively powerful. Even something as simple as allowing students to create their own math problems can be a revelation, as this focus group conversation I had with a high school algebra teacher several years ago illustrates:

> T: …when students get work, it's always coming from someplace else, either from a book or from the teacher. But if you tell them, you make up a problem, somehow they feel – how could I possibly do that? I mean, they don't think that they're capable of writing any equation of any kind

in the $y = mx + b$ form, and suddenly they say, 'I can do that?' and I say, yeah you can do that! Put down a three, now pick another number you want, any variable a through z, and they'll do that, now add some numbers to that and set it equal to something, suddenly they realize, you mean that's all there is to it? Yeah, you can actually create stuff yourself. So I had them creating homework problems for the class — you do one, you do one, you do one, then the whole class will do that set. They're [making up] their own homework...and doing it themselves...at my school, that's true power for the kids.

Me: It sounds like you felt empowered doing that?

T: Oh yeah, absolutely.

Me: And the students told you they did as well?

T: Yeah.[10]

Learner-generated content can also be used to improve access by producing openly available knowledge resources. For example, University of North Carolina at Pembroke professor Kenneth Mentor's students built a wiki site called cjencyclopedia, which consisted of encyclopedia-type articles on a variety of criminal justice topics. Students worked collaboratively to write the articles as class assignments and improve their writing skills in the process; the project was also intended to produce open access learning materials for other criminal justice students.[11]

Most papers that students write are seen by only two people: the student and the instructor. Fullerton College's student-generated content project engages students to gain greater exposure for the work they produce. Fullerton's use of iTunes as a repository for all its student-generated work provides an "international exposure" for that work and increases student excitement about seeing their projects online.[12] The synergistic effect of redefining knowledge, renegotiating authority, and redistributing access can make the production of learner-generated content, products, and knowledge a powerful teaching and learning experience.

Event-Anchored Learning

Imagine that you are a cybersecurity professional whose company's network is being relentlessly attacked by some of the best hackers in the world. Participants in the Mid-Atlantic Regional Collegiate Cyber Defense Competition (CCDC)[13] don't have to imagine this; for two days, they experience it intensely as members of student teams who try to manage and protect an existing network infrastructure from attacks by a volunteer "Red Team" of cybersecurity professionals who are also master hackers. The competition, which has been run since 2006 as part of CyberWatch, a National Science Foundation-funded Advanced Technological Education (ATE) center focused on cybersecurity and information assurance education,[14] determines the regional qualifier for the national CCDC. The event is also a powerful learning experience; numerous participants have reported that they learn more in two days from the experience than they do in an entire semester or year(s) of classroom work. In reality, though, the two experiences complement each other: classroom learning provides the chance to learn theory and skills, and the competition provides hands-on application of theory and skills to practice. The event is also the culmination of a months-long, intense learning experience during which teams prepare to participate in a virtual preliminary competition to determine the regional finalists. Virtualizing the preliminary competition also made it possible to increase the number of participants by reducing time and travel costs; the competition expanded from eight teams and 58 participants in 2009 to 23 teams and 224 participants in 2011. The entire process generates local campus interest in the field while also helping student participants develop collaboration, communication, and management skills.

Michigan State University Global Institute (MSUGI)'s Food Safety Knowledge Network (FSKN) project[15] exemplifies another emerging approach to event-anchored learning: use in-person events to enable participants to meet, interact, and initiate professional relationships, while at the same time capturing the event content and repurposing it as open educational resources which participants and others can use after the event. For example, the FSKN web site includes a structured online training course and other open learning resources organized by related competencies; much of the related content was generated by capturing presentations at live events and was downloaded thousands of times for training and related purposes.[16] MSUGI's approaches to event-centered learning have evolved from an earlier "event-centered, online-supported" model which also combined in-person events with ongoing access to online program activities such as course materials, audio interviews, newsletters, and other learning support resources. This model aligned learning experiences with organizational professional development needs and individuals' personal enrichment goals.[17]

Realizing the Dreams of Social and Individualized Learning

Cyberization holds the potential to realize a long-held dream of individualizing learning, while at the same time enhancing the social aspect of learning by individualizing both inputs and outcomes. Customized learning empowers learners by using different methods to accommodate different learning interests, needs, and paces.

Social Learning

Skeptics believe that one of online learning's biggest shortcomings is that it reduces the human element by isolating learners and hindering interaction, thereby negating the possibility of interpersonal presence. Joy Ventura Riach's online learning experience not only refutes these myths but also turns them on their head. The online master's program which Riach is completing through the Institute of Transpersonal Psychology (ITP) moves way beyond mere interaction; it is a "full spectrum psychology" which encompasses both functional and dysfunctional human behavior as well as a "serious scholarly interest in the immanent and transcendent dimensions of human experience" such as exceptional human functioning, non-ordinary states of consciousness, and fostering human potential fulfillment.[18] It doesn't get more interpersonal than that.

To some, Transpersonal Psychology is the very antithesis of an appropriate field to study online, but Riach's experience indicates otherwise. ITP's accredited blended master's program requires several in-person seminars. Riach described the first time her cohort of eight students met in Palo Alto, California: "It was a reunion of long-lost friends – we hugged, we shared our stories... listening deeply... we were such a close group, that other cohorts would come to our table to hang out and take part in our energy."[19] Cohort members had used their previous online interaction to forge close bonds with each other, which in turn *enhanced the in-person experience itself*. Far from being a hindrance, online interaction can enhance the entire learning experience when learners use it to their advantage, as Riach and her cohort did: "We continued to deepen our friendship through a healthy intimacy of honesty and trust, online and in-person...we flavored our individual work with Facebook, some email, a phone call now and then." So it only makes sense that learners who are studying how to advance the frontiers of human capacity in the interpersonal realm are finding online education to be an effective tool in this process.

Beyond compelling anecdotes like these, a substantial amount of conceptual and empirical research literature shows the value of social learning in online education, in particular the role of interpersonal interaction. Much of the existing research correlates instructor-student interaction and required student-student interaction with improved perceived student learning and satisfaction.[20] Social learning occurs through a variety of online learning practices such as discussion forums, collaborative projects, and communities of practice. Research has also found that students perceive asynchronous online discussions to be more equitable and democratic relative to in-person classroom discourse.[21] Multiple studies have found that teaching online enhances the teaching role by shifting instructors' responsibilities; for instance, one study found that instructors' cognitive role became deeper and more complex, while their managerial role required more attention to detail, structure, and student monitoring.[22]

Online open learning resources also support social learning. For instance, the OpenStudy web site focuses on "peers helping peers" to learn, according to CEO and cofounder Chris Sprague. OpenStudy aims to change perceptions about learning by providing a "community that is available 24/7" which engages students and enables them to become role models for each other.[23]

Individualized Learning

Individualized instruction in the form of private tutelage goes back at least as far as ancient Greece, for example Socrates or the tutors of Alexander the Great. In modern times, individualized instruction has long been viewed as a viable alternative to the shortcomings of classroom instruction and especially to the lecture method, which sacrifices individual learning for the efficiency, convenience, and cost savings of mass broadcast delivery. For more than five decades dating back to Benjamin Bloom in the mid 1950s, research findings have indicated that individualized instruction is a highly effective and cognitively efficient approach for most learners and that it is far superior to classroom-style learning because instructional content and style can be continuously adapted to best meet learner needs.[24] Individualized instruction has taken many forms during that period, including the Skinner box, Audio-Tutorial, Keller Personalized System of Instruction, and computer-based systems.[25]

Computer-based instructional systems have been around for several decades. Early versions used programmed instruction, in which the programs determined the learning sequence. Eventually, adding features such as branching and mastery learning enabled learner responses to help determine the learning sequence; these features also helped students learn by doing and from making mistakes.[26] Intelligent tutoring systems extend adaptive capabilities by collecting learner progress information and using domain knowledge bases to specify appropriate content and instructional strategies. One well-established example is LON-CAPA (LearningOnline Network/Computer-Assisted Personalized Approach), a "free open source distributed learning content management and assessment system" which Michigan State University has used since 1992. LON-CAPA enables faculty to augment courses with individualized homework and other exercises within an online content management system which also handles grading, communication, group work, and enrollment. More than 150 institutions worldwide use LON-CAPA for middle school to graduate level courses in a wide variety of disciplines.[27]

Over the past 20 years, intelligent tutoring systems and other types of computer-based instructional systems have become even more sophisticated in enabling individualized inputs. Several courseware products use various types of learning analytics for this purpose. For instance, Carnegie-Mellon's OLI courseware collects continuous, real-time student performance data, which makes it possible to track the level of assistance students need as they move through the course content. OLI courseware also includes an instructor dashboard that enables teachers to differentiate or adjust instruction based on student progress data.[28]

Increasing learner control is another strategy for individualizing learning. Some courses now allow students to *select delivery modes* for an entire course, or for course assignments and activities. For example, Western Kentucky University professor Judith Szerdahelyi provides instructions and feedback to students in her advanced online English composition courses based on their reported media preferences: text, audio, or video+text format. Szerdahelyi believes that "feedback is crucially important for revision and student learning" in English composition, so she also provides text, audio, and video files which provide instructions and feedback for each reading assignment to "individualize teaching and improve students' learning satisfaction."[29]

Enabling learners to *select activities and assignments* also increases learner control. Although giving students more say in choosing what to study has long been recognized as an effective way to motivate learners,[30] it remains an underutilized strategy. One high school algebra teacher who used online resources to support classroom instruction found that

> ...allowing my students to have a choice or a say in activities they did, problems they did, and sometimes in the way they were assessed...really got a lot of students more involved – it was amazing in my classes, whenever they felt they had a say or a choice in what they were going to do, that changed their performance.[31]

Online open learning resources also make it easier to students to individualize their learning by enabling them to choose activities and assignments that supplement or replace their formal education activities. The availability of these resources is expanding rapidly, and so is their use; for example, the Khan Academy has delivered over 80 million lessons from its extensive library of over 2,600 videos, along with practice exercises and assessments.[32]

Cyberized education can enable greater learner control not just over learning events, but also *over the learning process itself.* The flexibility and convenience of "anywhere, anytime" learning is recognized as one of the great strengths of online education, and it enables learners to exercise more self-discipline as described previously. Another important but usually overlooked aspect of learner control is simple physical freedom: particularly in asynchronous learning environments, online learners have much more control over when, where, and how long they will study and what to do with their bodies during the process. Online learners are subject to far fewer physical limitations, in stark contrast to traditional classroom environments where most physical self-expressions – motions, laughter, loud speech or other sounds, even doodling – are considered disruptive and so are tightly controlled. In teacher-centered environments, such expressions distract from the intended focus on the "lesson" and from the teacher as center of attention. While traditional classroom environments actively promote separation of mind from body, online education gives learners greater freedom in maintaining control over that connection.

As valuable as each of these approaches can be, they also suffer from an important limitation: they stop short of being truly individualized learning, which customizes both the inputs[33] and the results. Customized outcomes are commonplace at the advanced end of the formal learning experience in the form of doctoral dissertations and other graduate work. At the other end of the spectrum, kindergarten still allows for a fair amount of variety in learning outcomes, although the relentless push of standards-driven curriculum has started to change this as well. Customizing learning recognizes that the teaching and learning process is not an assembly line product, but one that leverages learners' unique talents, needs, interests, perspectives, and performance.

Strategies for supporting customized outcomes

Formal education already customizes learning to some extent. Learners choose what they learn from the available curriculum, so different learners learn different things. Learners learn things in slightly different ways and have unique understandings of what they learn. Because learners create their own learning experience, each individual has a "unique and visible pattern of achievement and readiness."[34] Cyberized education vastly increases the potential to personalize learning at much greater scale and depth. For instance, computer-based instructional systems make it much easier to enable, track, and assess personalized learning outcomes. The power of digital technologies to automate processes at scale also removes barriers which previously hampered the implementation of outcomes-based frameworks. For example, eLumen's outcomes-based framework[35] provides new capabilities for customizing learning and assessment:

- *Tracking outcomes attainment at the program level* allows a single assignment or activity to be used to assess multiple outcomes, and multiple activities can be used to assess larger outcomes. This departs from the traditional practice in higher education of treating courses as separate universes and spending little attention to tracking outcomes attainment across courses.

- *Assessing student work using faculty-created rubrics with explicit quality criteria* can replace the common practice of using implicit or undisclosed criteria to grade student work, saving students much time and energy trying to figure out what is expected of them.

- *Defining learning outcomes through collaborative faculty decision-making* at both the academic program and institutional level also allows faculty to create assessment rubrics for evaluating those outcomes. This contrasts with customary academic practice which makes individual instructors entirely responsible for determining assessment criteria for student work.

- *Tracking individual outcomes attainment* treats student learning outcomes as both individual student attributes and organizational attributes.

Learners can also have a say in choosing their own learning objectives. This requires a significant renegotiation of authority, but as Portland State University assessment expert Gary Brown asserts, "Students can't engage in learning if faculty hoard the responsibility for determining their learning goals and outcomes. Students also need to have a generative role in their own learning,"[36] and when learners can choose, form, and otherwise personalize their own objectives, customized outcomes are the inevitable result.

Inquiry-based learning is another method which supports collaboratively negotiated learning objectives. In well-designed inquiry-based learning environments, learning objectives emerge from a set of real-world problem solving tasks in the context of a social community of practice. The inquiry process itself forms the objectives, which change and develop their own character during the process. When learners choose their own learning objectives, the entire process requires greater use of reflection, critical thinking, and other metacognitive skills.[37] It also enhances the teacher role by emphasizing facilitation, guidance, and use of knowledge expertise to help students make the connection between their chosen objectives and the field of inquiry.

Blending the Individual and the Social

The tension between the individual and society is also one of the defining tensions of education. Advocates sometimes overemphasize an individual or social approach to the teaching and learning process. For instance, socio-cognitive learning theories assert that all learning is social[38] and that learners construct knowledge through social interactions. As a result, some social learning advocates insist on required interaction among learners in every online course. However, this requirement often increases learner interactivity at the expense of learner autonomy by decreasing flexibility, convenience, and learner control over the time, place, and pace of learning. Many learners prefer a more individualized, self-paced approach, and the research literature also supports self-paced, tutorial, and other more individualized approaches which do not require student-student interaction.[39] On the other hand, purely individualized learning has its own limitations, and many learners report feeling too isolated in online courses.

A better approach is to improve both social and individualized learning, since it is difficult to separate the individual and the social components of many learning environments in practice. *Personal learning environments* and *personal learning networks* are one example of how the two are combined, as they are the individual and social side of the same coin: a personalized, user-driven approach to learning. The term *personal learning environment* (PLE) describes the collections of resources such as tools, services and communities which learners build and use to pursue their individual learning and educational goals. In most educational experiences, including most current online education, learners use 'off-the-shelf' learning resources which have been selected for them such as textbooks, materials on reserve in the library, or learning resources loaded into LMSs. PLEs represent a "do-it-yourself" model in which learners select, compile, and organize the resources they use.

Although the concept is an amorphous and evolving one, PLEs are commonly conceived as a distinct, web-based place which one can view and share with others. PLEs predate the Internet, of course; in the old days, it was a room in the house with walls of bookshelves and was called a "study." The Internet and the Web have vastly increased the capabilities of PLEs, but building one requires a certain skill set which includes technological proficiency, willingness to learn new web-based tools, information fluency, and the ability to self-direct one's learning. As with "do-it-yourself" projects of all sorts, building, maintaining and growing one's PLE also requires a certain level of commitment to engage in the ongoing process.[40]

Having a *personal learning network* (PLN) epitomizes the New Smart. A PLN is a large collection of people who help you learn by engaging with them, exchanging information, finding out about learning opportunities, or even having them guide your learning. PLNs have also been around a long time through contacts with friends, family, and colleagues[41] – remember the rolodex? Web-based tools such as blogs, wikis, and social networking sites expand one's capabilities to build and utilize a PLN that is far more powerful than a rolodex. PLNs vastly increase opportunities to ask questions and receive help from a global community compared to normal daily face-to-face interactions. PLNs are also personal and do-it-yourself: the individual decides what tools to use, whom to connect with, and how, what, and when to learn.[42]

Perhaps because of their learner-centered nature, it's fairly clear how PLEs and PLNs relate to lifelong learning and informal education,[43] but it's less clear how they relate to formal education. At present, there are many calls for their use in formal education, but actual examples are not easy to find. One view is that PLEs change the role that people and media play in teaching and learning,[44] as they support learner-generated content and knowledge by enabling learners to take an active role in selecting, assembling, and organizing learning resources. PLEs can also enable a greater emphasis on metacognitive skills since they encourage learners to actively consider and reflect upon the specific tools and resources that they use, which leads to a deeper engagement with the content. PLNs can perform similar functions if they are explicitly directed to that purpose. Both PLEs and PLNs shift authority to learners by giving them far more control and responsibility over the learning resources they use. PLEs and PLNs are often viewed as an either/or alternative to existing practices such as the use of LMSs. In practice, different varieties of PLEs and PLNs are likely to evolve which reflect varying degrees of learner input, involvement, and responsibility.

Human Hooks: Creativity, Curiosity

Curiosity [is] the heart of academic engagement.

– Todd Kashdan, author of Curious?[45]

Creativity and curiosity are the most important "human hooks" that lead to learner engagement. Business leaders recognize the importance of creativity and innovation; according to interviews with over 1,500 CEOs worldwide, creativity is *the* most important leadership characteristic.[46] A 2009 New Media Consortium report noted that the design of learning experiences "must reflect the growing importance of innovation and creativity as professional skills."[47] Research has also demonstrated the links between creativity and learner engagement in formal education.[48]

Unfortunately, creativity and curiosity tend to be perennial afterthoughts in most educational practice. They are conspicuous by their absence in the current standards-driven educational "reform" movement, and they are still relatively uncommon in online and other forms of cyberized education as well. Creativity consultant Kathy Kegley and her Clemson University colleague Tina Robbins are bucking this trend by introducing creativity training to online management and elective courses. Their research indicates that using "thinkertoys" and other methods of building creative abilities enabled course participants to show significant increases in both creative self-efficacy and demonstration of creative abilities.[49]

Inquiry-based online learning environments are also especially well-suited to supporting creativity and curiosity. Perhaps the most notable example is the WebQuest; developed by San Diego State University professor Bernie Dodge in 1995, WebQuests enable learners to follow their curiosity while engaging them in applying higher level thinking to authentic problems.[50] Intriguingly, some research findings also suggest that online courses induce more creativity by pushing students to compensate for the absence of in-person interaction with their instructor or classmates. In one study, students reported being more creative in their online courses because they wanted to increase the value of their work and because the work itself was more challenging and required more creative and strategic thinking to complete.[51] Cyberized education offers many excellent ways to design learning experiences which support curiosity and promote creativity.

Technohooks: Augmented Reality, Virtual Worlds, Gaming

One might think that the most promising ways to use the cyberization of education for learning-centered engagement would be to use the most cutting-edge technologies. In reality, prominent "technohooks" such as augmented reality, virtual worlds, and gaming appeal to a significant fraction of learners, but they certainly do not appeal to all learners. The benefits of these technologies are sometimes oversold, and they should be seen as important strategies rather than as comprehensive solutions.

Then again, you might arrive at a somewhat different conclusion after spending some time with Colorado Technical University professor and self-described "researcher geek" Cynthia Calongne. A technology evangelist and one-person dynamo, Calongne personifies how one can be thoroughly engaged in virtual worlds and the 'real' world simultaneously. As her numerous SlideShare presentations attest,[52] Calongne (also known as Lyr Lobo in Second Life) spends much of her time journeying on the frontiers of new teaching technologies for engaging learners such as virtual worlds, augmented reality, and game-based learning. Her message: we are just getting started with exploring the incredible potential of these technologies and of the ones yet to come. For example, virtual worlds, which replace a real world experience with a simulated one, are excellent venues for teaching writing because they promote interaction within settings which depict imaginative scenes and an unfolding story, creating a sense of presence. Augmented reality adds multimedia elements to a real world environment in ways that allow users to retrieve and manipulate information. Examples include simulations such as the University of Massachusetts's sickle hemoglobin molecule, which students can see and manipulate in ways not possible in the real world, and flight or surgical simulators which enable users to practice related motor skills.[53] Mobile augmented reality applications are another emerging technology which is likely to be used for future teaching and learning applications. Game-based learning applications such as Conspiracy Code[54] and Calculation Nation[55] enable students to develop skills and learn content in a situated, engaging environment. All of these technologies allow users to engage in learning experiences that remove the potentially harmful consequences of doing comparable 'real-world' actions.

Sensible Assessment of Learning and Teaching

Sensible assessment supports a variety of methods to measure learning and attainment by combining external, standardized, internal, and individualized measures of achievement. Sensible assessment is integrated into the teaching and learning process[56] and aligns with the elements of that process, including learning objectives, assignments, instruction, and personal reflection. Sensible assessment also supports the development of independent, self-initiating learners while informing and improving practice[57] in the process. Examples of sensible ways to assess learning and teaching are not hard to find:

- An undergraduate textile design class that includes industry professionals who provide 'ground truth' feedback about how taking the course improves students' employability (or not).

- An information assurance student who finds that the experience of participating in an intense cybersecurity competition validates her plan to pursue further education in the field, while another participant realizes that this is not the field for him after all.

- A human resources development student who uses feedback from her instructor and peers for a class assignment to refine a policies and procedures manual, which her employer subsequently adopts as company policy.

- A middle school student who takes a test and does more poorly than expected, then passes the test a week later after spending the additional time required to attain mastery.

Sensible assessment offers an important antidote to current assessment practices, which too often function as indoctrination or sorting mechanisms, rely excessively on standardized tests, treat students as passive receptacles, reduce teachers to test preparation technicians, and treat assessment itself as an afterthought or as an autopsy that tries to figure out what happened after the learning event has passed. Instead, sensible assessment makes knowledge attainment more measurable in meaningful ways by connecting the learning process with larger societal goals and with the learner's individual interests, goals, and life. Sensible assessment can accommodate a set of core standards which are assessed by standardized tests, so long as such standards reflect what is necessary for everyone to know and are attainable and assessable by different means. Integrated with individualized learning, individualized assessment increases access by providing multiple paths to documenting effective learning while recognizing that knowledge is contextual and constructed. Several sensible assessment approaches are emerging which reflect these aims.

Harvesting Diverse Feedback

Washington State University's Center for Teaching, Learning, and Technology developed a model which uses technology to "harvest" diverse feedback from faculty, students, and industry professionals as part of the assessment process. One of their main goals was to demonstrate how to use diverse feedback instead of standardized measures to meet and exceed accountability requirements. In one study, students worked on a semester-long design project which was assessed by departmental faculty, industry professionals, and the students themselves. Each group was asked to assess student learning outcomes, including critical and integrative thinking, as well as the overall employability of students in the field based on their projects. The results of the assessment provided valuable feedback to all participants about how the project improved both learning and potential employability in the field. The results also illustrated how to hold students to high, authentic standards through diverse teams, projects, and methods without the need for standardized measures. As the study's authors noted, "Responsible accountability is about improvement, not measurement." Leveraging the insights of key stakeholders takes advantage of their diverse viewpoints while also sending a clear message that teaching and learning is everyone's business, not just that of educators. According to study co-author Gary Brown, this approach also enables a more sophisticated form of assessment which "compares expectations and the means to achieve those expectations with accomplishments as determined by those in the community of practice," including faculty, practitioners, and students.[58]

Impact Assessment

Traditional learning assessment focuses primarily on institution-centered outcomes. Grades, course completion rates, and other student achievement measures are framed from an institutional point of view; results are used to serve institution-oriented needs such as comparing results with other courses or improving courses. Data collection processes are extractive, benefits to students are indirect, and the impact beyond this frame of reference is largely ignored.

To counteract these shortcomings, Towson University Professor Emeritus Joan McMahon developed an alternative approach to engage learners by supporting their capacity to value, reflect on, and make meaning from their learning. According to McMahon, impact assessment is an "insight-based process grounded in the adult learning principle of relevancy" with the purpose of "asking students to capture those 'aha' moments in learning." Impact assessment uses a guided reflection process that focuses on student responses to statements containing key "trigger words" which enable them to identify or generate insights that reveal the impact of their learning. The process also encourages students to step outside of the usual game-playing, hoop-jumping exercise which formal education too often becomes. In fact, McMahon has often been surprised by how honestly her students confront these statements during the impact assessment process. "Students will sometimes write in their impact assessment responses, 'I really could have done more on this assignment, or worked better with my teammates on that project.' They will self-assess their learning experience critically but constructively, and share that in ways which rarely happen with traditional assessments."[59]

The use of impact assessment is deceptively simple, but it is also rarely done. Just as the right amount of the right spice can transform a bland, forgettable dish into a tasty, memorable one, the subtle but purposeful change in focus which impact assessment offers can make the learning experience a lot more rewarding for its participants. For example, the student who turned a class assignment into a company's policies and procedures manual used an impact assessment process. The act of paying conscious attention to impact sends learners the simple but powerful message that what they are learning is important beyond the educational experience itself. It also encourages them to rediscover the power of asking these simple questions: What does this learning experience mean to me? How has it affected my academic career, my work career, future plans, life? How could it have been better for me? How could I have been better in it?

Impact assessment's emphasis on relevancy engages students more deeply and helps them practice skills they will need to face the challenges of the future, such as reflection, analysis, synthesis, and evaluation. The impact assessment process also makes the teaching experience more rewarding by enabling instructors to discover more about the benefits of their labors, through learning what their students value about what they have learned.

E-portfolio Assessment

An e-portfolio is a collection of student work that is stored in a Web-accessible or other digital format, that can be stored in a web-based information management system with its attendant capabilities, and that supports assessment and other important teaching and learning activities.[60] E-portfolio systems can be implemented at the school, career, or course level; a student e-portfolio consists of artifacts which reflect a body of work from a course, a series of courses, or an entire school career. E-portfolios can be used for a variety of assessment-related purposes, including student reflection, higher order assessment, and performance-based assessment.

E-portfolios enable the self-reflection process by facilitating the collect-ing, considering, sharing, and presenting of learning outcomes within a larger learning cycle that integrates theory, action, self-reflection, and assessment.[61] In higher education, e-portfolios have enabled students to reflect on their growth in different areas over time.[62] Higher order assessment extends standardized forms of assessment by assessing higher order thinking skills, by including student-selected outcomes, and by supporting attainment of deep understanding. E-portfolios are especially well-suited to assessing attainment of higher order thinking skills; for instance, many school districts in Rhode Island have used individualized student digital portfolios to assess students' problem solving and reasoning skills.[63] "Constructivist" approaches to e-portfolio development enable students to include items that reflect learning from their perspective, which can be readily integrated with items selected by teachers and other stakeholders and which reflect their standards and interests.[64] E-portfolios can also engage students in creating performances and applying their skills and knowledge to solving "real-world" problems while producing assessable work such as artifacts, attestations, and productions.[65] E-portfolios are not panaceas; they can become a misused tool, and implementation and usage can be difficult and expensive. Done well, however, e-portfolios can help tremendously with sensible assessment.

Growing Self-Initiating Learners

Improving student skills has been a concern for decades. The desired skill sets go by various labels such as 21st century skills, higher order thinking, metacognitive skills, and complex thinking. They typically consist of a set of cognitive skills (e.g., critical thinking, reflection, analysis, synthesis), communication skills (e.g., oral and written communication), and interpersonal skills (e.g., sharing responsibility, negotiation, teamwork).

Beyond developing learners with higher skills is an even loftier aspiration, based on the need to adapt to the tumultuous changes in American society and elsewhere. In the work world, new types of workers and work environments are emerging such as micropreneurs and other free agents,[66] federated support networks,[67] and telecommuting. Business leaders and organizations are increasingly looking for employees who do more than simply wait for directions to follow: they want employees who can solve identified problems and who use their initiative to find potential problems and create solutions.

Change has swept across every other aspect of Americans' lives as well. Over the past several decades, Americans have faced a much wider array of choices across the entire range of their lives – home ownership, financial planning, lifelong education, lifestyle choices, family arrangements, sexual and romantic relationships, multicultural settings, citizenship, ethnic cuisines, you name it. The elements common to each of these developments – greater complexity, abstraction, freedom, choice, and responsibility — demand a new kind of education and a new kind of learner: self-directed and self-reliant. In a world of seven billion people with several billion more on the way, we live fundamentally interdependent lives, but our abilities to be effective learners start from within — with the ability to be *self-initiating learners*.

Andragogy (adult-centered education) has recognized the importance of the independent, autonomous, self-directed learner[68] for several decades; at the other end of the age scale, two-year-old children are now seen as becoming "independent, self-initiating learners" who develop "personal methods of inquiry."[69] In between, however, pedagogy has long been defined in very different terms, reflecting a view of education as something which is *done to* learners. This needs to change if education is to play a meaningful role in preparing people for the future they face.

The need to grow self-initiating learners appears to be gaining greater recognition in undergraduate, high school, and even earlier education. Implementing strategies for re-empowering learning and teaching — learning-centered engagement, learner-generated content and knowledge, event-anchored learning, individualized and social learning, human hooks and technohooks, and sensible assessment — can go a long way toward making this happen. However, there are also changes that need to happen at the institutional level.

CHAPTER 11

Strategies for Revitalizing the Educational Enterprise

Revitalizing the Educational Enterprise

There is a widespread perception that American education is losing its vitality: failing, falling behind, in need of "fixing." The reality is that American education has improved substantially over the past forty years but not nearly fast enough to meet its many institutional challenges. These challenges include the usually cited issues such as increasing graduation rates, keeping students in the education "pipeline," and reaching an increasingly diverse learner population, but the foundational shifts of redefined knowledge, redistributed access, and renegotiated authority also pose challenges to institutions. The task of improving American education to meet these challenges, and to restore its vitality in the process, is an enterprise in the larger sense of the word: an undertaking which is large in scope, complicated, difficult, and risky. This chapter describes how the cyberization of education can support three important strategies for revitalizing the educational enterprise: expanding merit, re-empowering education's historic role as creator of knowledge, and adopting a sensible approach to assess the success of educational institutions.

Expanding Merit

Despite its many inequities, American education reflects a belief in meritocracy as a core principle that supports the pursuit of the American Dream. As Peter Smith argues in his book *Harnessing America's Wasted Talent*, making educational attainment ever more essential for individual and society's success drastically changes the mission of higher education: it reverses the educational challenge from sorting and judging merit toward creating and validating it.[1] Expanding the concept of merit is essential for meeting the challenge of redistributing access, and one way to ensure that more people have a chance for individual success is to expand the availability of possible paths for attaining and demonstrating merit.

Prior Learning Assessment

Prior Learning Assessment (PLA) is the process of granting academic credit for prior learning by evaluating college-level knowledge and skills gained outside of the classroom or from non-college instructional programs.[2] PLA recognizes that adults have many ways to engage in significant learning in their lives: training programs or in-service courses, employment, military training or service, independent reading and study, volunteer service, cultural and artistic pursuits, community or religious activities, organizational memberships, travel and study abroad, even hobbies and recreational pastimes. Institutional PLA programs commonly use several different methods to award credit for prior learning which can be used in various ways depending on student and program characteristics, although the best PLA programs offer all these options:[3]

- The *American Council on Education's College Credit Recommendation Service (CREDIT)*[4] recommends academic credit for formal courses and examinations taken outside traditional degree programs, including professional certifications, corporate training curricula, and military service school curricula.

- Some individual colleges *evaluate local training* to assess and award credit for recognized proficiencies achieved through locally available non-collegiate instructional programs.

- *Standardized exams* such as the College Level Examination Program, Advanced Placement, and the U.S. Department of Defense's DANTES program allow learners to receive credit for prior learning by demonstrating sufficient knowledge to pass the equivalent of a comprehensive examination for selected courses.

- Some institutions also have their own *challenge exams* which provide the opportunity to earn academic course credit for competencies gained outside the classroom.[5]

- *Credit by portfolio* involves translating prior learning into college credit by enabling students to develop individualized portfolios which document learning and which faculty or subject matter experts assess to determine awarding of educational credit.

The credit by portfolio option also highlights the difference between learning and education, since the criteria commonly used to guide portfolio development also differentiate learning from college-level education. Many institutions with strong PLA programs use these four criteria recommended by the Council for Adult and Experiential Learning (CAEL):

- **Learning should include both a theoretical basis and practical application to demonstrate understanding of a subject.** For example, a business owner who researched and prepared a business plan could show evidence of understanding business development principles.

- **Learning should apply outside of the specific area in which it was learned.** For example, learning gained from a policy seminar about a specific industry should apply to policies in other types of industries.

- **Learning should relate to a subject area eligible for higher education credits.** Students can relate their learning experiences to college course syllabi, for instance.

- **Faculty experts should identify the learning as college level.** Faculty who teach the courses evaluate the depth and the quality of the learning detailed in the Portfolio.

Credit by portfolio programs often have two other key characteristics: **ability to write at a college level** and **demonstration of learning attainment** as evidenced by a portfolio or other work product. Some institutions include additional criteria related to their particular policies. Most institutions limit the amount of credit which can be obtained through PLA to ensure that any degrees awarded reflect the institution's distinctive qualities.

Despite these restrictions, PLA lowers barriers to re-entering college by giving adult learners a kick-start toward degree completion, which reduces the time needed to earn a degree and lowers the cost of obtaining that degree. CAEL conducted a comprehensive study of over 62,000 adult undergraduates at 48 colleges and universities and found that students who received academic credit for PLA programs were more likely to persist, and more than twice as likely to graduate, relative to peer students who had not earned credit via PLA. These results were found for almost all types of institutions and demographic categories represented in the study. Reducing time to degree resulted in significantly reduced costs; for 15 PLA credits earned, the savings in tuition costs alone ranged from about $1,600 at a large public university to about $6,000 at other institutions.[6]

PLA has been around for many decades, but the Web's capacity to increase access, convenience, and flexibility is making the PLA process far easier, more fluid, and more transparent. PLA has also long been a favored strategy by the U.S. military to help service members be more successful with college degree completion through its Servicemembers Opportunity Colleges program. Started in 1972, SOC's 1,900 institutional members enroll hundreds of thousands of servicemembers, their family members, and veterans annually in degree programs at all levels.[7]

Still, PLA remains a relatively unknown and underutilized strategy. Although over half of all U.S. colleges award some kind of credit for prior learning, very few offer it on a significant scale[8] or utilize multiple PLA methods. Students, colleges and policy makers often lack awareness of PLA programs, which is one obstacle to greater adoption. As CAEL's Senior Director for Online Programs Susan Kannel notes, adult students, employers, and state funding sources would "utilize these options to the max" if they were better known.[9] However, most colleges are less motivated to adopt PLA programs, although this is changing since more states or regions have now mandated PLA programs. Other obstacles include establishing policies which enable institutional readiness for PLA programs and training institutions how to implement the PLA process effectively.

To address these issues, CAEL has partnered with several other organizations to build a national virtual PLA center called Learning Counts. This online assessment service is designed to enable institutions nationwide to assess adults' prior learning using the variety of available methods. The goal is to help increase access for adult learners and increase institutional participation by making the service available in ways previously not possible.[10] For example, the Learning Counts service helps reduce the costs of training faculty and staff to establish a PLA process at small colleges and universities.[11]

Supported Opportunity: Student Success Systems

Another way to expand merit is to focus less on sorting and judging merit and more on creating it instead. Reflecting a gradual paradigm shift from providing instruction to producing learning,[12] many colleges and universities are focusing more on results such as successful course, program, or degree completion. Although commonly described in terms of increasing retention rates or reducing attrition, *student success* is an even better descriptor. Much of the effort to improve student success is happening in online education, partly because its rapid growth has highlighted the need for institutions to scale needed services to meet increased demand.

One emerging approach involves building student success systems which change the emphasis from simple opportunity to what might be called *supported opportunity*. For instance, the driving assumption behind J. Sargeant Reynolds Community College's initiative "The Ripple Effect" is that

> The full definition of access in the academic context is not limited to merely providing students with the opportunity to pursue their college and career goals. More importantly, true and meaningful access includes the provision of resources and services that help students to succeed in their efforts.[13]

JSRCC is implementing a Quality Enhancement Plan which is designed to improve student success for distance learners by building and coordinating three key components into a systemic approach: student readiness, student orientation, and faculty training.

Student success systems in online education have been around in various forms for some time, and sometimes simple changes can make big differences. For example, while at University of Maryland University College, former Director of Academic Success Sharon Morgenthaler developed a student academic success program for UMUC's School of Undergraduate Studies which implemented several simple but commonly ignored principles:[14]

- **Use 'at-risk' status as a starting point to improve student success, not an end point**. Most institutions give up on students who cite reasons for withdrawal that are out of the institution's control. Morgenthaler's program built support service structures to help at-risk students learn to be successful rather than succumbing to the obstacles that impede their progress.

- **Bring support staff to the students, not the other way around.**
  While many institutions rely on students to seek and find tutors, the
  UMUC program makes tutors available in selected online high-enroll-
  ment entry courses. Students can post questions to tutors at any time
  throughout the course and can also read responses posted to classmates'
  questions.[15]

- **Increase opportunities for involvement and sense of community.** Research shows that involved students are more likely to persist
  in their studies and that online students also want social and professional
  networking opportunities, so UMUC hired several learning coaches to
  develop and support online communities. UMUC's online students have
  access to a variety of student clubs online, virtual guests and lecturers, and
  even nationally recognized honor societies for eligible students. Findings
  show that UMUC students value the opportunity for peer engagement
  and discussion of career-related issues with faculty and outside experts.

- **Make student success a bigger part of the faculty's job** by making
  it clear that supporting student success is part of a faculty's job description; this includes providing faculty professional development on how to
  support student success.

- **Build a culture of student success.** UMUC has developed more visible means of recognizing and supporting high achieving students, such as
  the dozens of student, alumni, and faculty success stories featured promi-
  nently on their web site.

Many institutions make similar efforts for their online programs in various
related areas, including student readiness, orientation, and early intervention.
Institutions with high completion rates in their online courses also cite a variety
of factors which contribute to their programs' success, including a strong faculty
support system, robust course development capabilities, and institutional strategic
commitment to student success.[16] Effective student success systems which start
as online or distance learning initiatives often quickly spread to serve students on
campus. For example, when JSRCC expanded its pilot online tutoring program to
all subject areas, it also opened up the service to campus-based students. JSRCC
also made its online peer advisors available to campus students on a trial basis by
adding online student peer advisors to its campus-based ones when it expanded its
peer advising program. Building online student success system components which
reach an entire campus's students is also becoming more common.

Online courses can also be an integral part of an institution's entire student success support system, especially because "campus" and "online" students are often the same students at some institutions. At the Rochester Institute of Technology, for example, campus-based students comprised almost sixty percent of its total online student population in 2007-2008. RIT found that students in their 2001 freshman class who took at least one online course while at RIT were far more likely to graduate in six years (79.2 percent vs. 54.8 percent) than those who did not take an online course. Investigation of subsequent freshmen classes confirmed this relationship and also found that year-to-year retention rates remained consistently better for students who took one or more online courses.[17] Another recent study found that students' likelihood of staying in college correlated to their perception of whether online or web-based communication was seen as an excellent medium for social interaction.[18] In a wired world, online education can provide models for how to encourage the social interaction which supports student retention.

Creating and Validating Merit in K-12 Education

Online education can also help with creating and validating merit in K-12 education by increasing available opportunities for institutions to offer courses for dual enrollment (high school and college) credit. Students who participate in dual enrollment courses are more likely to maintain "academic momentum" and persistence through the second year of college.[19] Virtual schools and well-designed online credit recovery programs can enable school systems to offer effective alternatives for at-risk and other students who have not succeeded in demonstrating merit through traditional schooling methods.[20]

From Pipeline to Interstate: Serving Swirlers, Stopouts, Stay-Longers, & Savvy Explorers

Pathways to higher education degrees tend to treat students as if they were in a pipeline, flowing homogeneously from Point A (matriculation) to Point B (degree attainment) on a relatively direct, uniform schedule. In practice, however, college students navigate their way through the process in a wide variety of ways, and they make numerous decisions which affect their choice of study even in programs where navigational flexibility is quite limited.[21] As the proportion of traditional students continues to decrease, a new breed of students is emerging in their place:

Swirlers are students who attend multiple institutions during their collegiate career, taking courses from different institutions in the same semester, transferring frequently between or among different types of higher education institutions, or transferring between programs within institutions.[22] The concept of swirlers has been around for a while (the term was coined about 20 years ago),[23] and the available statistics are not that new either. A 2005 National Center for Education Statistics report found that forty percent of students who entered college in the 1995-1996 academic year attended at least two institutions in the following six years, and that almost sixty percent of 1999–2000 college graduates had attended more than one institution.[24] This means that about 2.5 million college students transfer each year. Although more recent statistics are not available, the proliferation of online education over the past ten years suggests that the percentage of swirlers has likely increased significantly.[25]

Many swirlers also become *stopouts*: students who drop in and out of college, pausing their education rather than dropping out of college permanently. Stop-outs have been around for even longer; a 1971 survey suggested that as many as one-third of college students paused their education to work, travel, or simply take a break from their education.[26] However, today's stopouts are much more likely to be nontraditional students who are adult, employed, and enrolled part-time, so they tend to take longer to complete degrees because their periods away from education tend to be longer and more frequent.[27] In practice, it is essentially impossible to distinguish between dropouts and stopouts except by self-report, especially since it is not uncommon for working adults to take as many as seven years to complete an associates degree.[28]

Stay-longers also confound traditional enrollment patterns by taking longer to pass through the pipeline, except that they never stop out; they simply take fewer courses per term. As Colorado Mountain College Instructional Chair for Online Learning Lisa Cheney-Steen observes, "We see many students who take one or two courses every semester, stretching a two-year degree into five years."[29] CAEL has stopped describing the associate degree programs it cosponsors as "two-year degrees" because it views the term as both inaccurate and demeaning; the implied time expectation ignores the realities which confront most working adults who are pursuing their education.

Savvy explorers are a newer phenomenon: students who are finding their own paths to attaining a college education which go beyond swirling, stopping out, or simply staying longer. Types of savvy explorers include *autodidacts, do-it-youselfers, and New Global Students*. Autodidacts, or self-taught learners, have been around for centuries; their relationships with formal education vary, but the growing availability of online programs and other alternative means of earning educational credit makes it more possible for autodidacts to attain educational degrees if they so choose. Do-it-yourselfers have also been around for decades,[30] although they are still relatively few in number. Digital technologies have made it much easier for intrepid do-it-yourselfers to assemble their own educational program. Anya Kamenetz's book *DIYU* is designed to help such students create their own degree paths.[31] Maya Frost's book *The New Global Student* outlines another savvy path to a college education: spend a year abroad during high school, then use a variety of underappreciated strategies such as community college, GED, and credit for study abroad to accelerate one's undergraduate career. Although Frost's strategies do not depend directly on digital technologies, she offers an excellent Web-based strategy for planning a global learning experience,[32] for which taking online courses could be used as a supplemental strategy. Savvy explorers are still a relatively rare breed, but their numbers and influence are likely to grow as nontraditional, online, lifelong education increases the variety of available alternatives.

The pipeline metaphor and its supporting infrastructure do not work very well for this emerging breed of students.[33] Swirling commonly results in loss of transfer credits, which tends to increase the cost of education and student indebtedness.[34] Stopping out is difficult and discouraging for overstressed adults who need support to continue their education. Staying longer also requires considerably more persistence and ongoing support. Savvy explorers who succeed do so despite a system which is not designed to accommodate their needs or recognize their accomplishments.

To serve these learners, we need a new metaphor for starters: how about an interstate highway instead? This metaphor describes a path which serves users who:

- Choose among multiple entry and exit points rather than passively following a prescribed path

- Vary greatly in their rate of 'flow,' traveling at different speeds on different schedules

- Get on and off the road more frequently

- Often prefer alternate routes and would benefit from 'roadmaps' which identify these routes

- Pursue multiple destinations over the course of their educational journeys

- Move bidirectionally sometimes, such as learners with bachelor's or advanced degrees who return to community college to jump start a career change.

Fortunately, there are several emerging strategies whose greater adoption would better serve these new types of learners and revitalize the educational enterprise in the process.

Stackable Credentials

Building more 'on' and 'off' ramps to higher education gives stopouts and career changers more opportunities to earn credentials by making it easier for them to leave and re-enter the process. One strategy for doing this is called *stackable credentials*, which refers to "a clearly-defined system of competencies and industry-recognized credentials that are linked to employment opportunities and advancement."[35] Stackable credentials typically consist of a series of certificates that are linked to job levels of increasing complexity and tied to particular job families or career maps. Stackable credentials break the degree attainment process down into smaller steps by enabling students to build certificate by certificate toward degrees – lower-level certificates leading to associate's degrees, then on to higher level certificates leading to a bachelor's degree.

Stackable credentials increase a student's value in the workplace,[36] and well-designed systems also identify opportunities to develop generalizable skills such as critical thinking, collaboration, and creativity which apply across the entire range of vocations. For example, the National Association of Manufacturers (NAM) launched a Manufacturing Skills Certification System (MSCS) which identifies the core skills required for entry-level workers in all manufacturing sectors, including personal effectiveness and foundational academic competencies, along with general workplace and industrywide technical skills.[37] The MSCS is grounded on the National Career Readiness Certificate, a credential that measures the essential skills of workers re-entering the workforce or transitioning into new occupations.[38]

As a flexible delivery system, online learning is well suited to support greater use of stackable credentials, which also enable the world of work to have a greater role in defining educational knowledge when appropriate.

Road Maps: Making Educational Paths More Transparent

Many vacationers like to have their itineraries planned for them: cruise ships, guided bus tours, rafting or cycling trips. Many other travelers who prefer to plan their own journeys tend to rely on a few essentials such as road maps, guide books, and the advice of travelers who have gone before them. Educational journeys are very similar; those learners who make more choices, take alternate routes, and pursue multiple destinations would benefit from 'road maps' and other resources which make the journey easier to navigate and more transparent.

Models such as NAM's MSCS make career paths more transparent by mapping, articulating and visualizing the alignments between career, education, and certification. For instance, the MSCS is also aligned with the Advanced Competency Manufacturing Model,[39] a framework which uses career ladders and lattices to help people visualize and learn about available job options associated with progression through a career.[40] Developed through a collaborative industry-government effort, the initial model aligns education, certification, and career pathways in the welding industry, and there are plans to expand the model to a variety of other sectors including aerospace, construction, energy, life science, and several others.[41]

The need for more transparent connections to career paths in K-12 education is also being recognized in a few fields. Through its SECURE IT initiative, the University of Maryland College of Education's Educational Technology Policy, Research, and Outreach unit runs information assurance and cybersecurity education programs at all K-12 levels: high school summer programs, afterschool programs for elementary and middle school students, and the Cool Careers in Cybersecurity Conference program for middle school girls. These programs reflect the philosophy that even younger students need to be informed about cybersecurity fields and careers; waiting until high school may already be too late.[42] Although these programs are offered in person, the SECURE IT initiative relies heavily on its web site and social media pages to disseminate information and support collaborative activities. The National Science Foundation's Computing Education for the 21st Century program also focuses on creating pathways which excite middle and high school students and attract them to the field.[43]

Career road maps and other resources have their limitations; for example, projections of future job growth sometimes fail to materialize, as has happened in various fields such as science, aerospace engineering, and information technology.[44] Road maps and other resources must also deal with the perennial tension between generalizable and career-specific education. Career-specific education tends to have more immediate practical utility but is more limiting for long-term choices. General education tends to have less immediate practical utility but often has better long-term value because it is often more widely applicable to a variety of jobs and careers. More transparent educational paths would make these distinctions more explicit and help learners better understand the value of both general and career-specific education.

Learners would also benefit from road maps which extend beyond the cluster of education, certification, and employment. Few good resources currently exist which make more transparent connections with academic careers, informed citizenship, or even personal development, and the available knowledge is often obscure. Education needs to do a better job of articulating the learning experiences it offers and how those experiences relate to these other desired outcomes. Digital technologies make it much easier to make the related knowledge less obscure by mapping, articulating, and sharing paths which show the connections between these outcomes.

Greater Granularity: Rethinking the Credit Hour and Carnegie Unit

The core structures that formal education uses to validate merit and convey knowledge – the credit hour and Carnegie unit – pose a considerable obstacle to change. In theory, the credit hour serves as a common currency which helps support the unrivaled institutional and curricular diversity of American higher education by serving as a credit transfer mechanism. In practice, credit transfer policies vary greatly, in part because credit transfer decisions are made by a host of faculty curriculum review committees who determine the credit worthiness of courses taken elsewhere.[45] Even within a single university system, transfer of course credit can be bewilderingly inconsistent. In one particularly complicated example, a Bronx Community College student who completed BCC's Technical Mathematics I course and tried to transfer those credits or "equivalent" course credits to one of the City University of New York system's 11 senior colleges could experience one of eight or more different outcomes.[46]

Credit hours are relatively large, unwieldy, and expensive units for delivering education, so the credit hour structure makes it very difficult for higher education to provide timely, right-sized certifiable knowledge. A credit hour typically represents around 12-13 hours of seat time in a classroom course, but students often only need to fill a few gaps in their knowledge or a brief skills 'brush-up,' not an entire credit hour or three. Many practitioners believe that the long-standing relationship between the credit hour and "seat time"[47] is now outdated; for example, National Center for Academic Transformation President Carol Twigg has characterized the concept of a credit hour based on seat time as a "relic." Seat time is a poor measure of learning and performance because it presumes that "seat" presence equates with time on task, level of effort, rate of learning, and efficacy of effort, when in fact all of these can vary greatly by student in most learning environments. The "time" part of "seat time" is also problematic; as Twigg noted, "we've got hundreds of years of understanding of what a credit hour represents" whether or not one attends a class, but "the fact that it's called 'hour' is a problem."[48] The growing use of instructional techniques that can accelerate the learning process, and the proliferation of asynchronous online education, have made time-based learning measures even more irrelevant.

Some practitioners believe that competency-based approaches eliminate the need for the credit hour as currency, and even for courses themselves. As eLumen Collaborative Chief Innovation Officer David Shupe argues, the credit hour system ignores learner progress unless a course is completed, subverts the teaching and learning process by equating attainment with earning credits, and focuses institutions on attending to aggregate data at the expense of individual student development. Shupe advocates the use of student learning outcomes that demonstrate what learners know and can do as a preferable currency for measuring learner achievement.[49]

Despite its voluminous faults, however, the credit hour endures because it is closely tied with using courses to deliver instruction and because it is deeply embedded into other institutional components such as academic progress, faculty workload, faculty pay, and facilities scheduling, and to larger system components such as compliance with federal student aid programs.[50] Because of its capacity for enforcing uniformity and equilibrium, the credit hour has also been a powerful employee training mechanism, conditioning future workers for time-measured performances such as punching a time clock or coming to work regularly from 9 to 5. Hours-for-credit correlates much more strongly with hours-for-pay than with learning. The credit hour also provides a well-established proxy for gauging the expected amount of course content or level of student effort, despite its inadequacies for measuring outcomes.

At the same time, as swirling, stopping out, staying longer, and savvy learning become more commonplace, the balance is shifting toward granting students a greater role in defining and developing creditworthy learning experiences, and cyberized education offers many ways to enable this approach within a credit hour structure. Online courses which are delivered synchronously simply use the existing credit hour structure, as do blended courses which include a proportion of time-based assignments comparable to traditional classroom seat time. Recent federal regulations have reaffirmed the opportunity to establish credit hour equivalencies that are demonstrable by "learning outcomes and verified achievement."[51] Many credit for prior learning methods such as equivalency exams or credit by portfolio externalize time requirements by assuming that students have already put in the time elsewhere. Online education providers have also employed a variety of practices which provide reasonable approximations of time spent, such as models which equate effort with time by calculating activity-based time estimates, or pilot study methodologies which calculate time estimates based on learner behavior.[52]

Competency-based systems push the envelope even farther by asserting that learning outcomes and verified achievement can be demonstrated without using time or effort-based measures. Higher education will continue to adopt competency-based systems slowly because of their unfamiliarity. There are also considerable challenges in moving from an hours-based to a competency-based system, such as defining competencies and recalibrating various institutional components such as academic progress, faculty workload, and student aid. However, the rise of institutions which use competency-based approaches, such as Western Governors University, suggests that it will become more common in higher education. Although K-12 education has lagged behind in adopting competency-based approaches, some changes are starting to happen there as well. For instance, a July 2011 iNACOL report described several strategies for moving beyond traditional time-based systems such as redefining Carnegie units from seat time to competencies, using seat time waivers, and enabling greater credit flexibility. According to the report, a few states seek to advance competency-based learning through policies which provide a basis for designing more comprehensive state policy frameworks that support more widespread adoption.[53]

There are also signs that the work environment itself is moving away from its long-ingrained time-based orientation. Best Buy's Results-Oriented Work Environment is a human resource management strategy which bases employee compensation on results rather than number of hours worked,[54] and this approach has spread to other organizations.[55] Much of the job growth in the U.S. is now the result of small businesses and individual entrepreneurs, many of whom work in environments which are much less based on time or effort, aided by the same technologies (computers, Web, smartphones, etc.) which are cyberizing society.

Rethinking the credit hour and Carnegie unit does not have to mean dispensing with the concept of time altogether, however. Some learning activities require a discrete and generous amount of time, and time-based learning measures can be useful for many purposes such as making it easier to structure collaborative, group-based, and some other types of learning activities. Time-based measures also help education institutions exercise their legitimate interest in retaining control over their offerings. Still, accepting the role of time as a proxy for learning outcomes in a creditable learning experience, while providing reasonable alternatives to the strictures and distortions of the credit hour and Carnegie unit, can be a useful strategy for expanding merit.

Re-Empowering the Knowledge Creation Function

Creating knowledge has historically been one of the most important functions of higher education, but this function is under threat from a variety of sources:

- Higher education no longer has a monopoly on knowledge creation and production, thanks to the proliferation of knowledge outside the campus, including on the Web.
- The cost of higher education is becoming prohibitive for more students and their families, and support is waning for subsidizing scholars who have little contact with students and whose work seems to be disconnected with the rest of the world.
- Most college students attend institutions or programs where creation of knowledge is a lesser or nonexistent priority relative to other ones such as career preparation.
- Student exposure to the knowledge creation process has declined even at institutions where knowledge creation is still a high priority; for example, many institutions no longer use active researchers to teach introductory courses, so their students lose contact with the faculty and graduate students who are producing knowledge.

Much of higher education is now disconnected from its knowledge creation function, so it is not surprising that most degree seekers show little interest in becoming creators of knowledge, and most key stakeholders don't understand the importance of this issue.

Some may argue that the historical function of universities as knowledge creators is now passé. A better approach is to *re-empower the knowledge creation function* within higher education by reinventing how it preserves, transmits and creates knowledge as well as how it produces creators of knowledge. Re-empowering the knowledge creation function increases higher education's value and the value of knowledge creation itself, bolstering its importance to society.

Expanding the Knowledge Creation Function

If relatively few students seem interested in becoming knowledge creators, perhaps that's because the role has been too narrowly defined and the related career path too difficult to achieve. Competition is fierce for the relatively few available academic posts which define knowledge creation as a significant part of the job. Most other students and many faculty are cut out of the process altogether. What if higher education defined knowledge creation in a way which connected more students and faculty to the process? This could be done in several ways:

Integrate knowledge creation into the teaching and learning process. Murray Turoff believes that undergraduates should learn early in their college careers how to create knowledge and "experience the joys that are associated with that sort of achievement"[56] and that educators who are themselves knowledge creators are the ones who can best show students how it's done. Greater use of previously described strategies such as learner-generated content and impact assessment can help students experience the knowledge creation process more deeply at all education levels.

Create knowledge creation networks. Networks increase their value exponentially by increasing the number of interconnected nodes, and connecting networks to other networks accelerates their growth.[57] Academia needs to continue its transition from a sole source of knowledge creation to a network which interconnects with other knowledge creation networks such as workplace practitioners, professional organizations, research institutes, and government agencies. Individual institutions become interdependent vital nodes in the network instead of stand-alone entities. Knowledge creation becomes a more inclusive, participatory process which reflects the comparable changes in society related to knowledge, access, and authority.

Restore the relevance between knowledge creation and society. Academic work has become what New York University professor Lawrence M. Mead calls scholasticism: hyper-specialized, methodologically driven, non-empirical, and self-referential, resulting in the pursuit of "refinement at the expense of substance," removed and remote from the larger world.[58] One way to restore relevance is to *connect knowledge creation with other life contexts,* as is often done in professional graduate programs which enable students to create knowledge which applies to their work and career. This can be extended in various forms to undergraduate, high school, and even younger students, as well as to other life pursuits. The trend toward incorporating popular culture into academic study and scholarship is another way to make knowledge creation more relevant. Once anathema to academia and still reviled in many collegiate quarters, the study of popular culture has gained legitimacy while providing instant relevance. Popular culture is a rich source of new knowledge simply because most of the world's culture – its wealth, infrastructure, even its people – is also a relatively recent creation. Formal education is the logical place to connect past knowledge with the present ferment of popular culture and knowledge production.

Another way to promote greater relevance is to *generate new knowledge domains*. New fields are emerging which are rapidly creating knowledge and require an educational infrastructure to systematize that knowledge. This provides an opportunity for higher education to expand its traditional role as generator and certifier of new knowledge domains. Professional education, continuing education, and community colleges are pretty good at developing programs in emergent fields, but higher education's capacity to absorb new practice-generated knowledge domains is lagging at the bachelor's and graduate levels. As Weber State University Program and Technology Development Manager Luke Fernandez notes, there is "a delay between the material changes in the world outside academe and academe's ability to create disciplines that could make sense of these changes."[59] The organizational sector's parallel infrastructure of corporate universities, product-specific and field-specific certification programs is collectively insufficient to meet the need. In fact, professional organizations and businesses often want to have their educational programs legitimized by the existing higher education structure rather than creating their own certification pathways.

Digital technologies can be instrumental in re-empowering knowledge creation. Beyond the obvious networking capabilities of the Internet and Web, online technologies such as lecture capture, event webcasting, content management systems, multimedia creation and editing software are making it much easier to capture, create, organize, and share knowledge in various forms. Such knowledge capture systems make knowledge more permanent, more accountable, and less evanescent. Virtual conferences, work teams, and webinars enable collaborative knowledge creation and sharing while offering greater convenience at lower cost.

Learning to Play Nicely: Inter-Institutional Collaboration and Knowledge Creation

Faculty have long collaborated extensively with their colleagues at other institutions to do research or share knowledge, and there are numerous examples of inter-institutional collaboration in higher education.[60] Historically, however, institutional autonomy and complex bureaucratic structures have hampered the ability of colleges and universities to collaborate. The cyberization of education is helping to change this by supporting numerous forms of inter-institutional collaboration which could also be used to support knowledge creation and sharing.

Institutions are collaborating to *share degree and certificate programs*, sometimes also collaboratively developing these programs through *curricular partnerships*. The Great Plains Interactive Distance Education Alliance is perhaps the most successful example in U.S. higher education which combines the two. Founded in 1994, Great Plains IDEA is a collaborative alliance of 11 major research universities which offers fully online graduate courses and programs in high-demand professional fields. Curricula are developed by inter-institutional faculty teams and offered jointly by multiple institutions; each institutional member awards its own academic credit and degrees for the programs in which it participates.[61] The Sloan Semester initiative was an extraordinary but temporary example of inter-institutional collaborative course sharing; over 150 institutions offered more than 1,300 courses to over 1,500 students whose institutions were closed for an entire semester by Hurricanes Katrina and Rita in fall 2005. Although this collaboration vanished after the fall 2005 semester, it serves as a proof of concept for more permanent collaborations focused on large scale, inter-institutional course sharing.[62]

Another especially innovative example of inter-institutional program sharing is the U.S. Army's eArmyU program, whose mission is to encourage active duty soldiers to stay in the Army by subsidizing their education while they serve. Launched in 2001, this program has used online learning to transform traditional army education by offering unprecedented access, choice, and flexibility; in the process, it is developing technology-savvy soldiers who are prepared for the challenges of 21st century soldiering. eArmyU's network of 30 education institution partners provides over 140 online degree or certificate programs and has delivered more than 3,000 online courses to more than 250,000 students. Soldiers in the program have earned more than 5,300 degrees, and the program has also been successful in boosting retention, as 25 percent have either extended their service period or reenlisted to maintain program eligibility.[63] eArmyU has also extended the reach of the Servicemembers Opportunity Colleges program.

Colleges and universities are also collaborating to *share courses* within one or more programs, also sometimes involving curricular partnerships. One notable example is the Web-based Information Science Education (WISE) Consortium, which uses a collaborative model to increase the quality, access, and diversity of online opportunities in Library and Information Science (LIS) education internationally. WISE's 14 member institutions in the U.S., Canada, Australia, and New Zealand use course sharing and cooperative pedagogical training to foster relationships among its institutions and their students.[64] WISE has also developed effective strategies for collaborating with over 20 professional library and information science organizations to develop, offer, and share specialty LIS courses.[65] Over its first four years, the WISE consortium offered more than 330 courses and enrolled more than 550 students.

Multiple institutions can also collaborate to provide *inter-institutional course offerings* through team teaching or course merging. For example, the University of Illinois at Springfield and Chicago State University collaboratively offered two of their courses online, resulting in many benefits: deepened learning through sharing of diverse perspectives in ways not possible in homogeneous classrooms, significant cost savings through resource sharing, and renewed faculty enthusiasm through collaborating in a new way with their colleagues.[66]

Sensible Institutional Assessment

Given the exploratory nature of democratic learning and living, why do we focus our reform efforts on acquiring greater certainty and control?

– Ruthanne Kurth-Schai and Charles R. Green,
Re-Envisioning Education and Democracy[67]

Many reform efforts which purport to focus on accountability and higher standards are really more about "acquiring greater certainty and control" – or more accurately, on chasing the illusion of certainty and control. The urge for clarity, simplicity, and certainty runs deep, which explains Americans' embrace of ranking systems such as U.S. News and World Report's as if they were actually a legitimate way to calibrate meaningful differences among colleges. There is a need for greater accountability, and performance- and accountability-based initiatives have a place in helping to revitalize the educational enterprise – if they don't strangle it in the process, that is. There is a very real danger that overreliance on simplistic institutional assessment will degrade the current system rather than improve it.

Sensible institutional assessment starts with seeking to preserve "the exploratory nature of democratic living and learning." Performance- and accountability-based approaches tend to measure institutional effectiveness based on prespecified, standardized, and ultimately sanitized outcomes, but part of the essence of a college education is **not** knowing what one will learn ahead of time. Each learner undergoes an individual journey which combines mastering the known and encountering the unknown, resulting in unique experiences with many unanticipated outcomes. K-12 education also produces variable outcomes for each learner, and greater customization will only produce more individualized outcomes. Thus, sensible institutional assessment is both broad and flexible, and it seeks to find an effective balance between measurement of outcomes which can be prespecified and ones which cannot.

Standards Sets

In the mid 1990s, the Western Interstate Commission for Higher Education developed the document *Best Practices for Electronically Offered Degree and Certificate Programs*, which described a set of standards for institutions to follow when assessing their distance education programs. Since then, other organizations have devised several other standards sets such as the American Distance Education Consortium's *Guiding Principles for Distance Teaching and Learning*, the National Education Association Quality Benchmarks, the Southern Regional Educational Board (SREB)'s *Principles of Good Practice and Criteria for Evaluating Online Courses*, and the Sloan Consortium's Quality Framework and Quality Scorecard.[68] These standards sets are not rule-based procedures for governing practice, enforcing compliance, or attaining greater certainty and control. Instead, many institutions have used one or more of them as guidelines to assess quality at the institutional and program levels, with the goal of supporting improvement by establishing supportive institutional norms, relationships, and policies.[69]

At the K-12 level, iNACOL developed national standards for quality online courses and quality online teaching,[70] based largely on SREB's previously developed standards for those areas. Although these standards are focused more on consistency than improvement, the broad array of criteria embedded in the related rubric indicates a focus on quality which supports a more sensible form of consistency than what is sought through test scores, rankings, or cross-institutional comparisons.

Embedded Assessment Systems

Traditional assessment is typically treated as something which happens outside the teaching and learning process. Embedded assessment moves beyond this common practice by providing a wide range of evaluative measures which not only integrate assessment into the teaching and learning process but also provide organized, immediate, and meaningful results to stakeholders institution-wide.[71] For example, Pace University has used IOTA Solutions's online embedded assessment products since 1999 to track the effectiveness of one of its online programs. This online feedback system provides reliable and valid evaluative measures, highlights potential problems, and provides continuous feedback which enables key stakeholders to make ongoing improvements.[72] The eLumen outcomes-based framework described in the previous chapter combines embedded assessment with several other components. eLumen's learning outcomes information structure integrates these components into existing student information systems, which gives institutions the capacity to selectively, incrementally, and voluntarily collect student learning outcomes data and distribute individual or institution-wide outcomes information.

Performance-Based Approaches

The appeal of performance-based approaches is understandable; they promise certainty and control through reliable consistency, ease of large-scale administration, and removal of potential bias.[73] Performance-based approaches tend to rely on standardized measures and cross-institutional comparisons to attain this aim. For instance, the Collegiate Learning Assessment (CLA) is a testing tool which enables institutions to compare performance on standardized analytic writing and performance tasks which measure various college-level skills such as critical thinking, analytic reasoning, problem-solving and written communication. The National Survey of Student Engagement enables institutions to compare performance based on five "benchmarks of effective educational practice": level of academic challenge, active and collaborative learning, student-faculty interaction, enriching educational experiences, and supportive campus environment.[74]

The use of learner analytics, which is the collection, analysis, and application of data to improve aggregate student success, is an increasingly common performance-based strategy. Learner analytics are designed to improve the quality of available information and analysis, which aids in detecting and remediating risk factors before they result in student failure or attrition. For example, the first round of EDUCAUSE's Next Generation Learning Challenges grant competition funded by the Gates Foundation identified learner analytics as one of four "challenge areas," with the ultimate goal of making "comprehensive, sophisticated learner analytics focused on improving student outcomes" pervasive in American higher education.[75]

Capella University's Career Learning & Career Outcomes web site illustrates the use of learner analytics to make learning outcomes more transparent and increase institutional accountability in the process. The web site describes intended program-level learning outcomes, learner attainment of those outcomes, alumni career outcomes results, and other indirect assessment results available to the public.[76] Capella also uses a management-focused analytics and reporting portal and quarterly Learning Outcomes Assessment Reports to help with implementing improvement-related decisions such as course and program revisions.[77] Capella is also implementing an assessment model which measures learner achievement of program outcomes and competencies; a future version will include personalized dashboards which will help learners track progress continuously throughout their program.

Another performance-based method is Action Analytics, a comprehensive approach which focuses on judgments, decisions, choices, and interventions which ultimately shape performance. The Action Analytics approach aims to develop an institutional culture of performance improvement by focusing on higher education's value propositions and by considering an extensive array of strategies for assessing and implementing institutional improvement.[78]

Student satisfaction is another common measure used for institutional assessment. Most student satisfaction-based assessment methods correlate performance with student satisfaction level (the higher, the better). A more sophisticated approach is based on research which suggests that student success correlates with a close relationship between students' expectations about their online educational experience and how they perceive their actual experience. The Noel-Levitz 2010 National Online Learners Priorities Report identifies "performance gaps" between these two factors and identifies areas of greater perceived importance to students, which helps institutions prioritize where to put limited resources to make improvements.[79]

Limitations of performance-based approaches

Performance-based approaches to institutional assessment have also raised numerous concerns about their limitations, such as their often excessive reliance on limited instruments such as standardized tests. As Association of American Colleges and Universities President Carol Schneider has noted, there is "strong disagreement about the validity of gauging colleges' effectiveness" based on the results of a single test taken by a small number of student volunteers, to judge "the quality of student achievement across the entire family of programs and majors."[80] Performance-based assessment approaches are also limited by their narrow focus on output measures such as grades, course or program completion, degree or certificate attainment, or simple persistence. This is problematic because focusing on the "what" (output measures) often neglects the "so what": impact or quality measures which give a more complete picture of institutional effectiveness.

Output measures also often fail to capture important outcomes. For example, a 2003 Student Goals Achievement Survey at Middlesex (MA) Community College found that over 90 percent of their students who left in good academic standing before earning a degree or certificate said that "they had completely or partially satisfied their primary educational goal."[81] In another study, 25 percent of 375 survey respondents dropped out of their online courses because they learned what they needed to know in order to do their job before the course ended.[82] In other words, sometimes dropping out is a sign of success for mature learners who exercise their authority to decide when they have achieved their learning objectives.[83] Another limitation of performance-based assessment is that it often ignores the role of institutional inputs in producing student learning outcomes; as assessment expert Gary Brown notes, too often assessment is treated almost exclusively as a lens to focus on student performance, rather than as a mirror for an institution to self-examine how it uses curricula, pedagogy, and other practices to support student performance.[84]

Performance-based approaches also often tend to have an almost relentless focus on employability preparation. For example, the 2011 *Disrupting College* report recommended allocation of federal aid to higher education based on a "Quality-Value Index" comprised of four measures: job or school placement rate, increase in students' earnings, retrospective student satisfaction, and student repayment rate.[85] Even though the report supported measuring attainment by using competencies rather than simple degree completion, the Q-V index measures focus almost exclusively on college as employability preparation.

Expanding the Realm of Acceptable Outcomes

An excessive focus on standardized tests, cross-institutional comparisons, and employability preparation undervalues the many other important outcomes which educational institutions produce. Informed local and global citizenship or maximizing human potential too often become afterthoughts. Developing creativity and curiosity are routinely ignored by so-called "value added" assessment approaches. Notions such as "learning for its own sake" have become almost quaint or reserved only for the most elite students.

Some initiatives use a broader set of measures to provide a more complete picture. Capella uses a mix of program and post-program outcomes, while NSSE measures a much broader array of student and institutional behaviors.[86] American Public University System (APUS) uses a Community of Inquiry Framework to assess a variety of institutional outcomes related to its programs, courses, instructors and retention patterns, as well as the results of institutional inputs such as instructional design efficacy and technology implementations. APUS uses this data to guide continuous quality improvement across all levels of the institution.[87]

Another approach is to *expand the criteria for acceptable outcomes* which signify institutional success. Institutions provide learning experiences which play a much greater role in student success than traditional measures of attainment indicate, for example learning to succeed from failure, enabling productive or even life-changing directions, or learning which realizes its value many years later. Institutions should get more credit for helping students attain these outcomes. Colleges and universities also need to focus more on their broader impact, including long-term and post-program impacts. Although some of this information is unknowable or difficult to find out without being excessively intrusive, e-portfolios, impact assessment techniques, and social networking tools are examples of useful cyber-tools for accomplishing this aim.

Another strategy is simply to do more widely what our most valued educational institutions already do: *aim for distinction and focus on intangibles.* Elite colleges and universities offer educational benefits which are much more valuable than completion of prespecified outcomes. Elite colleges tout their superiority based on the distinctive opportunities they offer, such as interdisciplinary courses and programs or knowledge production through undergraduate research. Elite K-12 private schools meet higher and often more diverse standards than those embodied in the Common Core Standards. If our most highly regarded institutions value such practices, it makes sense to apply this principle more broadly to more institutions as well.

In an age of greater accountability, the sensible approach is to broaden the range of institutional assessment in ways which add measurable value for education's key stakeholders. As the above examples indicate, cyberized education has already demonstrated its potential for enabling effective institutional assessment, which will help revitalize the educational enterprise.

CHAPTER 12

The Distant Scenario: Education Rules?

Behind the illusion of perpetual crisis in American education lies a different reality: a K-12 education system which has done a decent job of meeting the multiple demands which society has placed on it over the past century,[1] and a higher education system which retains an admirable diversity and remains among the world's most highly regarded. At the same time, incremental improvements have not enabled American education to keep up with the rising expectations which have accompanied its growing importance to society. We need to pick up the pace of improvement, and cyberizing education can help in numerous and substantial ways.

Beyond substantive improvement lies yet another possibility, a Seventh Future for Education: a future in which society acts as if everyone's education matters. Trends and movements such as compulsory primary and secondary education, the aspiration of universal higher education, No Child Left Behind and Education for All are attempts to move us in this direction – but we are still far, far away from making this future a reality.

Even if cyberized education produced a quantum leap improvement, it would not be enough to make everyone's education matter. Making this future happen is more than an educational issue; it is also a much larger cultural issue. Our overly free market-oriented society is based on creating winners and losers, which is incompatible with valuing everyone's education. We are far from knowing how to resolve the competing demands of equality and diversity. We are even farther from knowing how to balance individual rights with society's needs in a way that would make valuing everyone's education possible. We also face numerous other challenges which are beyond our current capabilities to handle effectively: educating children with autism and other complex developmental disabilities, or educating those with severe intellectual disabilities caused by genetic and environmental sources, or educating most of the nation's and world's poor, to name a few. Cyberized education can help reach these populations of learners and make their lives somewhat brighter, but it won't transform them in most cases. For these reasons, a future where everyone's education truly matters is the scenario that is least likely to be realized anytime soon, even though it is a future that is worth striving to attain.

In making these assertions, it is hard to avoid the feeling of lurching back and forth between deep cynicism and wild utopianism. It seems hopelessly naive to imagine a scenario where everyone's education matters, let alone discuss it seriously, in a nation still divided by savage educational inequalities, and in a world still plagued by war, hunger, and disease where so much "education" is indoctrination in how to hate others. Yet it sounds coldly cynical to admit the opposite: that we are on track to let millions upon millions of our fellow human beings in this country and worldwide fall by the wayside in society by depriving them of quality education.

A future in which everyone's education matters would look very different from what we have today. One key characteristic would be an education system which somehow has *moved beyond meritocracy*, because the concept of meritocracy is ultimately an ideology of inequality. Meritocracy ostensibly rewards those who earn it; the truly meritorious overcome obstacles to success by employing their superior talent, working harder, or being more virtuous. This Jeffersonian "aristocracy of talent" augmented by hard work and virtue is far preferable to aristocracies based on birthright, reincarnation, or the assertion of innate superiority, but it still presumes a class of people who are better than others. In practice, American education is a highly imperfect meritocratic system riddled by inequalities which have more to do social and cultural capital, racism, sexism, and socioeconomic status[2] than with performance-based merit. A K-12 education funding system which rewards affluence through dependence on local property taxes, and the "steep prestige hierarchy" in American higher education[3] which helps support the intergenerational transmission of inequality,[4] are among the more egregious examples.

There is no easy answer to this situation, which reflects the fundamental tension between equality and diversity. The ideal of equal educational opportunity which has been a guiding force in American education for the past several decades relies on a meritocratic concept of attainment. Standardization has been the preferred path to equality, as exemplified by curricular practices which standardize instruction such as lectures and whole class instruction, along with assessment practices such as standardized tests which aim to provide relatively objective measures of achievement. Standardized curriculum and assessment practices have their benefits; for example, standardized tests offer a useful counterpoint to the subjective judgments of teachers. Unfortunately, their proliferation has happened at the expense of diversity. Standardization offers an illusion of meritocracy by defining a common set of merit-based criteria, but in fact the very process of standardizing merit favors some over others. Specifically, it favors those who best fit the selected criteria or have the means to do so, as the long-standing strong correlation between SAT scores and household income demonstrates.[5] The new demands placed on education to reach everyone and to improve educational performance have not changed the emphasis on standardization. Standards-driven reform approaches pursue greater equality of results by imposing an educational straitjacket which tends toward fitting everyone into the same, mediocre size – except, of course, for those who can use their greater social and cultural capital to find superior alternatives.

Another clear implication is that *a future where everyone's education matters can only make sense in a society where everyone matters*. This is hardly the case in our current market-driven society which favors economic winners over losers, nor is it the case in our current educational system which has produced a new generation of pushouts, massive numbers of college dropouts, and the most highly indebted college graduates in history.[6] If education continues to be ever more tightly aligned with employment, it is hard to imagine a future where everyone's education matters without *a society where everyone's employment matter*s — that is, one which can offer gainful employment to any seeker who is not sidetracked by personal failures. Imagine, for example, if American education actually succeeded in leaving no child behind and produced many more millions of graduates prepared for high-skilled work. Even after filling the currently reported shortfall (assuming of course that this shortfall would persist), a shortage of high-skilled jobs in the workplace would still remain, resulting in millions of overqualified individuals who would lose in the competition for them. Would their education matter, or would it simply be a waste? This is really more of a labor market problem than an education problem, as past worker gluts in science and information technology[7] have demonstrated. At the same time, in a society filled with high-skilled workers, who's going to flip the burgers, clean the suites, and pick the fruit? Does such a society have to rely on immigrants to do its menial work? Or admit that some of its citizens' educations matter more than others?

A society where everyone matters also implies an educational system where *everyone's ability to learn to become informed local and global citizens, develop their potential, and contribute to the construction of a more democratic society also matter.* In present-day America's highly polarized and politicized social discourse, each of these ideas is commonly attacked as "socialist," "communist," or worse. This illustrates the vast distance between a "winners and losers"-based society and one which values everyone's education, and it will remain so until Americans can figure out how to resolve this fundamental incompatibility. Consider, for example, Stanford education professor Linda Darling-Hammond's list of requirements for making K-12 education accessible and equitable for all American children:

- Secure housing, food, and health care so that children can come to school ready to learn

- Supportive early learning environments

- Equitably funded schools which provide equitable access to high-quality teaching

- Well-prepared and well-supported teachers and leaders

- Standards, curriculum, and assessments focused on 21st-century learning goals

- Schools organized for in-depth student and teacher learning[8]

This seems to be a reasonable list of necessary requirements for a society which aspires to make everyone's education matter: one that is willing to contribute the needed resources and recognizes that taxes are the dues we pay to live in a civilized society[9] while understanding that simply "throwing money at the problem" is an ineffective strategy. Unfortunately, this does not describe present-day America, in which one of its two major political parties has fought fiercely against the expansion of health care for all children and against increasing taxes under any circumstances.[10] In today's political climate, the notion of providing "secure housing, food, and health care" for all children seems hopelessly naive, and its chances of attainment seem remote to say the least. The prospect of decisions which perpetuate inequalities seems much more likely, as illustrated by the South Carolina judge who ruled that the state was required to provide only "minimally adequate education," not "what is best" for children.[11] A society which enforces laws to provide "minimally adequate education" will never be one in which everyone's education matters.

Such issues raise the question of whether a future in which Education Rules would also be a disaster scenario if realized in the extreme. For instance, the current drive toward standardizing education employs social engineering techniques at the expense of the individual. The resulting system marginalizes creativity, curiosity, and diversity in favor of attainment on extremely narrow measures. A future in which education successfully organized itself around enabling all its students to pass the current batch of standardized tests would also be one in which very few people's education mattered. Applying a narrow set of one-size-fits-all "rigorous" standards to all students, or seeking to turn education into an employment and training enterprise, or hoping that free learning by itself will carry the day, or treating the onset of cybersymbiosis as a harbinger of doom, or simply holding a steady course and hoping this too will pass – none of these is an effective strategy for attaining a future where everyone's education matters.

A better starting point is to see the current challenge in its proper light. Trying to "fix" a "failing" or "broken" education system diminishes the real challenge we face, which is far more serious than returning to some prior level of success or reclaiming some imaginary lost paradise. The challenge we face, should we actually choose to accept it, is a historic, formidable, and worthy undertaking to create something which is unprecedented in human history: an education system which works for everyone in a large, heterogeneous society. It involves building things we don't know how to build yet, and probably some things we don't even know we need. It means learning how to resolve the fundamental tensions between individual and society, and between equality and diversity, which would realize the total redistribution of access, the mastering of redefined knowledge, and the constant renegotiation of authority among education's key participants, without descending into the rule of free markets, free learning, standards, cyberdystopia, or incremental change.

The best way to meet this challenge is not to seek a fix, but to seek massive improvement. This is not a semantic gimmick, but a crucial shift in how to approach the task. Seeking fixes oversimplifies and looks backward; it disrespects the task by trying to shrink it, and it ultimately aims for disengagement once the problem is "fixed" and the task "completed." Seeking massive improvement is different: it engages and sustains; it recognizes the complexity of the situation and the awesomeness of the task; it opens possibilities and moves us forward. Cyberization alone can't get us there, but it can help move us in the right direction. This book has proposed dozens of relatively simple strategies for movement, such as these:

- Aim beyond trying to equal classroom quality when using digital technologies.

- Incorporate the influences of key constituencies for positive change.

- Engage teachers and learners as agents in the educational process rather than as functionaries.

- Realign education with redefined knowledge.

- Continue to redistribute educational access universally with individual autonomy and dignity.

- Manage renegotiated authority to accommodate a self-initiated, negotiated, and shared model.

- Place greater value on student-produced content, their work products, and their time.

- Individualize student inputs *and* outcomes while enhancing teachers' roles in the process.

- Use rigorous *and* flexible methods to assess teaching, learning, and institutions.

- Employ strategies for creating and expanding merit, including expanding student success.

- Re-empower higher education's knowledge creation function.

Few of these are particularly new, but formal education has been relatively slow to adopt most of them. The proposed strategies are transformative but do not require the demolition of education as it is currently constituted, nor are they a comprehensive prescription for fixing perceived ailments. They are designed to enable education's key stakeholders to build on a point of common agreement: that improving education is a good and necessary thing to do.

People often think about education and its cyberization in either/or terms: if learning happens online, then teachers will disappear; if students have more authority over their learning, then they will rule; if uniform, rigorous standards are not applied to all students, then no meaningful standards are possible. These choices are not dichotomous ones. Cyberizing education is an incomparable opportunity to *enhance* the value of in-person interaction, enhance the value of both teachers *and* learners, apply rigorous *and* flexible standards which create and expand merit for ever more learners, and so on.

Each of the other futures described in this book can help make this happen. For every Free Market Rules-oriented company that treats education as little more than a business opportunity to be conquered profitably, there are dozens of businesses working to make education better by coevolving with it. The foolish consistency of Standards Rule with its futile search for certainty and control can be replaced by a more sensible consistency which uses standards to expand merit by broadening and more clearly defining the paths to achievement, while also preserving the exploratory nature of democratic living and learning. The desire for a new dawn of Free Learning to sweep away the wretched practices of formal education is best tempered by realizing that free learning is most influential in its roles as a resource, innovation source, and recourse: supplementing formal education, challenging it to improve, keeping it honest and on its toes. We can manage the dark side of embracing the steady parade of bedazzling technologies which are surely coming our way by employing a healthy caution: engaging in a process of *realtechnik* which acknowledges the costs of adopting new technologies, anticipates possible ramifications, and figures out workable responses to emergent problems and issues. Education can even maintain a steady course while embracing society's latest demands for change by using its considerable capacities to identify and conserve what's worth keeping.

Even if all this were to happen, one can safely predict that it will be a long time before Americans create a future where everyone's education matters. And even while we fall short of this ideal, the cyberization of education will have profound and far-reaching implications for how we educate, and thus inexorably for how we structure our society. Both education and society have a long way to go before a future where Education Rules would be a desirable one, but cyberizing education effectively will help Americans learn how to value education in proportion to its rising importance. Ultimately, cyberizing education is about humanizing education – leveraging our ever-increasing technological prowess to become more evolved and capable social creatures. The cyberization of education is a golden opportunity to magnify our human capacities in a way which channels that collective yearning for deeply meaningful change into effective action. It also allows us to embrace our humanity if we choose to do so.

References

Adkins, S. S. (2011). Personal communication, May 17-18, 2011.

Albright, P. (2006). *Open Educational Resources: Open content for higher education.* International Institute for Educational Planning, Forum 1 final report, February 2006. Retrieved from: http://www.unesco.org/iiep/virtualuniversity/media/forum/oer_forum_final_report.pdf

Allen, I. E. and Seaman, J. (2010a). *Class Differences: Online Education in the United States, 2010.* Babson Survey Research Group, November 2010. Retrieved from: http://sloanconsortium.org/sites/default/files/class_differences.pdf.

Allen, I. E. and Seaman, J. (2010b). *Learning on Demand: Online Education in the United States, 2009.* Babson Survey Research Group, January 2010. Retrieved from: http://sloanconsortium.org/publications/survey/pdf/learningondemand.pdf.

Allen, I., & J. Seaman. (2007). *Online Nation: Five Years of Growth in Online Learning.* Retrieved from: http://sloanconsortium.org/sites/default/files/online_nation.pdf

Allen, I. E., Seaman, J., and Garrett, R. (2007). *Blending In: The Extent and Promise of Blended Education in the United States.* Sloan-C, March 2007. Retrieved from: http://sloanconsortium.org/sites/default/files/Blending_In.pdf.

Alliance for Children (2010). *Common Core Standards: Why We Object to the K-3 Core Standards.* June 11, 2010. Retrieved from: http://www.allianceforchildhood.org/standards

Almansi, C., (2010). Why Unjoin Ning Networks That Won't Pay. *ETC Journal,* August 28, 2010. Retrieved from: http://etcjournal.com/2010/08/28/why-unjoin-ning-networks-that-wont-pay/

Almeda, M. B. and Rose, K. (1999). Instructor Satisfaction in University of California Extension's On-Line Writing Curriculum. In *Online Education: Learning Effectiveness and Faculty Satisfaction; Proceedings of the 1999 Sloan Summer Workshop on Asynchronous Learning Networks.* Nashville, TN: Center for Asynchronous Learning Networks, 2000.

Altbach, P. G. (1998) *Comparative higher education: knowledge, the university, and development.* Greenwich, CT: Ablex.

American Society of Mechanical Engineers Innovative Technologies Institute (2010). *A Risk Analysis Standard for Natural and Man-Made Hazards to Higher Education Institutions.* Washington, DC: ASME.

American Speech-Hearing-Language Association (2010). Pilot Study Orientation web page. Retrieved from: http://www.asha.org/ce/for-providers/admin/pilot_study_orientation.htm

Amrein-Beardsley, A. (2008). Methodological Concerns About the Education Value-Added Assessment System. *Educational Researcher*, 37(2), pp. 65–75.

Anderson, J. and Rainie, L. (2010). *Future of the Internet IV*. Pew Research Center's Internet and American Life Project, February 19, 2010. Retrieved from: http://www.pewinternet.org/Reports/2010/Future-of-the-Internet-IV/Part-1Google/Intelligence.aspx

Anderson, T., Rourke, L., Garrison, D.R., and Archer, W. (2001). Assessing teaching presence in a computer conferencing context. Seattle, WA: Paper presented at the annual meeting of the American Educational Research Association, 2001.

Archer, J. (2007). Digital Portfolios: An Alternative Approach to Assessing Progress. *Education Week*, 26(30), 38.

Associated Press (2010). Schools face big budget holes as stimulus runs out. *NewsOne for Black America*, February 15, 2010. Retrieved from: http://newsone.com/nation/associated-press/schools-face-big-budget-holes-as-stimulus-runs-out/

Attwell, G. (2007). Personal Learning Environments – the Future of eLearning? *eLearning Papers*, 2(1), January 2007.

Bacheldor, B. (2010). Packing Light. *EDTECH Focus on Higher Education*, December 31, 2010. Retrieved from: http://www.edtechmag.com/higher/november-december-2010/packing-light.html

Baek, Y. (2011). EDTECH 597: Introduction to Edutainment syllabus. Retrieved from: http://www.qdocuments.com/EDTECH-597-Introduction-to-Edutainment-Educational-Technology-at–doc.html

Baker, E. (1989). *Higher Order Assessment and Indicators of Learning*. Los Angeles: UCLA Center for Research on Evaluation, Standards and Student Testing, CSE Technical Report #295, 1989. Retrieved from http://www.cse.ucla.edu/products/Reports/TR295.pdf

Balfanz, R. (2009). Can the American High School Become an Avenue of Advancement for All? *America's High Schools,* 19(1), Spring 2009. Retrieved from: http://futureofchildren.org/futureofchildren/publications/journals/article/index.xml?journalid=30&articleid=35&sectionid=62&submit

Barr, R. B. and Tagg, J. (1995) From teaching to learning: A new paradigm for undergraduate education. *Change* (27), pp. 6. (Nov/Dec)

Barrett, H., (2007) Researching Electronic Portfolios and Learner Engagement: The REFLECT Initiative, *Journal of Adolescent and Adult Literacy*, 3:50(6) 436-449.

Batson, T. (2010). The IT Revolution Is Over; Now the Work Begins. *Campus Technology*, April 14, 2010. Retrieved from: http://campustechnology.com/articles/2010/04/14/the-it-revolution-is-over-now-the-work-begins.aspx

Batson, T. (2002). The Electronic Portfolio Boom: What's it All About? *Syllabus,* November 26, 2002. Retrieved from: http://campustechnology.com/articles/2002/11/the-electronic-portfolio-boom-whats-it-all-about.aspx

Beatty, B. (2008) Using the "HyFlex" Course and Design Process. Sloan-C Effective Practices Collection. Retrieved from: http://sloanconsortium.org/effective_practices/using-quothyflexquot-course-and-design-process

Bejou, D. (2010). Broken Promises. In Are They Students? Or 'Customers'? *New York Times*, January 3, 2010. Retrieved from: http://roomfordebate.blogs.nytimes.com/2010/01/03/are-they-students-or-customers/.

Bejou, D. (2005). Treating Students Like Customers. *BizEd*, March/April 2005. Retrived from: http://www.aacsb.edu/publications/Archives/MarApr05/p44-47.pdf

Benderly, B. L. (2010). The Real Science Gap. *Miller-McCune*, June 14, 2010. Retrieved from: http://www.miller-mccune.com/science/the-real-science-gap-16191/

Bennett, D.L., Lucchesi, A.R., and Vedder, R.K. (2010). *For-Profit Higher Education: Growth, Regulation, and Innovation.* Retrieved from: http://www.centerforcollegeaffordability.org/uploads/ForProfit_HigherEd.pdf.

Berg, I. (1970). *Education and Jobs: The Great Training Robbery*. New York: Praeger.

Betrus, A. (1995). *Individualized Instruction: A History of the Critiques.* Proceedings of the 1995 Annual Convention for the Association for Educational Communications and Technology. ED 383 308.

Bielick, S., Chandler, K., and Broughman, S. P. (2001). *Homeschooling in the United States: 1999.* U.S. Department of Education, Office of Educational Research and Improvement, NCES 2001–033. Retrieved from: http://nces.ed.gov/pubs2001/2001033.pdf

Bird, C. (1975). *The Case Against College.* New York: Bantam.

Bloom, B. S. (1984). The 2-Sigma Problem: The Search for Methods of Group Instruction as Effective as One-to-one Tutoring. *Educational Researcher*, 13: 4-16.

Bloom, B. S. (1956). *Taxonomy of Educational Objectives.* New York, NY, McKay.

Bloomberg Businessweek (2006). Smashing the Clock. *Bloomberg Businessweek,* December 11, 2006. Retrieved from: http://www.businessweek.com/magazine/content/06_50/b4013001.htm

Boettcher, J. V. (2006). The Rise of Student Performance Content. *Campus Technology*, February 28, 2006. Retrieved from: http://www.campustechnology.com/article.aspx?aid=40747

Bonk, C. (2009). *The World Is Open: How Web Technology Is Revolutionizing Education.* San Francisco: Jossey-Bass.

Blumenstyk, G. (2010). Beyond the Credit Hour: Old Standards Don't Fit New Models. *Chronicle of Higher Education*, January 3, 2010.

Boser, U. (2006). Calculating high school graduation rates. Center for Public Education. Retrieved from: http://www.centerforpubliceducation.org/Main-Menu/Policies/Calculating-high-school-graduation-rates-At-a-glance-/Calculating-high-school-graduation-rates-.html

Boston, W., Diaz, S.R., Gibson, A.M., Ice, P., Richardson, J., and Swan, K. (2009). An Exploration of the Relationship Between Indicators of the Community of Inquiry Framework and Retention in Online Programs. *Journal of Asynchronous Learning Networks*, 13 (3), October 2009, pp.67-83.

Bracey, G. (2004). Serious Questions About the Tennessee Value-Added Assessment System. *Phi Delta Kappan,* 85(9) (May 2004), p.716.

Bradshaw, T., and Nichols, B. (2004). *Reading at Risk.* National Endowment for the Arts, Research Division Report #46, Washington, DC, June 2004. Retrieved from: http://www.nea.gov/pub/ReadingAtRisk.pdf

Bratton, S. and Toffler, A. (2009). Alvin Toffler on the Road Race to the 21st Century Economy. *Dishy Mix with Susan Bratton,* Episode 106, July 7, 2009. Transcript and podcast retrieved from: http://personallifemedia.com/podcasts/232-dishymix/episodes/48389-alvin-toffler-road-race-21st-century

Brewster, C. and Fager, J. (2000). *Increasing Student Engagement and Motivation: From Time-on-Task to Homework.* Northwest Regional Educational Laboratory, October 2000. Retrieved from: http://home.comcast.net/~reasoned/4410/CRM%20Concept%20Map%20with%20Links/html-tdm-model-hyperlinke_files/motivationforstudents_13.pdf

Bridgeland, J. M., Dilulio, J. J., and Morison, K. B. (2006). *The Silent Epidemic: Perspectives of High School Dropouts.* Civic Enterprises and Peter D. Hart Research Associates, Mrch 2006. Retrieved from: http://www.gatesfoundation.org/united-states/Documents/TheSilentEpidemic3-06Final.pdf

Brooks, L. (2007). *Considering Open Source: A Framework for Evaluating Software in the New Economy.* EDUCAUSE Center for Applied Research, January 2, 2007. Retrieved from: http://net.educause.edu/ir/library/pdf/ERB0701.pdf

Brown, G. (2011). Personal communication, June 2011.

Brown, G., Desrosier, T., Peterson, N., Chida, M., Lagier, R. (2009). *Harvesting Feedback, Accountability, and Community.* The Center for Teaching, Learning, and Technology, Washington State University, March 2009.

Buddin, R. (2010). *How Effective Are Los Angeles Elementary Teachers and Schools?* August 2010. Retrieved from: http://documents.latimes.com/buddin-white-paper-20100908/

Burke, L. A. (2005). Transitioning to Online Course Offerings: Tactical and Strategic Considerations. *Journal of Interactive Online Learning,* Volume 4, Number 2, Fall 2005. ISSN: 1541-4914.

Buzzfocus.com (2010). Giveaway: BBC Wildlife Series - 'Life.' Buzzfocus.com, June 4, 2010. Retrieved from: http://www.buzzfocus.com/2010/06/04/giveaway-bbc-wildlife-series-life/

Caldwell, R. L. (2010). *Review of Scenarios for Higher Education: Background for Understanding Options for 2010-2015.* January 26, 2010. Retrieved from: http://cals.arizona.edu/dean/planning/January%202010%20Scenarios%20for%202020%20Higher%20Education.pdf

California Distance Learning Project (2005). What Is Distance Learning? web page, For Adult Educators web site. Retreived from: http://www.cdlponline.org/index.cfm?fuseaction=whatis&pg=3

California State University Monterey Bay (n.d.). Wireless Education and Technology Center web site. Retrieved from: http://wetec.csumb.edu/site/x17155.xml.

Campbell, S. (2009). Giving Up My iPod for a Walkman. *BBC News Magazine,* June 29, 2009. Retrieved from: http://news.bbc.co.uk/2/hi/8117619.stm

Capella University (2011). Capella Learning and Career Outcomes web page. Retrieved from: http://capellaresults.org/index.asp

Carey, K. (2011).The Quiet Revolution in Open Learning. *Chronicle of Higher Education,* May 15, 2011. Retrieved from: http://chronicle.com/article/The-Quiet-Revolution-in-Open/127545/

Carey, K. (2009). College for $99 a Month. *Washington Monthly*, September/October 2009. Retrieved from: http://www.washingtonmonthly.com/college_guide/feature/college_for_99_a_month.php

Carnegie-Mellon University (n.d.) Carnegie-Mellon Open Learning Initiative web site. Retrieved from: http://oli.web.cmu.edu/openlearning/initiative

Carney, R. N., and Levin, J. R. (2002). Pictorial Illustrations *Still* Improve Students' Learning From Text. *Educational Psychology Review*, 14(1), March 2002. Retrieved from: http://users.cdli.ca/bmann/0_ARTICLES/Graphics_Carney02.pdf

Carr, N. (2008). Is Google Making Us Stupid? What the Internet is doing to our brains. *The Atlantic*, July/August 2008. Retrieved from: http://www.theatlantic.com/magazine/archive/2008/07/is-google-making-us-stupid/6868/

Carnevale, A. (2010a). How do you measure educational "success"? Letter to the Editor, *Washington Post*, August 26, 2010. Retrieved from: http://www.washingtonpost.com/wp-dyn/content/article/2010/08/25/AR2010082506720.html

Carnevale, A. (2010b). *Ready or Not: The Jobs Recovery and Educational Requirements through 2018.* The Georgetown University Center on Education and the Workforce, March 2010.

Carnevale, A. (1991). *America and the New Economy*. Alexandria, VA and Washington, DC: American Society for Training and Development, and the United States Department of Labor, Employment and Training Administration.

Carter, D. (2011). $2 billion that could change online education. *eCampus News*, January 31, 2011. Retrieved from: http://www.ecampusnews.com/funding/2-billion-that-could-change-online-education/

Carter, D. (2009). Yale researchers examine online accreditation. *eCampus News*, September 29, 2009. Retrieved from: http://www.ecampusnews.com/top-news/yale-researchers-examine-online-accreditation/

Castells, M. (2000). *The Rise of the Network Society.* San Francisco: Wiley-Blackwell.

Cavanaugh, C. (2009). *Getting Students More Learning Time Online: Distance Education in Support of Expanded Learning Time in K-12 Schools.* Center for American Progress and The Broad Education Foundation, May 2009. Retrieved from: http://www.americanprogress.org/issues/2009/05/pdf/distancelearning.pdf

CBS New York (2011). Bloomberg: If I Had It My Way I'd Dump Half of NYC's Teachers. *CBS New York,com,* December 1, 2011. Retrieved from: http://newyork.cbslocal.com/2011/12/01/bloomberg-if-i-had-it-my-way-id-dump-half-of-nycs-teachers/

Center for Education Policy (2009). *Compendium of Major NCLB Studies*. Retrieved from: http://www.cep-dc.org/documents/RFR-CompendiumNCLB/CurriculumandInstruction.pdf

Center for Energy Workforce Development (n.d.). Get Into Energy Career Pathways for Skilled Utility Technicians. Retrieved from: http://www.cewd.org/documents/pathwayswhitepaper.pdf

Centre for Educational Research and Innovation (n.d.) Centre for Educational Research and Innovation (CERI) - The OECD Schooling Scenarios in Brief. Retrieved from: http://www.oecd.org/document/10/0,3343,en_2649_39263231_2078922_1_1_1_37455,00.html

Chairman of the Joint Chiefs of Staff (2006). *National Military Strategy for Cyberspace Operations (U)*. Chairman of the Joint Chiefs of Staff, December 2006. Retrieved from: http://www.bits.de/NRANEU/others/strategy/07-F-2105doc1.pdf

Cheney-Steen, L. (2010). Is the "New Normal" Anything But? NUTN Summit, Colorado Springs, CO, September 29, 2010.

Cheesman Day, J. and Newberger, E. C. (2002). *The Big Payoff: Educational Attainment and Synthetic Estimates of Work-Life Earnings*. Washington, D.C.: United States Bureau of the Census Current Population Reports, P23-210, July 2002.

Chichilnisky, G. (1998). The knowledge revolution. *Journal of International Trade and Economic Development*, 7(1), 39-54. Retrieved from: http://chichilnisky.com/pdfs/papers/170.pdf

Chivvis, D. (2010). No End in Sight for School Budget Cuts. *Aolnews.com*, March 21, 2010. Retrieved from: http://www.aolnews.com/2010/03/21/no-end-in-sight-for-school-budget-cuts/

Christian Science Monitor (2009). *Virtual ivy: why the US needs more e-colleges* editorial, August 31, 2009. Retrieved from: http://www.csmonitor.com/Commentary/the-monitors-view/2009/0831/p08s01-comv.html.

Christensen, C. M., Horn, M. B., Caldera, L, and Soares, L. (2011). *Disrupting College: How Disruptive Innovation Can Deliver Quality and Affordability to Postsecondary Education*. Washington, D.C. and Mountain View, CA: Center for American Progress and Innosight Institute, February 2011. Retrieved from: http://www.americanprogress.org/issues/2011/02/pdf/disrupting_college.pdf

Christensen, C. M., Horn, M. B., and Johnson, C. W. (2008). *Disrupting Class: How Disruptive Innovation Will Change the Way the World Learns*. New York: McGraw-Hill.

Cicognani, A. (2000). Concept Mapping as a Collaborative Tool for Enhanced Online Learning. *Educational Technology & Society* 3(3), 2000.

City Colleges of Chicago (2008). Benefits for Your Child web page. The Child Development Laboratory Center at Kennedy-King College. Retrieved from: http://www.udccenter.org/classrooms.php

Clark, D. R. (1995). B. F. Skinner. Big Dog and Little Dog's Performance Juxtaposition web site. Retrieved from: http://www.nwlink.com/~donclark/hrd/history/skinner.html

CNN.com (2005). Web surfing 'as addictive as coffee.' May 19, 2005. Retrieved from: http://edition.cnn.com/2005/BUSINESS/05/19/web.work/index.html

Cockroft, L. (2009). Facebook 'enhances intelligence' but Twitter 'diminishes it', claims psychologist. *The Telegraph,* September 7, 2009. Retrieved from: http://www.telegraph.co.uk/technology/twitter/6147668/Facebook-enhances-intelligence-but-Twitter-diminishes-it-claims-psychologist.html

Coleman, J. (1967). *The Concept of Equality of Educational Opportunity.* Education Resources Information Center, ED015157. Retrieved from: http://www.eric.ed.gov:80/PDFS/ED015157.pdf

Coles, P., Cox, T., Mackey, C., and Richardson, S. (2006). *The toxic terabyte: How data-dumping threatens business efficiency.* IBM Global Technology Services, July 2006. Retrieved from: http://www-935.ibm.com/services/no/cio/leverage/levinfo_wp_gts_thetoxic.pdf

Collins, A. and Halverson, R. (2009). *Rethinking Education in the Age of Technology: The Digital Revolution and Schooling in America.* New York: Teachers College Press.

Commission for Higher Education (1998). *Policy for Delivering Degree Programs through Distance Technology,* March 13, 1998. Retrieved from: http://www.in.gov/che/files/9803029B.pdf.

Cook, D., Levinson, A., Garside, S., & Dupras, D. (2008). Internet-based learning in the health professions: A meta-analysis. *JAMA,* 2008;300(10):1181-1196 (doi:10.1001/jama.300.10.1181). http://jama.ama-assn.org/cgi/content/full/300/10/1181.

Cooper, M. (2010). Breaking Free of the Technology Bungy: Delivering Untethered Learning for Today's Socially Wired World. NUTN Summit, Colorado Springs, CO, September 29, 2010.

Council for Adult and Experential Learning (2010). *Fueling the Race to Post-Secondary Success: A 48-Institution Study of Prior Learning Assessment and Adult Student Outcomes.* Retrieved from: http://www.cael.org/pdfs/PLA_Fueling-the-Race

Council for Adult and Experiential Learning (2007). *Enrollment Decisions and Persistence of On-Line Learners in NACTEL and EPCE.* Final Report B-2006-8. Retrieved from: http://www.cael.org/pdfs/SloanReport

Council for Higher Education Accreditation (2010). U.S. Department of Education Publishes Proposed Regulations Addressing Program Integrity and Student Aid Programs. *CHEA Federal Update #10,* June 28, 2010. Retrieved from: http://www.chea.org/Government/FedUpdate/CHEA_FU11.html.

Cross, J. (2007). *Informal Learning: Rediscovering the Natural Pathways That Inspire Innovation and Performance.* San Francisco: Pfeiffer.

Cross, J. and Hamilton, I. (2002). *The DNA of eLearning.* Retrieved from: http://www.internet-time.com/Learning/articles/DNA.pdf.

Cullinane, M. (2008). Creating Artists of Learning: Building the School of the Future. Retrieved from: http://marycullinane.com/Documents/NUTN%20Keynote.pptx

Cumming, C. S. (2011). *Enhancing Professional Learning through Aspects of Creativity.* 24th International Congress for School Effectiveness and Improvement. Retrieved from: http://www.icsei.net/icsei2011/Full%20Papers/0001.pdf

Cwikowski, M. (2010). Food Safety Knowledge: The Coca-Cola Food Safety Conference…A collaborative initiative. *New Food*, Issue 6, 2010, December 15, 2010. Summary retrieved from: http://www.newfoodmagazine.com/tag/marc-cwikowski/

Darling-Hammond, L. (2010). *The Flat World and Education: How America's Commitment to Equity Will Determine Our Future.* New York: Teacher's College Press.

Darling-Hammond, L. and Bransford, J. (2005). *Preparing Teachers for a Changing World: What Teachers Should Be Able to Know and Do.* San Francisco: John Wiley and Sons.

Davies, S. and Hammack, F. M. (2005). The Channeling of Student Competition in Higher Education: Comparing Canada and the U.S. *The Journal of Higher Education,* 76(1), pp. 89-106.

Davis, B. G. (1999). Motivating Students. From *Tools for Teaching.* San Francisco: Jossey-Bass. Retrieved from: http://teaching.berkeley.edu/bgd/motivate.html

Davis, N. and Rose, R. (2007). *Professional Development for Virtual Schooling and Online Learning.* North American Council for Online Learning. Retrieved from: http://www.inacol.org/research/docs/NACOL_PDforVSandOlnLrng.pdf

Dawley, L., Rice, K., and Hinck, G. (2010). *Going Virtual! 2010: The Status of Professional Development and Unique Needs of K-12 Online Teachers.* North American Council for Online Learning. Retrieved from: http://edtech.boisestate.edu/goingvirtual/goingvirtual3.pdf

Dede, C., (2008a). Transforming education for the 21st century: rethinking curriculum. Specialist Schools and Academies Trust, The road to transformation in education, iNet online conferences for educators 2008. Retrieved from: http://www.cybertext.net.au/inet_s4wk2/p11_28.htm

Dede, C. (2008b). A seismic shift in epistemology. *EDUCAUSE Review, 43*[3], 80-81. Retrieved from: http://net.educause.edu/ir/library/pdf/ERM0837.pdf

Deniston, R.D., and Gerrity, K. W. (2010). Elementary School Teachers' Perceptions of No Child Left Behind and Its Effect on Morale. *scholarlypartnershipsedu* 5(2), Article 4. Retrieved from: http://opus.ipfw.edu/cgi/viewcontent.cgi?article=1059&context=spe

Derbyshire, D. (2009). Social websites harm children's brains: Chilling warning to parents from top neuroscientist. *Mail Online,* February 24, 2009. Retrieved from: http://www.dailymail.co.uk/news/article-1153583/Social-websites-harm-childrens-brains-Chilling-warning-parents-neuroscientist.html#ixzz1XcQK8but

Diaz, D.P. (2002). Online drop rates revisited. *The Technology Source,* May/June 2002. Retrieved from: http://technologysource.org/article/online_drop_rates_revisited/

Digital Library Foundation (2005). 4.3 Pathways to E-Learning in Science and Beyond. Retrieved from: http://www.diglib.org/pubs/dlf106/DLF106part3c.html.

Discovery Channel (2011). Creating the Life Series (video). Discovery Channel, Life - Behind the Scenes web page. Retrieved from: http://dsc.discovery.com/videos/life-behind-the-scenes-videos/

Downes, S. (2010). The Role of the Educator. *The Huffington Post*, December 5, 2010. Retrieved from: http://www.huffingtonpost.com/stephen-downes/the-role-of-the-educator_b_790937.html

Drucker, P. (1999). Beyond the Information Revolution. *Atlantic Magaine*, October 1999. Retrieved from: http://www.theatlantic.com/doc/199910/information-revolution.

Duderstadt, J. (2007) The Future of the University: A Perspective from the Oort Cloud. Retrieved from: http://milproj.dc.umich.edu/publications/oort_cloud/index.html

Duffy, T., and del Valle, R. (2005). LTTS: A course management system for online inquiry learning. Presentation at the 21st Annual Conference on Distance Teaching & Learning, Madison, WI. Retrieved from: http://www.uwex.edu/disted/conference/Resource_library/handouts/05_1805P.pdf

Duffy, T. M. and Kirkley, J. R., eds. (2004). *Learner-Centered Theory and Practice in Distance Education: Cases from Higher Education.* Mahwah, NJ: Lawrence Erlbaum Associates.

Ede, A. (2006). Scripted Curriculum: Is It a Prescription for Success? *Childhood Education*, 83(1), p.29.

Education-Portal.com (2010). Scholars Grow More Comfortable with Online Research. Education-Portal.com, April 12, 2010. Retrieved from: http://education-portal.com/articles/Scholars_Grow_More_Comfortable_with_Online_Research.html

EDUCAUSE (2010). Next Generation Learning Challenges Wave 1: Building Blocks for College Completion; Request for Proposals – Rules and Guidelines. Retrieved from: http://nextgen-learning.org/sites/default/files/Final_RFP-1.1.pdf

EDUCAUSE (2009). Seven Things You Should Know about Personal Learning Environments. EDUCAUSE Learning Initiative, May 12, 2009. Retrieved from: http://net.educause.edu/ir/library/pdf/ELI7049.pdf

eLearninternational (2004). *The Edinburgh Scenarios: The Edinburgh Scenarios: Global Scenarios for the Future of eLearning*. Retrieved from: http://www.internettime.com/Learning/articles/eLearning%20Age%20pdf.pdf

Elert, G. (1992). SAT: Aptitude or Demographics? Retrieved from: http://hypertextbook.com/eworld/sat.shtml#income

Evergreen Freedom Foundation. (2001). Value added assessment. *School Directors Handbook, VA-1*. Retrieved from: http://www.myfreedomfoundation.com/pdfs/Value-Added.pdf

Fagan, A. (2007). Teach your children well; with new resources, home-schooling numbers grow. *The Washington Times*, November 26, 2007.

Fairleigh Dickinson University (2010). *GVF Program*. Retrieved from: http://staging.fdu.edu/default.aspx?id=267.

FairTest.org (n.d.) *College Admissions Test Scores by Family Income: 1997*. Retrieved from: http://fairt-est.org/college-admissions-test-scores-family-income-1997

Farber, J. (1969). The Student and Society: An Annotated Manifesto. In *The Student As Nigger*. New York: Pocket Books.

Farenga, P. (n.d.). What Is Unschooling? Holtgws.com. Retrieved from: http://www.holtgws.com/whatisunschoolin.html

Fasse, R., Humbert, J., and Rappold, R. (2009). Rochester Institute of Technology: Analyzing Student Success. *Journal of Asynchronous Learning Networks,* (13) 3, October 2009.

Fehlen, D.J. (2011). Apples to Oranges: Are PISA Tests Fair? *Education-portal.com*, February 9, 2011. Retrieved from: http://education-portal.com/articles/Apples_to_Oranges_Are_PISA_Tests_Fair.html

Felch, J. et al. (2010a). Los Angeles Teacher Ratings: FAQ & About. *Los Angeles Times online*. Retrieved from: http://projects.latimes.com/value-added/faq/#what_is_value_added

Felch, J. et al. (2010b). Top 100 "Value-Added" Teachers. *Los Angeles Times online*. Retrieved from: http://projects.latimes.com/value-added/rank/top-100/ela/

Fendrich, L. (2009). The Dystopia of Distance Learning. *Chronicle of Higher Education,* September 13, 2009. Retrieved from: http://chronicle.com/blogPost/The-Dystopia-of-Distance/8020

Fernandez, L. (2009). Sloan-C listserv discussion posting, September 10, 2009.

FinAid (2011). Tuition Inflation web page. Retrieved from: http://www.finaid.org/savings/tuition-inflation.phtml

Fitch, D., Reed, B., Peet, M., & Tolman, R. (2008). The Use of E-Portfolios in Evaluating the Curriculum and Student Learning. *Journal of Social Work Education*, 44(3), 37-54. Retrieved from http://www.ied.edu.hk/obl/files/out23.pdf

Florida, R. (2007). *The Flight of the Creative Class: The New Global Competition for Talent*. New York: HarperCollins.

Friedman, T. (2007). *The World Is Flat: a Brief History of the 21st Century*. New York: Macmillan.

Friesen, N. (2011). *The Lecture as Trans-Medial Pedagogical Form: An Historical Analysis*. Draft retrieved from: http://learningspaces.org/n/papers/lecture_as_transmedial.pdf

Fromm, E. (1971). *Escape From Freedom*. New York: Avon Books, 11th edition.

Frost, M. (2009). *The New Global Student*. New York: Three Rivers Press.

Fuller, B. (1962). *Education Automation*. Carbondale, IL: Southern Illinois University Press.

Gabriel, T. (2011). More Pupils Are Learning Online, Fueling Debate on Quality. *New York Times*, April 5, 2011. Retrieved from: http://www.nytimes.com/2011/04/06/education/06online.html?_r=1&pagewanted=2

Garrison, D. R., Anderson, T., & Archer, W. (2000). Critical inquiry in a text-based environment: Computer conferencing in higher education. *The Internet and Higher Education*, 2(2-3), 87-105.

Gates, B. (2010). *2010 Annual Letter from Bill Gates: Online Learning*. Bill and Melinda Gates Foundation. Retrieved from: http://www.gatesfoundation.org/annual-letter/2010/Pages/education-learning-online.aspx

Gehringer, E.F. and Miller, C.S. (2009). Student-generated active-learning exercises. *SIGCSE 2009, Fortieth Technical Symposium on Computer Science Education*, Chattanooga, Mar. 4-7, 2009, in *Inroads: SIGCSE Bulletin* 41:1 (March 2009), 81–85.

Gehringer, E. F., Ehresman, L. M., Conger, S. G., and Wagle, P. A. (2007). Reusable learning objects through peer review: The Expertiza approach. *Innovate—Journal of Online Education* 3:6, August/September 2007.

Geith, C., Vignare, K., Thiagarajan, D., and Bourquin, L. (2010). Designing Corporate Training in Developing Countries Using Open Educational Resources. *Journal of Asynchronous Learning Networks,* 14(3), November 2010.

Gleick, J. (1999). *Faster: The Acceleration of Just About Everything*. New York: Pantheon.

Glenn, M. (2008). *The Future of Higher Education: how technology will shape learning.* Economist Intelligence Unit, October 2008. Retrieved from: http://www.nmc.org/pdf/Future-of-Higher-Ed-(NMC).pdf

Goldsmith, D. (2007). Enhancing learning and assessment through e-portfolios: A collaborative effort in Connecticut. *New Directions for Student Services*, (119), 31-42. doi:10.1002/ss.247.

Goodnow, C. (2007). Teens buying books at fastest rate in decades; new 'golden age of young adult literature' declared. *Seattle Post Intelligencer,* March 7, 2007. Retrieved from: http://www.seattlepi.com/books/306531_teenlit08.html?source=mypi

Great Plains Interactive Distance Education Alliance (n.d.) About Great Plains IDEA web page. Retrieved from: http://www.gpidea.org/index.html

Green, C. (2011). Publishers Criticize Federal Investment in Open Educational Resources. *Changes Next Exit blog,* May 26, 2011. Retrieved from: http://blog.oer.sbctc.edu/2011/05/publishers-criticize-federal-investment.html

Greenfield, D.N. (2002). Lost in cyberspace: the web @ work. Retrieved from: http://www.virtual-addiction.com/pdf/lostincyberspace.pdf

Griffths, R. T. (2002). History of the Internet, Chapter Two: From ARPANET to World Wide Web. Retrieved from: http://www.let.leidenuniv.nl/history/ivh/chap2.htm

Guess, A. (2007). Open Courses Open Wider. *Inside Higher Ed*, December 12, 2007. Retrieved from: http://www.insidehighered.com/news/2007/12/12/openyale

Gunawardena, C. and Zittle. F. (1997). Social presence as a predictor of satisfaction within a computer mediated conferencing environment. *American Journal of Distance Education* 11: 8–26.

Hamilton, D.W. (2004). *The Morrill Land Grant Act of 1862.* encyclopedia.com. Retrieved from: http://www.encyclopedia.com/topic/Morrill_Land_Grant_Act_of_1862.aspx

Harasim, L. (2006). A History of E-learning: Shift Happened. *The International Handbook of Virtual Learning Environments*. Springer Netherlands: 2006. Abstract Retrieved from: http://www.springerlink.com/content/k7g58wtm11114811/.

Harasim, L., Hiltz, S. R., Teles, L., and Turoff, M. (1995). *Learning Networks: A Field Guide to Teaching and Learning Online*. Cambridge, MA: MIT Press, 1995.

Harasim, L. (1990). *On-line Education: Perspectives on a New Environment*. New York: Praeger.

Harding, A., Kaczynski, D., & Wood, L. (2005). Evaluation of blended learning: Analysis of qualitative data. *Proceedings of the Blended Learning in Science, Teaching and Learning Symposium*, University of Sydney, Australia, September 30, 2005.

Hartman, J. (2010a.) Personal communication, September 26, 2010.

Hartman, J. (2010b). The Promise and Practice of Blended Learning. Sloan-C Blended Learning Conference, Chicago, April 19, 2010. http://sloanconsortium.org/sites/default/files/webform/2010bldPresentations/hartman_sloanc_Blended.pdf.

Havenstein, H. (2007). Wiki becomes textbook in Boston College classroom. *Computerworld*, August 15, 2007. Retrieved from: http://www.computerworld.com/s/article/9030802/Wiki_becomes_textbook_in_Boston_College_classroom

Hayles, K. (1999). *How We Became Posthuman: Virtual Bodies in Cybernetics, Literature, and Informatics*. Chicago: University of Chicago Press.

Higgins, A. (2010). Have we become posthuman digital zombies? *Pittsburgh Post-Gazette*, January 24, 2010. Retrieved from: http://www.post-gazette.com/pg/10024/1030468-109.stm

Hiltz, S. R., and Goldman, R. eds. (2005). *Learning Together Online: Research on Asynchronous Learning Networks*. Mahwah, NJ: Lawrence Erlbaum, 2005.

Hiltz, S. R., Y. Zhang, and M. Turoff. (2002). Studies of effectiveness of learning networks. In *Elements of Quality Online Education: Learning Effectiveness, Cost Effectiveness, Access, Faculty Satisfaction, Student Satisfaction*, J. Bourne & J. C. Moore (Eds.). Needham, MA: Sloan Center for Online Education, 2002.

Hiltz, S. R. (1994) *The Virtual Classroom: Learning without Limits via Computer Networks*. Norwood, NJ: Ablex, 1994.

Holt, J. (1974). *Escape from Childhood: The Needs and Rights of Children*. New York: Ballantine.

Holzer, H. J. (2010). Postsecondary Credentials for Adults: How States Can Move Ahead. Increasing Postsecondary Credential Attainment by Adults: An Institute for State Policymakers, National Governors Association, Washington, DC, March 24, 2010.

Hoover, E. (2010). Application Inflation: When Is Enough Enough? *New York Times*, November 5, 2010. Retrieved from: http://www.nytimes.com/2010/11/07/education/edlife/07HOOVER-t.html

Horn, M. B. (2009). Education Innovations overseas. *Disrupting Class blog*, November 5, 2009. Retrieved from: http://disruptingclass.mhprofessional.com/apps/ab/?s=%22university+of+the+people%22

Howell, S.L., Williams, P.B., and Lindsay, N.K. (2003). Thirty-two Trends Affecting Distance Education: An Informed Foundation for Strategic Planning. *Online Journal of Distance Learning Administration*, 6(3), Fall 2003. Retrieved from: http://www.westga.edu/~distance/ojdla/fall63/howell63.html

Hughes, L. (2006). Improvement of Classroom Teaching through Online Course Development. *Focus Microbiol. Educ.* 12(3):7–9.

Husser, W.M., and Bailey, T.J. (2008). *Projections of Education Statistics to 2017*. National Center for Education Statistics. Retrieved from: http://nces.ed.gov/pubs2008/2008078.pdf

IBM Institute for Business Value (2010). *Capitalizing on Complexity: Insights from the Global Chief Executive Officer Study*. Somers, NY: IBM Global Business Services, May 2010. Retrieved from: http://public.dhe.ibm.com/common/ssi/ecm/en/gbe03297usen/GBE03297USEN.PDF

Ice, P. (2010). Using the Community of Inquiry Framework Survey for Multi-Level Institutional Evaluation and Continuous Quality Improvement. Retrieved from:

http://sloanconsortium.org/effective_practices/using-community-inquiry-framework-survey-multi-level-institutional-evaluation-an

Illich, I. (1971). *Deschooling Society*. New York: Harper & Row.

iNACOL (2010a). *National Standards of Quality for Online Courses* (updated August 2010). Retrieved from: http://www.inacol.org/research/nationalstandards/NACOL%20Standards%20Quality%20Online%20Courses%202007.pdf

iNACOL (2010b). *National Standards for Quality Online Teaching* (updated August 2010). Retrieved from: http://www.inacol.org/research/nationalstandards/NACOL%20Standards%20Quality%20Online%20Teaching.pdf

Institute of Transpersonal Psychology (n.d.) What Is Transpersonal Psychology? Retrieved from: http://www.itp.edu/about/transpersonal.php

Institute for Alternative Futures (n.d.). *The Future Belongs to Those Who...A Guide for Thinking about the Future*. Alexandria, VA: Institute for Alternative Futures.

Institute for the Future (2006). *2006-2016 Map of Future Forces Affecting Education*. Knowledge Works Foundation. Retrieved from: http://resources.knowledgeworks.org/map/

Institute of Museum and Library Services (2008). August 2008: 15 Library Schools Share Quality Online Courses via WISE Consortium. Retrieved from: http://test.imls.gov/news/prisource/Aug08.shtm

International Astronomical Union (n.d.). Questions and Answers about Planets. Press Release iau0603. Retrieved from: http://www.iau.org/public_press/news/release/iau0603/questions_answers/

Iowa State University (2009). ISU study finds college students are online regularly and reading more overall. *ISU News Service*, March 24, 2009. Retrieved from: http://www2.iastate.edu/~nscentral/news/2009/mar/readingstudy.shtml

Jarmon, C. G., ed. (2002). Pew Project Updates: Round III, Ohio State University: Statistics. *The Pew Learning and Technology Program Newsletter*, 4 (3), September 2002. http://www.thencat. org/PCR/PewNews/PLTP13.html.

Jarvik, E. (2009). "Universities will be 'irrelevant' by 2020, Y. professor says", *The Deseret News*, April 20, 2009.

Jaschik, S. (2010). A Jobs Mismatch. *Inside Higher Ed*, June 15, 2010. Retrieved from: http://www. insidehighered.com/news/2010/06/15/jobs

Jaschik, S. (2007). Could RateMyProfessors.com Be Right? *Inside Higher Ed,* June 5, 2007. Retrieved from: http://www.insidehighered.com/news/2007/06/05/rmp

Jeffries, M. (n.d.) Research in Distance Education. http://www.digitalschool.net/edu/DL_history_mJeffries.html

Jensen, B., and Chamberlin, S. (2009). Featured Story: Fullerton College: Dean Bob Jensen and Dr. Sean Chamberlin (video interview). Studentgenerated.com web site, May 2, 2009. Retrieved from: http://www.studentgenerated.com/Main/Main.html

Johnson, L., Levine, A., Smith, R., and Smythe, T. (2009). *The 2009 Horizon Report: K-12 Edition.* Austin, Texas: The New Media Consortium. Retrieved from: http://eskillslearning.net/uploads/2009-Horizon-Report-K12%20with%20summary.pdf

Johnson, N., Oliff, P., and Williams, E. (2011). An Update on State Budget Cuts: At Least 46 States Have Imposed Cuts That Hurt Vulnerable Residents and the Economy. Center on Budget and Policy Priorities, February 9, 2011. Retrieved from: http://www.cbpp.org/cms/index. cfm?fa=view&id=1214

Johnson, N. (2007). *Simply Complexity: A Clear Guide to Complexity Theory.* Oxford: One World Press. Retrieved from: http://www.oneworld-publications.com/pdfs/simply_complexity.pdf

Johnstone, S. M. (2005). Open Education Resources Serve the World. *EDUCAUSE Quarterly*, 28(3), 2005. Retrieved from: http://www.educause.edu/EDUCAUSE+Quarterly/EDUCAUSEQuarterlyMagazineVolum/OpenEducationalResourcesServet/157357

Jones International University (n.d.). JIU History web page. Retrieved from: http://www.international.edu/about/history

Jorgensen, J. (2009). Student loan lenders brace for rise in defaults. *Boston Globe*, May 6, 2009.

Junco, R., Heiberger, G., and Loken, E. (2011). The effect of Twitter on college student engagement and grades. *Journal of Computer-Assisted Learning,* 27(2), April 2011, pp. 119-132.

Kahn, R.L., and Prager, D.J. (1994). Interdisciplinary Collaborations Are a Scientific and Social Imperative. *The Scientist*, 8(14), July 11, 1994, p.1. Retrieved from: http://notes.utk.edu/bio/unistudy.nsf/3f16569267bd2644852566fe00625b46/bcb1c3cad59f101b852566fe0063ad5f?OpenDocument

Kamenetz, A. (2010). *DIY U: Edupunks, Edupreneurs, and the Coming Transformation of Higher Education.* White River Junction, VT: Chelsea Green.

Kannel, S. (2010). Private conversation, March 2010.

Karabel, J. (1972). Open Admissions: Toward Meritocracy or Democracy? *Change*, May 1972, pp.38-43.

Kashdan, T. (2010). Curiosity: The Heart of Academic Engagement. Extraordinary Lives Colloquium, Fort Worth, TX, June 7, 2010.

Kass, L. (2006). A Warfighting Domain (slide presentation). Headquarters US Air Force, AF Cyberspace Task Force, September 26, 2006. Retrieved from: http://www.au.af.mil/info-ops/usaf/cyberspace_taskforce_sep06.pdf

Kassop, M. (2003). Ten Ways Online Education Matches, or Surpasses, Face-to-Face Learning. *The Technology Source*, May/June 2003. Available online at http://technologysource.org/article/ten_ways_online_education_matches_or_surpasses_facetoface_learning/

Katz, M. S. (1976). *A History of Compulsory Education Laws*. Fastback Series #75, Bicentennial Series. Bloomington, IN: Phi Delta Kappa. Retrieved from: http://www.eric.ed.gov:80/PDFS/ED119389.pdf

Katz, M.B. (1971). *Class, Bureaucracy, and Schools: The Illusion of Educational Change in America*. New York: Praeger.

Keeton, M.T., B.G. Scheckley, and Krecji-Griggs, J. (2002). *Effectiveness and Efficiency in Higher Education for Adults*. Council on Adult and Experiential Learning. Chicago: Kendall-Hunt, 2002.

Kelderman, E. (2009). Most Colleges Avoid Risk Management, Report Says. *Chronicle of Higher Education*, June 25, 2009. Retrieved from: http://chronicle.com/article/Most-Colleges-Avoid-Risk/47806.

Kessleman, J. R. (1976). The Care and Feeding of Stop-Outs. *Change*, 8(4), May 1976, pp. 13-15.

Kidd, J. J., O'Shea, P. M., Kaufman J., Baker, P. B., Xiao, Y., & Allen D. W. (2009). *Traditional Textbook vs. Student-authored Wikibook: A Quasi-Experimental Study of Student Attitudes and Behaviors*. Paper presented at annual meeting of American Educational Research Association, San Diego, CA, April 2009.

Klima, S. (2007). The Children We Leave Behind: The Effects of High-Stakes Testing on Dropout Rates. *Review of Law and Social Justice* 17(1), pp.8-10. Retrieved from: http://lawweb.usc.edu/why/students/orgs/rlsj/assets/docs/issue_17/07_Klima_Macro.pdf

Klingensmith, K. (2009). PLN: Your Personal Learning Network Made Easy. Once a Teacher... blog, May 5, 2009. Retrieved from: http://onceateacher.wordpress.com/2009/05/05/pln-your-personal-learning-network-made-easy/

Klor de Alva, J. (2010). *For Profit Colleges and Universities: America's Least Costly and Most Efficient System of Higher Education: Case Study—University of Phoenix*. Nexus Research Institute, August 2010. Retrieved from: http://nexusresearch.org/1/NexusStudy8-31-10.pdf

Kohn, A. (2010). Debunking the Case for National Standards: One-Size-Fits-All Mandates and Their Dangers. *Education Week,* January 14, 2010. Retrieved from: http://www.alfiekohn.org/teaching/edweek/national.htm

Kohn, A. (2002). The 500-Pound Gorilla: The Corporate Role in the High-Stakes Testing Obsession & Other Methods of Turning Education into a Business. October, 2002. Retrieved from: http://www.reclaimdemocracy.org/weekly_article/corporate_influence_education_kohn.html

Kolowich, S. (2010). Tuition-free, online education? Try University of the People. *USA Today*, February 22, 2010. Retrieved from: http://www.usatoday.com/news/education/2010-02-22-IHE_University_of_the_People_ST_N.htm

Kozol, J. (1992). *Savage Inequalities: Children in America's Schools*. New York: Harper Perennial.

Knapp, L.G., Kelly-Reid, J. E., and Ginder, S. A. (2010). *Postsecondary Institutions and Price of Attendance in the United States: Fall 2009, Degrees and Other Awards Conferred: 2008–09, and 12-Month Enrollment: 2008–09: First Look.* National Center for Education Statistics, Institute of Education Sciences. Retrieved from: http://nces.ed.gov/pubs2010/2010161.pdf

Knowles, M. (1984). *The Adult Learner: A Neglected Species,* Houston: Gulf Publishing, 3rd edition.

Kortemeyer, G. (2010). The LearningOnline Network with CAPA web page. Retrieved from: http://www.lon-capa.org/history.html]

Krashen, S. (2008). The 'Decline' in reading in America: Another case of the "Shock Doctrine"? *Substance News*. Retrieved from: http://www.substancenews.net/articles.php?page=255

Kuh, G. (2006). *Student Engagement: A Means to Many Desirable Ends.* A National Dialogue: The Secretary of Education's Commission on the Future of Higher Education Indianapolis, Indiana April 7, 2006. Retrieved from http://www2.ed.gov/about/bdscomm/list/hiedfuture/4th-meeting/kuh.pdf.

Kumari, D.S. (2001). Connecting Graduate Students to Virtual Guests through Asynchronous Discussions - Analysis of an Experience. *Journal of Asynchronous Learning Networks*, 5(2), September 2001, pp. 53-63.

Kurth-Schai, R., and Green, C. G. (2006). *Re-Envisioning Education and Democracy.* Greenwich, CT: Information Age Publishing.

Lataif, L.E. (2011). Universities on the Brink. *Forbes.com*, February 2, 2011. Retrieved from: http://www.forbes.com/2011/02/01/college-education-bubble-opinions-contributors-louis-lataif.html

Lauerman, J., and Deprez, E.E. (2010). Apollo, Education Shares Slide on Bleak Enrollment Outlook. *Bloomberg.net*, October 14, 2010. Retrieved from: http://www.bloomberg.com/news/2010-10-14/apollo-group-s-forecast-withdrawal-drags-down-for-profit-education-shares.html

Lave, J., & Wenger, E. (1991). *Situated Learning: Legitimate peripheral participation.* New York, NY, USA: Cambridge University Press.

Lazowska, E. (2009). E-Science as a Lens on the World. WCET conference, October 2009. Retrieved from: http://www.slideshare.net/guest43b4df3/e-science-as-a-lens-on-the-world-lazowska

Lederman, D. (2010). The "Prior Learning Edge", *Inside Higher Ed,* March 1, 2010. Retrieved from: http://www.insidehighered.com/news/2010/03/01/prior

Lederman, D. (2008). The Competition to Be Transparent. *Inside Higher Ed*, September 29, 2008. Retrieved from: http://www.insidehighered.com/news/2008/09/29/vsa.

Lederman, D. (2005). Adding Up the Damage. *Inside Higher Ed*, November 14, 2005. Retrieved from: http://www.insidehighered.com/news/2005/11/14/gulf

Lenzenr, R., and Johnson, S. S. (1997). Seeing things as they really are (interview with Peter Drucker), *Forbes*, March 10, 1997. Retrieved from: http://www.forbes.com/forbes/1997/0310/5905122a_7.html

Levie, W. H., and Lentz, R. (1982). Effects of Text Illustrations: A Review of the Research, *Educational Communication and Technology Journal* 30 (Winter 1982): 195–232.

Lewin, T. (2010). Scrutiny Takes Toll on For-Profit College Company. *New York Times*, November 9, 2010. Retrieved from: http://www.nytimes.com/2010/11/10/education/10kaplan.html

Lipka, S. (2010). Academic Credit: Colleges' Common Currency Has No Set Value; Colleges resist regulators' calls for consistency. *Chronicle of Higher Education*, October 17, 2010

Lipka, S., and Coddington, R. (2010). One Math Course, Variously Valued Within a Single University System. *Chronicle of Higher Education*, October 15, 2010. Retrieved from: http://chronicle.com/article/One-Math-Course-Variously/125002/

Liu, Y. W. (2002-03). The Cyberization of Education and the Reformation of Class Education. *Journal of Educational Science of Hunan Normal University*, 2002-03. Abstract retrieved from: http://en.cnki.com.cn/Article_en/CJFDTOTAL-FLJY200203004.htm

Lok, C. (2008). Interdisciplinary science: Harvard under review. *Nature* 454, pp, 686-689, August 6, 2008. doi:10.1038/454686a. Retrieved from: http://www.nature.com/news/2008/080807/full/454686a.html

Lorenzo, G. (2006). The Sloan Semester Brought An Academic Lifeline to Hurricane-Affected Students, But Not Without Its Set of Challenges and Lessons Learned for the Future of Higher Ed Disaster Preparedness. Sloan Consortium, 2006. Retrieved from: http://sloanconsortium.org/sites/default/files/pages/SloanSemester.pdf

Lucas, L. W. (1994). Say "YES" to Telephone Lines in the Classroom. ERIC Digest, December 1994. ED377829. Retrieved from: http://www.ericdigests.org/1995-2/yes.htm

Lynch, M., Engle, J., and Cruz, J.L. (2010) *Subprime Opportunity: The Unfulfilled Promise of For-Profit Colleges and Universities*. The Education Trust, November 2010. Retrieved from: http://www.edtrust.org/sites/edtrust.org/files/publications/files/Subprime_report_1.pdf

Lytle, R. (2010). *Private Sector Post-Secondary Schools: Do they deliver value to students and society?* The Parthenon Group, February 2010. Retrieved from: http://phx.corporate-ir.net/External.File?item=UGFyZW50SUQ9NDcxMzl8Q2hpbGRJRD0tMXxUeXBlPTM=&t=1

Malopinsky, L., Kirkley, J. R., Duffy, T. (2002). Building Performance Support Systems to Assist preK-12 Teachers in Designing Online, Inquiry-Based Professional Development Instruction. Paper presented at the Annual Meeting of American Educational Research Association, New Orleans, LA.

Manufacturing Instiute (2011). Skills Certification System web page. Retrieved from: http://www.themanufacturinginstitute.org/Education-Workforce/Skills-Certification-System/Skills-Certification-System.aspx

Marquardt, P. J. (2010). Comment posted on article by Lederman, D. (2010). The "Prior Learning Edge", *Inside Higher Ed*, March 1, 2010. Retrieved from: http://www.insidehighered.com/news/2010/03/01/prior

Marsh, G., Carlson, N.L., and Irons, E.J. (2010). A Comparison of the Aftermath of Hurricanes Rita and Ike: University Administrator's Perspectives. *National Social Science Journal* 35(1), pp. 86-92. Retrieved from: http://www.nssa.us/journals/2010-35-1/pdf/35-1%2011%20Marsh.pdf

Martin, G. (2010). Ivory Tower definition web page. *The Phrase Finder*. Retrieved from: http://www.phrases.org.uk/meanings/210800.html

Maryland State Department of Education (2010). State Board Agrees to Limited Waiver Process Due to Winter Weather. *Maryland Education Bulletin*, March 4, 2010. Retrieved from: http://msde.state.md.us/MSDEBulletins/2010/march_04/

Masie, E. (2000). Blended learning: the magic is in the mix. In *The ASTD E-Learning Handbook*, A. Rossett (ed.), New York: McGraw-Hill.

Matkin, G. (2002). The Whys and Hows of Online Education at UC: A Dean's Perspective. Retreived from: http://www.ucop.edu/tltc/news/2002/06/matkin.php

Mathews, J. (2011). Michelle Rhee's early test scores challenged. Class Struggle blog, *Washington Post*, Feburary 8, 2011. Retrieved from: http://voices.washingtonpost.com/class-struggle/2011/02/michelle_rhees_early_test_scor.html

Mayadas, A. F. (1997). Asynchronous Learning Networks: A Sloan Foundation Perspective. *Journal of Asynchronous Learning Networks*, 1(1), March 1997.

Mayer, R. E. (2001). *Multimedia learning*. Cambridge: Cambridge University Press.

McCurdy, S. and Schroeder, R. (2006a). Achieving Diversity Through Online Inter-Institutional Collaborations. *Journal of Asynchronous Learning Networks*, 10(1), February 2006.

McCurdy, S. and Schroeder, R. (2006b). Inter-Institutional Collaborations in the Delivery of Online Learning. Proceedings of the 21st Annual Conference on Distance Teaching and Learning, February 2006. Retrieved from: http://www.uwex.edu/disted/conference/Resource_library/proceedings/05_1829.pdf

McLeod, S., admin. (2011). Education Blogs by Discipline. Moving Forward wiki. Retrieved from: http://movingforward.wikispaces.com/Education+Blogs+by+Discipline

McMahon, J. (2011). Personal communication, July 2011.

McMahon, K. (2010). Testing Kindergarten: Young Children Produce Data—Lots of Data. *EducationNews.org,* January 14, 2010. Retrieved from: http://www.educationnews.org/ed_reports/education_organizations/30160.html

McNamee, G. (2008). Walt Kelly's Pogo, Sixty Years On. *Encyclopedia Brittanica Blog*, October 15, 2008. Retrieved from: http://www.britannica.com/blogs/2008/10/walt-kellys-pogo-sixty-years-on/

McNamee, S.J.. and Miller, R. K. (2009). The meritocracy myth. In *The American Dream: Origins and Prospects*. Lanham, MD: Rowman & Littlefield, 2009. Retrieved from: http://www.rci.rutgers.edu/~jdowd/meritocracy.pdf

McPherson, P., and Shulenburger, D. (2008). *University Tuition, Consumer Choice and College Affordability: Strategies for Addressing a Higher Education Affordability Challenges*. National Association of State Universities and Land-Grant Colleges, November 2008. Retrieved from: https://www.aplu.org/NetCommunity/Document.Doc?id=1296

Mead, L. M. (2010). The Other Danger...Scholasticism in Academic Research. *Academic Questions*, 23(4), pp. 404-419.

Metros, S. (2003). *E-Learning: From Electronic-Learning to Engaged-Learning*. Retrieved from: www.adec.edu/nsf/Susan.ppt

Middlesex Community College (2010). Disclosure Statements: Student Completion Rate web page. Retrieved from: http://www.middlesex.mass.edu/DisclosureStatements/.

Miller, D. (2008). Podcasting: Enhancing University Courses, Visibility, and Student Life. American Association of Collegiate Registrars & Admissions Officers, July 11, 2008. Retrieved from: http://handouts.aacrao.org/tech08/finished/F1115a_D_Miller.pdf

Miller, D. (2007). Beyond Lecturecasting: Using Podcasts for Discussion and Student Content Creation. Sloan Consortium Effective Practices, Student-Generated Content Collection. Retrieved from: http://sloanconsortium.org/effective_practices/beyond-lecturecasting-using-podcasts-discussion-and-student-content-creation

Miller, D. (2006). Podcasting at the University of Connecticut: Enhancing the Educational Experience. *Campus Technology*, October 18, 2006. http://campustechnology.com/articles/2006/10/podcasting-at-the-university-of-connecticut-enhancing-the-educational-experience.aspx.

Miller, G. (2011a). Personal communication, May 16, 2011.

Miller, G. (2011b). Sloan-C listserv discussion posting, February 22, 2011.

Miller, G. (2010a). Collaboration versus Competition: Trends in Online Learning for Workforce Development. Retrieved from: http://sloanconsortium.org/node/2350

Miller, G. (2010b). Organization and Technology of Distance Education. in Cleveland-Innis, M. and Garrison, R., eds. (2010), *An Introduction to Distance Education: Understanding Teaching and Learning in a New Era*. New York: Taylor & Francis.

MIT iCampus (2004). What is TEAL? Retrieved from: http://icampus.mit.edu/teal/content/?whatisteal

Minaei-Bidgoli, B. (2004). *Data Mining for a Web-based Educational System.* Doctoral Dissertation, Michigan State University. Retrieved from: http://www.lon-capa.org/papers/BehrouzThesisRevised.pdf

Mintu-Wimsatt, A., Sadler, T., and Ingram, K. (2007). Creativity in Online Courses: Perceptions of MBA Student. *MERLOT Journal of Online Learning and Teaching,* 3(4), December 2007. Retrieved from: http://jolt.merlot.org/vol3no4/mintu-wimsatt.htm

Mitchell, M. (2009). *Complexity: A Guided Tour.* New York: Oxford University Press.

Moe, T. M., and Chubb, J. E. (2009). *Liberating Learning: Technology, Politics, and the Future of American Education.* San Francisco: Jossey-Bass.

Mokhtari, K., Reichard, C., and Gardner, A. (2009). The Impact of Internet and Television Use on the Reading Habits and Practices of College Students. *Journal of Adolescent & Adult Literacy,* 52(7), April 2009, pp.609-619.

Moloney, J., and Oakley, B. II. (2006). Scaling Online Education: Increasing Access to Online Education. *Journal of Asynchronous Learning Networks,* 10(3), July 2006.

Moore, J. C. (2002). *Elements of Quality: The Sloan-C Framework, Pillar Reference Manual.* Needham, MA: Sloan Consortium.

Moore, M. G. (1989). The Three Types of Interaction. *American Journal of Distance Education,* 3(2).

Moran, M., Seaman, J., and Tinti-Kane, H. (2011). *Teaching, Learning, and Sharing: How Today's Higher Education Faculty Use Social Media.* Retrieved from: http://www.pearsonlearningsolutions.com/educators/pearson-social-media-survey-2011-bw.pdf

Morgenthaler, S. (2007). SUS Retention Efforts: Supporting Students at a Distance. DE Oracle @ UMUC web page, September-October 2007. Retrieved from: http://deoracle.org/online-pedagogy/student-issues/school-of-undergraduate-retention-efforts-supporting-students-at-a-distance.html

Muegge, S., Mora, M., Hassin, K., and Pullin, A. (2008). A Flat Network for the Unflat World: Open Educational Resources in Developing Countries. *Open Source Business Resource,* August 2008: Education. Retrieved from: http://learn.creativecommons.org/wp-content/uploads/2008/08/muegge.pdf

Mullane, L. (2009). When Stopping Out Doesn't Mean Dropping Out: How Colleges and Universities Are Bringing Stop-Out Students Back to the Classroom. ACE CenterPoint web page, American Council on Education, January 9, 2009. Retrieved from: http://www.acenet.edu/AM/Template.cfm?Section=Home&TEMPLATE=/CM/ContentDisplay.cfm&CONTENTID=30756

Muncrief, D. (2005). The Great Red River Raft. January 8, 2005. Retrieved from: http://www.okgenweb.org/~okmurray/Murray/stories/great_red_river_raft.htm

Nagel, D. (2011). Online Learning Set for Explosive Growth as Traditional Classrooms Decline. *Campus Technology*, January 26, 2011. Retrieved from: http://campustechnology.com/articles/2011/01/26/online-learning-set-for-explosive-growth-as-traditional-classrooms-decline.aspx

National Association of Manufacturers (2009a). Manufacturing Institute Receives Gates Foundation Grant For National Skills Certification System. Press release, May 27, 2009. http://www.nam.org/Communications/Articles/2009/05/ManufacturingInstituteGatesFoundation.aspx

National Association of Manufacturers (2009b). New NAM Mfg Skills Certification System Will Help New & Transitioning Workers. Press release, March 4, 2009. Retrieved from: http://news.thomasnet.com/companystory/NAM-partners-to-launch-skills-certification-system-557091

National Center for Education Statistics (2009). *Table 103. High school graduates, by sex and control of school: Selected years, 1869-70 through 2018-19.* Digest of Education Statistics, National Center for Education Statistics. Retrieved from: http://nces.ed.gov/programs/digest/d09/tables/dt09_103.asp

National Center for Education Statistics (2005). *Table 8. Percentage of persons age 25 and over and 25 to 29, by race/ethnicity, years of school completed, and sex: Selected years, 1910 through 2005.* Retrieved from: http://nces.ed.gov/programs/digest/d05/tables/dt05_008.asp

National Center on Education Statistics (n.d.). College Enrollment - Fast Facts. Retrieved from: http://nces.ed.gov/fastfacts/display.asp?id=98

National Center for Education Statistics (n.d.). Nontraditional Undergraduates: Definitions and Data. Retrieved from: http://nces.ed.gov/pubs/web/97578e.asp

National Center for Supercomputing Applications (n.d.). About NCSA Mosaic web page. Retrieved from: http://www.ncsa.illinois.edu/Projects/mosaic.html

National Endowment for the Arts (2007). *To Read or Not to Read: A Question of National Consequence.* National Endowment for the Arts, Research Division Report #47, Washington, DC, November 2007. Retrieved from: http://www.nea.gov/research/toread.pdf

National Postsecondary Education Cooperative (2010). *Suggestions for Improving the IPEDS Graduation Rate Survey Data Collection and Reporting.* (NPEC 2010–832) Prepared by Brenda Albright for Coffey Consulting. Washington, DC. Retrieved from: http://nces.ed.gov/pubs2010/2010832.pdf

National Science Foundation (2010). Computing Education for the 21st Century (CE21). Program Solicitation NSF 10-619. Retrieved from: http://www.nsf.gov/pubs/2010/nsf10619/nsf10619.htm

National Survey of Student Engagement. 2010. *Major Differences: Examining Student Engagement by Field of Study. Annual Results 2010.* Retrieved from: Retrieved from: http://nsse.iub.edu/NSSE_2010_Results/pdf/NSSE_2010_AnnualResults.pdf

National Survey of Student Engagement (2009). *Assessment for Improvement: Tracking Student Engagement Over Time. Annual Results 2009.* http://nsse.iub.edu/NSSE_2009_Results/pdf/NSSE_AR_2009.pdf.

National Survey of Student Engagement (2008). *Promoting Engagement for All Students: The Imperative to Look Within. 2008 Results.* http://nsse.iub.edu/NSSE_2008_Results/docs/withhold/NSSE2008_Results_revised_11-14-2008.pdf.

National Survey of Student Engagement (n.d.). Benchmarks of Effective Educational Practice. Retrieved from: http://nsse.iub.edu/pdf/nsse_benchmarks.pdf.

Nelson, C. (2008) Foreword. in Bosquet, M. *How the University Works: Higher Education and the Low-Wage Nation.* New York: NYU Press. Excerpt retrieved from: http://marcbousquet.net/reviews.html

New Leadership Alliance (2010). *Expanding the Reporting on Student Learning Outcomes On- and Off-Campus to Ensure Transparency and Accountability.* New Leadership Alliance, October 11, 2010. Retrieved from: http://www.newleadershipalliance.org/images/uploads/listings/Capella_University-3.pdf

New Jersey Institute of Technology (n.d.). Computerized Conferencing and Communications Center: Report Title List. Robert W. Van Houten Library. Retrieved from: http://library.njit.edu/archives/cccc-materials/index.php

Nichols, S. E., (1997) A Toolkit for Developing Critically Reflective Science Teachers. *Journal of Science Teacher Education*, 8(2), 77-106.

Nineplanets.org (2011). The Nine Planets Solar System Tour. Retrieved from: http://nineplanets.org/

Noel-Levitz (2010). The 2010 National Online Learners Priorities Report. Retrieved from: https://https://www.noellevitz.com/papers-research-higher-education/2010/2010-adult-and-online-learner-satisfaction-priorities-reports

Norris, D. M., and Baer, L. (2009). Linking Analytics to Lifting out of Recession. National Symposium on Action Analytics, September 4, 2009. Retrieved from: http://www.strategi-cinitiatives.com/documents/Linking_Analytics_26sep09.pdf

North Central Regional Educational Laboratory (n.d.) Integrated Learning Systems web page. Retrieved from: http://www.ncrel.org/sdrs/areas/issues/content/cntareas/reading/li3lk59.htm

Oliver, K. & Raubenheimer, D. (2006). Online Concept Mapping in Distance Teacher Education: Two Case Studies. In C. Crawford et al. (Eds.), Proceedings of Society for Information Technology & Teacher Education International Conference 2006, pp. 114-119. Chesapeake, VA: AACE.

Ombudsman.com (n.d.). Credit Information web page. Retrieved from: http://www.ombudsman.com/measurable_results/credit_information.aspx.

O'Shea, P. M., Baker, P. B., Allen, D. W., Curry-Corcoran, D. E., & Allen, D. B. (2007). New levels of student participatory learning: A WikiText for the introductory course in education. *Journal of Interactive Online Learning*, 6[3], 228−235.

Overdrive Interactive (2011). Social Media Map for Social Marketing. Retrieved from: http://www.ovrdrv.com/social-media-map/index.asp

Packer, D. J. (2010). Los Angeles Teacher Ratings: Debra J. Packer. *Los Angeles Times* online. Retrieved from: http://projects.latimes.com/value-added/v1/teacher/debra-j-packer/

Parry, M. (2009a). Colleges Will Be 'Torn Apart' by Internet, Law Professor Predicts. *Chronicle of Higher Education*, September 14, 2009.

Retrieved from: http://chronicle.com/blogPost/Colleges-Will-Be-Torn-Apart/8035/

Parry, M. (2009b). New Tuition-Free 'University of the People' Tries to Democratize Higher Ed. *Chronicle of Higher Education - Wired Campus*, August 26, 2009. Retrieved from: http://chronicle.com/blogPost/New-Tuition-Free-Universit/7831/

Patrick, S., and Sturgis, C. (2011). *Cracking the Code: Synchronizing Policy and Practice for Performance-Based Learning*. International Association for K-12 Online Learning, July 2011. Retrieved from: http://www.inacol.org/research/docs/iNACOL_CrackingCode_full_report.pdf

Patrick, S., and Powell, A. (2009). *A Summary of Research on the Effectiveness of K-12 Online Learning*. International Association for K-12 Online Learning, June 2009. Retrieved from: http://www.inacol.org/research/docs/NACOL_ResearchEffectiveness-lr.pdf

Pels, M. (2004). History of Caddo Parish: City of Shreveport. Retrieved from: http://www.caddohistory.com/shreveport_1830s_1860.html

Peter, K. and Forrest Cataldi, E., (2005). *The Road Less Traveled? Students Who Enroll in Multiple Institutions*. Washington, DC: U.S. Department of Education, Institute of Education Sciences, NCES 2005–157. Summary retrieved from: http://nces.ed.gov/das/epubs/2005157/; complete report retrieved from http://nces.ed.gov/pubs2005/2005157.pdf.

Phipps, R., and Merisotis, J. (1999). *What's the difference? A review of contemporary research on the effectiveness of distance learning in higher education*. Institute for Higher Education Policy. Retrieved from: http://www.ihep.org/assets/files/publications/s-z/WhatDifference.pdf

Picciano, A.G. & Seaman, J. (2009). *K-12 online learning: A 2008 follow-up survey of U.S. school district administrators*. Needham, MA: The Sloan Consortium.

Picciano, A.G. & Seaman, J. (2007). *K-12 online learning: A survey of school district administrators*. Needham, MA: The Sloan Consortium. Retrieved from: http://www.sloanconsortium.org/publications/survey/pdf/K-12_Online_Learning.pdf

Pink, D. (2009). *Drive: The Surprising Truth about What Motivates Us*. New York: Riverhead Books.

Pink, D. (2001). *Free Agent Nation: The Future of Working for Yourself*. New York: Warner.

PLATO Learning Corporation (n.d.). Our History web site. Retrieved from: http://www.plato.com/About-Us/Our-Company/History.aspx

Poole, D. M. (2000). Student participation in a discussion-oriented online course: a case study. *Journal of Research on Computing in Education*, 33 (2), 162-177, 2000.

Porter, D. (2010). "Nowhere near critical mass." *Convivality* blog, August 16, 2010. Retrieved from: http://conviviality.ca/2010/08/nowhere-near-critical-mass/

Powell, W. W, and Owen-Smith, J. (1998). Universities and the Market for Intellectual Property in the Life Sciences. *Journal of Policy Analysis and Management*, Vol. 17, No. 2, 253–277.

Powell, W. W. and Snellman, K. (2004). The Knowledge Economy. *Annu. Rev. Sociol.* 2004, 30:199–220 doi: 10.1146/annurev.soc.29.010202.100037. Retrieved from: http://www.stanford.edu/group/song/papers/powell_snellman.pdf

Prensky, M. (2008). Shaping Tech for the Classroom. *Edutopia,* July 20, 2008. Retrieved from: http://www.edutopia.org/adopt-and-adapt

Pruitt-Mentle, D. et al. (2010). *SECURE IT: Strategies to Encourage Careers in CyberSecurity and Information Technology.* Retrieved from: http://www.edtechpolicy.org/cyberk12/SecureIT/SECUREITCurrDevelopmentDraft_Section1_6.pdf

Rampell, C. (2009). SAT Scores and Family Income. *New York Times,* August 27, 2009. Retrieved from: http://economix.blogs.nytimes.com/2009/08/27/sat-scores-and-family-income/

Rasmus, D. (2008). Scenario planning and the future of education. *Innovate 4* (5). Retrieved from: http://www.microsoft.com/education/highered/whitepapers/scenario/ScenarioPlanning.aspx#copyright

Ravid, G., Kalman, Y. M., & Rafaeli, S. (2008). Wikibooks in higher education: Empowerment through online distributed collaboration. *Computers in Human Behavior*, 24, pp. 1913-1928.

Ravitch, D. (2010). *The Death and Life of the Great American School System: How Testing and Choice Are Undermining Education.* New York: Perseus.

Rawson, J., and Thomes, C. (2008) Open Educational Resources. *DE Oracle @ UMUC*, September-October 2008. Retrieved from: http://deoracle.org/online-pedagogy/emerging-technologies/open-educational-resources.html

Reimer, E. (1971). *School Is Dead.* Retrieved from http://arvindguptatoys.com/arvindgupta/dead.pdf

Reiten, K. (2007). Astronomers Measure Mass of Largest Dwarf Planet. *National Aeronautics and Space Administration, Hubble News,* June 14, 2007. Retrieved from: http://www.nasa.gov/mission_pages/hubble/news/eris.html

Rhodes, G. L., and Brasington, D. F. (2010). *The Ripple Effect: Transforming Student Success in Distance Learning, One Student & One Instructor at a Time.* J. Sargeant Reynolds Community College. October 2009; revised March 2010. Retrieved from: http://www.jsr.vccs.edu/QEP/projectdocs/JSRCC%20QEP%20Revised%203-16-10.pdf

Riach, J. V. (2011). Personal communication, October 1, 2011.

Richardson, J. & Swan, K. (2001). *An examination of social presence in online learning: students' perceived learning and satisfaction*. Seattle, WA: Paper presented at the annual meeting of the American Educational Research Association.

Rimer, S. (2007). At 71, Physics Professor Is a Web Star. *New York Times*, 12/19/07. Retrieved from: http://www.nytimes.com/2007/12/19/education/19physics.html?ex=1355720400&en=78ff7cfea904d7b1&ei=5088&partner=rssnyt&emc=rs"

Rischard, J.R. (2002). *High Noon: 20 Global Problems, 20 Years to Solve Them*. New York: Basic Books.

Robbins, T. L., and Kegley, K. (2009). Playing with Thinkertoys to build creative abilities through online instruction. *Thinking Skills and Creativity, 5*(1), pp. 40-48.

Rourke, L., Anderson, T. Garrison, D. R., & Archer, W. (2001). Assessing social presence in asynchronous, text-based computer conferencing. *Journal of Distance Education*, 14(3), 51-70.

Russell, T. (1999). *The No Significant Difference Phenomenon: A Comparative Research Annotated Bibliography on Technology for Distance Education*. Montgomery, AL: IDECC.

Sachs, D. (2007). Access to Online Support Services. Sloan-C Effective Practices Collection. Retrieved from: http://sloanconsortium.org/effective_practices/access-online-support-services

Saltman, K. J. (2010). "Value-Added" Assessment: Tool for Improvement or Educational "Nuclear Option"? *Truthout*, September 14, 2010. Retrieved from: http://firgoa.usc.es/drupal/node/47424

Sanders, R. (2002). UC Berkeley's first entirely online course could lead way to more classes without a classroom. University of California Campus News Media Relations Press Release, August 22, 2002. Retrieved from: http://berkeley.edu/news/media/releases/2002/08/22_class.html

San Millan Maurino, L. (2006). Looking for Critical Thinking in Online Threaded Discussions. *e-Journal of Instructional Science and Technology* (e-JIST) Vol. 9 No. 2, September 2006. Retrieved from: http://www.ascilite.org.au/ajet/e-jist/docs/vol9_no2/papers/full_papers/maurino.pdf

Schroeder, R. (2011a). *Recession Realities in Higher Education* blog. Retrieved from: http://recessionreality.blogspot.com/

Schroeder, R. (2011b). Fueling Online Learning blog. Retrieved from: http://fuelingonline.blogspot.com.

SchWeber, C. (2005). A Tipping Point for Online Education. *Sloan-C View, Perspectives in Quality Online Education* 4(3). Retrieved from: http://www.sloan-c.org/publications/view/v4n3/coverv4n3.htm

Seaman, J. (2011). Personal communication, May 17-18, 2011.

Seaman, J. (2009a). *Online Learning as a Strategic Asset, Volume I: A Resource for Campus Leaders*. American Public and Land-Grant Universities, August 2009. http://sloanconsortium.org/sites/default/files/APLU_online_strategic_asset_vol1-1.pdf

Seaman, J. (2009b). *Online Learning as a Strategic Asset, Volume II: The Paradox of Faculty Voices: Views and Experiences with Online Learning*. American Public and Land-Grant Universities, August 2009.

Retrieved from: http://sloanconsortium.org/sites/default/files/APLU_online_strategic_asset_vol2-1.pdf.

Sener, J. (2011). Standardized tests prove I'm better than Michael Jordan. *Washington Post,* April 8, 2011. Retrieved from: http://www.washingtonpost.com/opinions/standardized-tests-prove-im-better-than-michael-jordan/2011/03/29/AF4sdL4C_story.html

Sener, J. (2010a). Chill Out at a Tailgating Party. *Educational Technology and Change Journal,* June 10, 2010. Retrieved from: http://etcjournal.com/2010/06/10/4417/

Sener, J. (2010b). Why Online Education Will Attain Full Scale. *Journal of Asynchronous Learning Networks,* 14(4), December 2010.

Sener, J. (2009a). Is a Virtual Revolution Brewing in Colleges? *Educational Technology and Change Journal,* September 14, 2009. Retrieved from: http://etcjournal.com/2009/09/14/2341/

Sener, J. (2009b). Book Review of 'Disrupting Class.' *eLearn Magazine,* December 23, 2009. Retrieved from: http://www.elearnmag.org/subpage.cfm?section=reviews&article=13-1

Sener, J. (2009c). The 15th Annual Sloan-C Conference: A Review. *Educational Technology and Change Journal,* November 6, 2009. Retrieved from: http://etcjournal.com/2009/11/06/15th-annual-sloan-c-conference-a-review/

Sener, J. (2009d). Interview with Mike Abbiatti: Issues and Advancing the Field. Retrieved from: http://www.academiccontinuity.org/?q=node/329

Sener, J. (2008a). Why It's Good to Forecast the Future Even Though It's Impossible. Retrieved from: http://senerknowledge.com/blogs/why-its-good-forecast-future-even-though-its-impossible.

Sener, J. (2008b). Academic Continuity and Institutional Resilience in Higher Education. academiccontinuity.org, May 12, 2008. Retrieved from: http://www.academiccontinuity.org/node/288

Sener, J. (2007a). Enshrining Authoritarian Education into Law: Justice Thomas's Opinion on Morse v. Frederick. Retrieved from: http://senerknowledge.com/blogs/enshrining-authoritarian-education-law-justice-thomass-opinion-morse-v-frederick

Sener, J. (2007b). Open Yale Courses and the Cult of the Magical Sage. Retrieved from: http://senerknowledge.com/blogs/open-yale-courses-and-cult-magical-sage-part-1

Sener, J. (2007c). In Search of Student-Generated Content in Online Education, *e-mentor,* 4(21), 2007. Retrieved from: http://www.e-mentor.edu.pl/_xml/wydania/21/467.pdf

Sener, J. (2007d). Event-Centered, Online-Supported Delivery Model. Sloan Consortium Effective Practices web site. Retrieved from: http://sloanconsortium.org/effective_practices/event-centered-online-supported-delivery-model.

Sener, J. (2005). From Skeptical to Satisfied: Online Teaching as a Conversion Experience. *Educational Pathways* (4), May 2005. Retrieved from: http://www.edpath.com/2005/0505/050502.htm?zoom_highlight=conversion.

Sener, J. (2004a). Escaping the Comparison Trap: Evaluating Online Learning on Its Own Terms. *Innovate*, 1(2), Winter 2004. Retrieved from: http://innovateonline.info/pdf/vol1_issue2/Escaping_the_Comparison_Trap-_Evaluating_Online_Learning_on_Its_Own_Terms.pdf

Sener, J. (2004b). Discovering Our Inner Chefs: A Strategy for Advancing Blended Learning. *Educational Pathways*, 3(5), May 2004. Retrieved from: http://www.edpath.com/2004/0504/050403.htm

Sener, J. (2004c). Asynchronous instructor-led online learning: turning a blind spot into a sweet spot. In J. Nall & R. Robson (Eds.), *Proceedings of World Conference on E-Learning in Corporate, Government, Healthcare, and Higher Education 2004* (pp. 934-939). Chesapeake, VA: AACE.

Sener, J., and Hawkins, R. (2007). Factors Affecting Completion Rates in Asynchronous Online Facilitated Faculty Professional Development Courses. *International Journal of Instructional Technology and Distance Learning*, 4(12), December 2007. Retrieved from: http://itdl.org/Journal/Dec_07/article03.htm

Servicemembers Opportunity Colleges (2009). Servicemembers Opportunity Colleges Principles and Criteria, 2009-2011. Retrieved from: http://www.soc.aascu.org/socconsortium/SOCPrinCriteria.html

Sewell, W.H. (1971). Inequality of Opportunity for Higher Education. *American Sociological Review*, 36(5), October 1971. Retrieved from: http://www2.asanet.org/governance/PresidentialAddress1971.pdf

Shah, A. (2008). Children as Consumers", Global Issues: Social, Political, Economic, and Environmental Issues That Affect Us All. Retrieved from: http://www.globalissues.org/article/237/children-as-consumers.

Shavelson, R. J., Klein, S., and Benjamin, R. (2009), The Limitations of Portfolios, *Inside Higher Ed*, October 16, 2009. Retrieved from: http://www.insidehighered.com/views/2009/10/16/shavelson

Shea, C. (2001). Taking Classes to the Masses. *Washington Post Magazine*, September 16, 2001, p. W25ff.

Shea, P., Swan, K., Fredericksen, E., and Pickett, A. (2002). *Student satisfaction and reported learning in the SUNY learning network.* In Bourne, J., and Moore, J. (Eds.), Elements of Quality Online Education. (pp.145-56). Needham, MA: Sloan Center for OnLine Education.

Shelton, K. (2010). A Quality Scorecard for the Administration of Online Education Programs. Retrieved from: http://sloanconsortium.org/effective_practices/quality-scorecard-administration-online-education-programs

Shortridge, A. (2001). Using Concept Mapping as an Interactive Learning Tool in Web-based Distance Education. In C. Montgomerie & J. Viteli (Eds.), Proceedings of World Conference on Educational Multimedia, Hypermedia and Telecommunications 2001, pp. 1723-1724. Chesapeake, VA: AACE.

Shupe, D. (2011). Student Learning Outcomes as Innovative Currency for Tracking Student Achievement. Presentation at NUTN Network Conference, Fort Worth, TX, September 28, 2011.

Shupe, D. (2007). Significantly Better: the Academic Benefits for an Institution Focused on Student Learning Outcomes. *On The Horizon*, 15 (2), May 2007. Retrieved from: http://www.elumen.info/media/eLumenWhitepaper.pdf

Shuttleworth Foundation and Open Society Institute (2007). Cape Town Open Education Declaration FAQ web page. Retrieved from: http://www.capetowndeclaration.org/faq

Siemens, G. (2008). "Cute Kitten Syndrome: Open Educational Resources" *Connectivism: Networked and Social learning* blog, April 29, 2008. Retrieved from: http://www.connectivism.ca/?p=111

Siemens, G. (2004). Connectivism: A Learning Theory for the Digital Age. elearnspace, December 12, 2004. Retrieved from: http://www.elearnspace.org/Articles/connectivism.htm.

Simba Information (2010). *Moving Online: K-12 Distance Learning Market Forecast 2010* web page. Retrieved from: http://www.simbainformation.com/pub/2522707.html

Skinner, B.F. (1958). Teaching Machines. *Science*, 128(3330), October 24, 1958, pp. 969-977. Retrieved from: http://www.bfskinner.org/BFSkinner/Articles_files/teaching_machines.pdf

Sjoberg, S. (2007). PISA and "Real-Life Challenges": Mission Impossible? Retrieved from: http://folk.uio.no/sveinsj/Sjoberg-PISA-book-2007.pdf

Sloan Consortium (2011). Sloan-C Endorses Quality Scorecard for Measuring Quality of ONline Education Programs. Sloan-C Press Release, April 5, 2011. Retrieved from: http://sloanconsortium.org/news_press/april2011_sloan-c-endorses-quality-scorecard-measuring-quality-online-college-education-p

Sloan Consortium (2008). About Academic Continuity. academiccontinuity.org, May 11, 2008. Retrieved from: http://www.academiccontinuity.org/node/272

Sloan Consortium (n.d.) The Sloan Semester. http://sloanconsortium.org/sloansemester.

Smick, D. M. (2009). *The World Is Curved: Hidden Dangers to the Global Economy.* New York: Penguin.

Smith, P. (2010). *Harnessing America's Wasted Talent*. San Francisco: Jossey-Bass.

Smith, S.D., Salaway, G., and Caruso, J.B. (2009). Key Findings, The ECAR Study of Undergraduate Students and Information Technology, 2009. EDUCAUSE Center for Applied Research, October 2009. Retreived from: http://net.educause.edu/ir/library/pdf/EKF/EKF0906.pdf

Smith Bailey, D. (2003). 'Swirling' changes to the traditional student path. *Monitor on Psychology*, December 2003, 34(11), p.36. Retrieved from: http://www.apa.org/monitor/dec03/swirling.aspx

Snyder, T.D., Dillow, S.A., and Hoffman, C.M. (2008). *Digest of Education Statistics 2007* (NCES 2008-022). National Center for Education Statistics, Institute of Education Sciences, U.S. Department of Education. Washington, DC. Tables 187, 217 and 181. http://nces.ed.gov/pubs2008/2008022.pdf

Southern Association of Colleges and Universities (2010). Distance and Correspondence Education: Policy Statement, June 2010. Retrieved from: http://www.sacscoc.org/pdf/Distance%20 and%20correspondence%20policy%20final.pdf.

Southern Regional Education Board (2008). Professional Development for Online Teachers. SREB Online Teachers web site. Retrieved from: http://www.srebonlineteachers.org/profession-alDevelopmentLinks.html

Staples, G. B. (2011). Homework sites home grown. *Atlanta Journal-Constitution*, August 29, 2011. Retrieved from: http://www.ajc.com/lifestyle/homework-sites-home-grown-1150758. html

Star, J. and Cross, J. (2004). Scenario Planning: Learning the New Rules for 2014. Emergent Learning Forum. Retrieved from: http://www.elearningforum.com/archives/meet-ings/2004/january/index.html.

StateUniversity.com (n.d.) Lifelong Learning. Retrieved from: http://education.stateuniversity. com/pages/2181/Lifelong-Learning.html

Steinberg, J. (2010) Plan B: Skip College. *New York Times*, May 15, 2010. Retrieved from: http:// www.nytimes.com/2010/05/16/weekinreview/16steinberg.html

Stevens, R., O'Connor, K., Garrison, L., Jocuns, A., & Amos, D. M.(2008). Becoming an Engineer: Toward a Three Dimensional View of Engineering Learning. *Journal of Engineering Education*, 97(3), pp.355-368.

Stewart, B.S. (2006). *Value-Added Modeling. The Challenge of Measuring Educational Outcomes.* Carnegie Corporation.

Stoll, C. (1995). The Internet? Bah! *Newsweek*, February 27, 1995. Retrieved from: http://www. newsweek.com/id/106554

Strauss, V. (2010). The problem(s) with the Common Core standards. *The Answer Sheet, Washington Post*, March 10, 2010. Retrieved from: http://voices.washingtonpost.com/answer-sheet/ national-standards/the-problems-with-the-common-c.html

Swan, K. (2010). Personal communication, September 26, 2010.

Swan, K. (2003). Learning Effectiveness: What the Research Tells Us. *Elements of Quality Online Education: Practice and Direction,* J. Bourne & J. C. Moore (Eds.). Needham, MA: Sloan Center for Online Education.

Swanson, J. (2008). *An Analysis of the Impact of High School Dual Enrollment Course Participation on Post-Secondary Acadmic Success, Persistence, and Degree Completion.* Retrieved from: http://www. nacep.org/confdownloads/swanson_executive_summary.pdf

Swisher, D.J. (2007). *Does Multimedia Truly Enhance Learning? Moving Beyond the Visual Media Bandwagon Toward Instructional Effectiveness.* Retrieved from: http://www.sal.ksu.edu/facultys-taff/Swisher_ProfessionalDay07_paper.pdf

Szerdahelyi, J. (2010). Personal communication, December 2, 2010.

Teaching and Learning Centre (2007). Community of Inquiry model web page. Retrieved from: http://communitiesofinquiry.com/model

Teachout, Z. (2009). A Virtual Revolution Is Brewing. *Washington Post*, 9/13/2009. Retrieved from: http://www.washingtonpost.com/wp-dyn/content/article/2009/09/11/AR2009091104312.html?referrer=emailarticle

Teitelbaum, M. S. (2003). Do we need more scientists? *The Public Interest*, Fall 2003. Retrieved from: http://web.archive.org/web/20040804010915/http://www.thepublicinterest.com/archives/2003fall/article2.html

Tennessee Higher Education Commission (2010). 2010 Outcomes Based Funding Formula Model Presentation. Retrieved from: http://www.tn.gov/thec/Divisions/Fiscal/funding_formula_presentation.html

Theroux, J. (2009). Real-Time Case Method: Analysis of a Second Implementation. *Journal of Education for Business*, 84(6), p.367-373.

Theroux, J. and Kilbane, C. (2004). The Real-Time Case Method: A New Approach to an Old Tradition. *Journal of Education for Business*, 79(3), p.163-167.

Theroux, J. (2004) Real-Time Case Study. Retrieved from: http://intra.som.umass.edu/theroux/about.html

Thomas, C. (2007). Concurring Opinion, *Morse v. Frederick*. United States Supreme Court, June 25, 2007. Retrieved from: http://www.law.cornell.edu/supct/pdf/06-278P.ZC

Thomas, D. and Brown, J.S. (2011). *The New Culture of Learning: Cultivating the Imagination in a World of Constant Change*. CreateSpace.

Thomas Edison State College (n.d.) Prior Learning Assessment FAQs web page. Retrieved from: http://www.tesc.edu/4842.php

Tiersten, S. (2010). College Catalogs Increase Their Menu of Online Course Offerings. *San Diego Business Journal*, March 22, 2010.

Tobin, D. L. (1998). Building Your Personal Learning Network. Retrieved from: http://www.tobincls.com/learningnetwork.htm

Toffler, A. and Toffler, H. (2006). *Revolutionary Wealth: how it will be created and how it will change our lives*. New York: Knopf.

The Trustees of Indiana University (2011). About NSSE web page. Retrieved from: http://nsse.iub.edu/html/about.cfm

Turkle, S. (2011). *Alone Together: Why We Expect More from Technology and Less from Each Other*. New York: Basic Books.

Turoff, M. (2010). The facts of life. Sloan-C listserv discussion posting, February 25, 2010.

Turoff, M. (1997). *Alternative futures for distance learning: The force and the dark side*. Retrieved from: http://eies.njit.edu/~turoff/Papers/darkaln.html

Turoff, M. (1980). Natural Language and Computer Interface Design. Retrieved from: http://acl.ldc.upenn.edu//P/P80/P80-1037.pdf

Turoff, M. and Hiltz, S. R. (2011). Private communication, May 6 - June 13, 2011.

Turoff, M., and Hiltz, S.R. (2001). Effectively Managing Large Enrollment Courses: A Case Study. In *Online Education, Volume 2: Learning Effectiveness, Faculty Satisfaction, and Cost Effectiveness.* Proceedings of the 2000 Sloan Summer Workshop on Asynchronous Learning Networks, 2001.

United Nations Education, Scientific, and Cultural Organization (2010). Education For All Goals web page. Retrieved from: http://www.unesco.org/new/en/education/themes/leading-the-international-agenda/education-for-all/efa-goals/

United States Census Bureau (2010a). A Half-Century Of Learning: Historical Census Statistics On Educational Attainment in the United States, 1940 to 2000: Detailed Tables., Tables 1 and 2. Retrieved from: http://www.census.gov/hhes/socdemo/education/data/census/half-century/tables.html.

United States Census Bureau (2010b). Census Bureau Reports Nearly 6 in 10 Advanced Degree Holders Age 25-29 Are Women. Press Release CB10-55, April 20, 2010. Retrieved from: http://www.census.gov/newsroom/releases/archives/education/cb10-55.html

United States Bureau of the Census (1990). We Asked...You Told Us: Telephone and Vehicle Availability. Census Questionnaire Content, 1990 CQC-26. Retrieved from: http://www.census.gov/apsd/cqc/cqc26.pdf.

United States Department of Education (2009a). *Evaluation of evidence-based practices in online learning: A meta-analysis and review of online learning studies.* U.S. Department of Education, Office of Planning, Evaluation, and Policy Development, Washington, DC. 2009. Retrieved from: http://www2.ed.gov/rschstat/eval/tech/evidence-based-practices/finalreport.pdf.

United States Department of Education (2009b). *Preparing for the Flu: Department of Education Recommendations to Ensure the Continuity of Learning for Schools (K-12) during Extended Student Absence or School Dismissal.* Retrieved from: http://www2.ed.gov/admins/lead/safety/emergencyplan/pandemic/guidance/continuity-recs.pdf

United States Department of Education (2004a). *Toward A New Golden Age In American Education—How the Internet, the Law and Today's Students Are Revolutionizing Expectations.* Washington, DC: United States Department of Education. Retrieved from: http://www2.ed.gov/about/offices/list/os/technology/plan/2004/plan.pdf

United States Department of Education (2004b). NCLB Overview Executive Summary web page. Retrieved from: http://www2.ed.gov/nclb/overview/intro/execsumm.html

United States Department of Education (1997). National Standards of Academic Excellence. Retrieved from: http://www2.ed.gov/updates/PresEDPlan/part2.html

United States Department of Labor (2010a). Advanced Competency Manufacturing Model web page, Competency Model Clearninghouse. Retrieved from: http://www.careeronestop.org/CompetencyModel/pyramid.aspx?HG=Y

United States Department of Labor (2010b). Career Ladder/Lattice General Instructions web page, Competency Model Clearinghouse. Retrieved from: http://www.careeronestop.org/CompetencyModel/CareerPathway/CPWCllInstructions.aspx

United States Department of Labor (2009). Career Guide to Industries, 2010-11 Edition. Bureau of Labor Statistics, Educational Services. Retrieved from: http://www.bls.gov/oco/cg/cgs034.htm.

United States Senate (2010). *Emerging Risk?: An Overview of Growth, Spending, Student Debt and Unanswered Questions in For-Profit Higher Education.* United States Senate Health, Labor, Education, and Pensions Committee, Tom Harkin, Chairman, June 24, 2010. Retrieved from: http://harkin.senate.gov/documents/pdf/4c23515814dca.pdf.

University of California, San Diego (2011). UCSan Diego Extension Online web page. Retrieved January 3, 2011 from: http://extension.ucsd.edu/online/index.cfm

University of Illinois Online (2011). Making the Virtual Classroom a Reality (MVCR) Reaches Largest Enrollment. *University of Illinois Online Newsletter*, Spring 2011. Retrieved from: http://www.online.uillinois.edu/

University of Illinois Springfield (2010). UIS sets a record with 5,174 students enrolled. *News @ Illinois Springfield.* http://news.uis.edu/2010/09/uis-sets-record-with-5174-students.html.

University of Maryland (2010). Electronic Access to Scholarly Material web page. University Libraries - University of Maryland. Retrieved from: http://www.lib.umd.edu/ETC/ejournalfaq.html

University of Maryland University College (2010). Admissions, Frequently Asked Questions web page. Retrieved from: http://www.umuc.edu/admissions/faq.shtml

University of Maryland University College (2008). *UMUC Classroom Interruption Planning Guide.* August 8, 2008. Retrieved from: http://www.umuc.edu/faculty/facsupport/facservices/upload/planninguide.pdf

University of Maryland University College School of Undergraduate Studies. (2010). Department of Student Success: Mentors and Tutors. Retrieved from: http://www.umuc.edu/student-success/mentors.shtml

University of Melbourne (2009). Freedom to surf: workers more productive if allowed to use the internet for leisure. *University of Melbourne News,* April 2, 2009. Retrieved from: http://newsroom.melbourne.edu/news/n-19

University of Pennsylvania, School of Arts and Sciences (n.d.). Ivar Berg, Ph.D. web page. Retrieved from: http://sociology.sas.upenn.edu/ivar_berg

University of the People (2010). News Center, Press Releases web page. Retrieved from: http://www.uopeople.org/groups/news_center

University of Phoenix (2009). A 20-Year Legacy of Innovation. University of Phoenix Office of the President, September 23, 2009. Retrieved from: http://www.phoenix.edu/colleges_divisions/

office-of-the-president/articles/university-of-phoenix-online-20-year-legacy-innovation. html

University of Washington. (n.d.) Academic continuity toolkit (ACT). Retrieved from http:// www.washington.edu/itconnect/emergency/act.

University of Wisconsin (2006). Select Public University President/Chancellor Salaries and Institution Enrollment. Retrieved from: http://www.wisconsin.edu/news/2006/06-2006/ jun09_chanc-pres-salaries-WI-IA-IL-MN.pdf

Vedder, R. (2010). A Pampered Population. In Are They Students? Or 'Customers'? *New York Times*, January 3, 2010. Retrieved from: http://roomfordebate.blogs.nytimes.com/2010/01/03/ are-they-students-or-customers/

Vien, C. (2010). The New Gold Standard? Online Learners Outperform On-site students. *UOPX Knowledge Network*, January 13, 2010. Retrieved from: http://www.phoenix.edu/uopx-knowledge-network/articles/current-conversations/online-learners-outperform-on-site-students.html.

Vignare, K., and Sener, J. (2005). Successful Online Bioterrorism Courses Meet Needs of Learners. *Journal of Asynchronous Learning Networks* 9(4): 83-99, December 2005. Retrieved from: http:// sloanconsortium.org/sites/default/files/v9n4_vignare_1.pdf

Vollmer, T. (2010). Flat World Knowledge's Eric Frank: Open Education and Policy. *Creative Commons CC Talks With Weblog,* November 4, 2010. Retrieved from: http://creativecommons. org/weblog/entry/24191

Wallace, B. (2010). From Crackberry to iCrack: Stanford students are crazy about their iPhones. *Today's iPhone*, March 10, 2010. Retrieved from: http://www.todaysiphone.com/2010/03/ from-crackberry-to-icrack-stanford-students-are-crazy-about-their-iphones/

Wang, C. (2009). Comprehensive Assessment of Student Collaboration in Electronic Portfolio Construction: An Evaluation Research. *Tech Trends: Linking Research & Practice to Improve Learning*, *53*(1), 58-66. doi:10.1007/s11528-009-0238-1.

Wang, G, Foucar-Szocki, D, Griffen, O., O'Connor, C. and Sceiford, E. (2003). *Departure, Abandonment, and Dropout of E-learning: Dilemma and Solutions*. James Madison University, October 2003. Retrieved from: http://independent.academia.edu/TJTaylor/Papers/1396490/Departure_ Abandonment_and_Dropout_-_Dilemma_Solutions_-_James_Madison_University_2003

Washburn, J. (2006). *University, Inc.: The Corporate Corruption of Higher Education*. New York: Basic Books.

Waters, S. (2011). PLN Yourself! web site. Retrieved from: http://suewaters.wikispaces.com/

Watson, J. (2008). *Blended learning: The convergence of online and face-to-face education*. Vienna, VA: The North American Council for Online Learning. Retrieved from: http://www.inacol.org/ research/promisingpractices/NACOL_PP-BlendedLearning-lr.pdf

Watson, J., and Gemin, B. (2008). *Promising Practices in Online Learning: Using Online Learning for At-Risk Students and Credit Recovery*. International Association for K-12 Online Learning, June

2008. Retrieved from: http://www.inacol.org/research/promisingpractices/NACOL_CreditRecovery_PromisingPractices.pdf

WBGH Educational Foundation (1999). Timeline of Farming in the U.S. American Experience web site. Retrieved from: http://www.pbs.org/wgbh/amex/trouble/timeline/index.html

WCET (n.d.) No Significant Difference Phenonemon web site. www.nosignificantdifference.org.

Wedemeyer, C. A. (1981). *Learning at the Back Door: Reflections on Non-Traditional Learning in the Lifespan.* Madison, WI: University of Madison Press.

Wicks, M. (2010). A National Primer on K-12 Online Learning, Version 2. International Association for K-12 Online Learning, 2010. Retrieved from: http://www.inacol.org/research/docs/iNCL_NationalPrimerv22010-web.pdf

Wiener, N. (1948). *Cybernetics: Or Control and Communication in the Animal and the Machine.* Hermann & Cie Editeurs, Paris, The Technology Press, Cambridge, Mass., John Wiley & Sons Inc., New York, 1948.

Wiggins, G. P. (1993). *Assessing student performance.* San Francisco: Jossey-Bass Publishers.

Wikipedia (2011a). Eris (dwarf planet). *Wikipedia;* last modified September 5, 2011. Retrieved from: http://en.wikipedia.org/wiki/Eris_(dwarf_planet)

Wikipedia (2011b). Corporal Punishment in the United States. Retrieved February 27, 2011 from: http://en.wikipedia.org/wiki/File:Corporal_punishment_in_the_United_States.svg

Wikipedia (2011c). University of the People. Retrieved September 10, 2011 from: http://en.wikipedia.org/wiki/University_of_the_People

Wikipedia (2011d.) Link Rot. Retrieved May 28, 2011 from: http://en.wikipedia.org/wiki/Link_rot

Wikitionary (2009). Cyberize (definition). *Wikitionary;* last modified June 23, 2009. Retrieved from: http://en.wiktionary.org/wiki/cyberize

Wiley, D. (2008) "Openness and the Disaggregated Future of Education," presentation at E-Learn, 2008. Retrieved from: http://www.slideshare.net/opencontent/openness-and-the-disaggregated-future-of-higher-education-presentation?type=powerpoint

Williams, R. (2009) Distributed cognition. Retrieved from: http://www.education.com/reference/article/distributed-cognition/

Williamson, J. (2009). The History of Distance Education. Distance Education.org, February 11, 2009. http://www.distance-education.org/Articles/The-History-of-Distance-Education-113.html.

Willis, B. (1993). *Distance Education: a practical guide.* Englewood Cliffs, NJ: Educational Technology Publications.

Wilson, J. (n.d.) Shreveport, Louisiana: Shreveport history, facts, Red River, Texas Trail. Retrieved from: http://jayssouth.com/louisiana/shreveport/

Wire, S. (2010). Missouri colleges told to prepare for deep cuts. *Southeast Missourian,* February 19, 2010. Retrieved from: http://www.semissourian.com/story/1612373.html

Wise, B., and Rothman, R. (2010). The Online Learning Imperative: *A Solution to Three Looming Crises in Education*. Alliance for Excellent Education Issue Brief, June 2010. Retrieved from: http://www.all4ed.org/files/OnlineLearning.pdf

WISE Consortium (2011). What is WISE? web page. Retrieved from: http://www.wiseeducation.org/students/whatiswise.aspx

World Future Society (2008). The Futurist Interviews Andrew Keen, author and Internet guru. *The Futurist*, January-February 2008, Vol. 42. Retrieved from: http://www.wfs.org/node/343

Wright, G. (2009). SHRM Poll: More U.S. Employers Welcoming Candidates with Online Degrees. *HR News*, September 29, 2009.

wtop.com (2009). Flu less virulent than feared; Md. schools reopen, *wtop.com*, May 6, 2009. Retrieved from: http://www.wtop.com/?sid=1665829&nid=25

Zemsky, R., and Massy, W. F. (2004). *Thwarted Innovation - What Happened to e-learning and Why*. The Learning Alliance for Higher Education, 2004. Retrieved from: http://www.irhe.upenn.edu/WeatherStation.html

Zuboff, S. and Maxmin, J. (2002). *The Support Economy:Why Corporations Are Failing Individuals and the Next Episode of Capitalism*. New York: Penguin.

Notes

Introduction

1. When I first started writing this book in late 2009, the only reference to "cyberization of education" I could find online was a 2002 journal article written in Chinese called "The Cyberization of Education and the Reformation of Class Education" (Liu 2002).
2. Nelson, in Bosquet (2008).
3. Kozol (1992).
4. U.S. Department of Education (2004a).

Chapter 1: Cyberized

1. Wallace (2010).
2. Allen and Seaman (2010a).
3. Personal communication with Jo Cazes, September 15, 2010.
4. Wikitionary (2009).
5. Chairman of the Joint Chiefs of Staff (2006), p.3.
6. Kass (2006), slide 14.
7. Chairman of the Joint Chiefs of Staff (2006), p.9.
8. Pels (2004).
9. Muncrief (2005); Wilson (n.d.).
10. Cyber Innovation Center: http://www.cyberinnovationcenter.org/
11. CNN.com (2005).
12. University of Melbourne (2009); Greenfield (2002).
13. Hayles (1999), in Higgins (2010).
14. The Borg is a fictional cybernetic life form (from the television series Star Trek: The Next Generation) which seeks to subjugate other species by assimilating them. See http://www.startrek.com/database_article/borg for a complete description.
15. Bonk (2009); Cross (2007).
16. Marsh et al. (2010).
17. Smith et al. (2009).
18. For example, see Lucas (1994).
19. Tiersten (2010).
20. Picciano and Seaman (2009), p.14.

Chapter 2. Shifting Foundations: The Changing Nature of Knowledge

1. Anderson and Rainie (2010).
2. Toffler and Toffler (2006), p.64.
3. Chichilnisky (1998).

4. Drucker (1999).
5. Batson (2010).
6. The use of the term "Ivory Tower" to refer to academia and its "sheltered and unworldly intellectual isolation" is a relatively recent invention, dating back to the early 20th century (Martin 2010).
7. For example, see Powell & Owen-Smith (1998); Kahn & Prager (1994).
8. University of Maryland (2010).
9. Education-Portal.com (2010).
10. Picciano and Seaman (2009), p.20.
11. Powell and Snellman (2004).
12. Wikipedia (2011a); Reiten (2007).
13. International Astronomical Union (n.d.)
14. nineplanets.org (2011).
15. Lazowska (2009).
16. Coles et al. (2006), p.2.
17. Dede (2008a).
18. Cross (2007).
19. Dede (2008b).
20. Toffler and Toffler (2006), p. 8.
21. A web search (Google) on the term "interdisciplinary programs" conducted January 6, 2011 yielded about 411,000 results, including descriptions of numerous programs at U.S. colleges and universities.
22. Lok (2008).
23. Siemens (2004).
24. Williams (2009).
25. People networks are probably the best resource; I could have probably gotten a similarly quick answer from the Mac Help function or from a web search, but I wouldn't have gotten the exact screen capture I needed, nor become acquainted with another resource in my personal network.
26. Friesen (2011).
27. Campbell (2009).
28. A commonly cited statistic is that U.S. television presented 3,600 images per minute per channel in the late 1980s, based on a Nielsen report (Castells 2000, p.361). Watching the dim flicker of television lights through a house's windows after dark is now a lot like watching a fireworks show, only without the sound.
29. For example, see the NEA reports *Reading at Risk* (Bradshaw and Nichols 2004) and *To Read or Not to Read* (National Endowment for the Arts 2007); also Krashen (2008).
30. Krashen (2008) debunks the NEA's *To Read or Not to Read* report and cites data which indicate that young people are reading as much or more than ever. A 2006-2007 Iowa State University study found that college students are reading "considerably" more then than they were ten years previously (Mokhari, Reichard, and Gardner 2009; Iowa State University 2009).
31. Goodnow (2007).
32. Carr (2008).

33. For example, see the University of Connecticut's New Literacies Research Team web site, which describes related activity in this area from 1999-2009: http://www.newliteracies.uconn.edu/

34. The effects on combining pictures with text simultaneously has been well-documented for over 30 years (Carney and Levin 2002; Levie and Lentz 1982). Richard Mayer's work (Mayer 2001; in Swisher 2007) extended this to combining narration and animation, although his "redundancy principle" asserts that adding text to narration and animation inhibits learning.

35. Discovery Channel (2011); Buzzfocus.com (2010).

36. For a detailed resource on the topic of edutainment software, see the syllabus for Boise State professor Young Baek's EDTECH 597: Introduction to Entertainment course (Baek 2011).

Chapter 3. Shifting Foundations: Access, Authority

1. Coleman (1967).
2. Katz (1976), p.22.
3. Darling-Hammond (2010), pp. 74-78.
4. The calculation of high school diploma attainment (Figure 3-1) is a convoluted and sometimes contentious process. Reported high school graduation rates vary widely by source because the methods for calculating this metric are much more varied and complicated than they may at first appear (for example, see Boser (2006)). The statistics used here are based on U.S. Census data from the following sources: 1900 data, National Center for Education Statistics (2005), Table 8; 1960 data, United States Census Bureau (2010a); 2009 data, United States Census Bureau (2010b). Some sources believe that U.S Census and U.S. Department of Education (NCES) data undercount dropout rates and overestimate attainment rates; for example, see Klima (2007), National Postsecondary Education Cooperative (2010).
5. WBGH Educational Foundation (1999).
6. Cheesman Day and Newberger (2002).
7. Carnevale (1991).
8. Carnevale (2010a).
9. Jaschik (2010); Carnevale (2010b).
10. Darling-Hammond (2010), p.2.
11. See Berg (1970), and University of Pennsylvania, School of Arts and Sciences (n.d.).
12. Bird (1975).
13. See Steinberg (2010). This article confuses the issue by equating "college degree" with "bachelor's degree.
14. United Nations Education, Scientific, & Cultural Organization (2010).
15. Rischard (2002), pp.101-102.
16. Bonk (2009), pp.11-15, 51.
17. National Center for Education Statistics (n.d.), Nontraditional Undergraduates.
18. Snyder et al. (2008).
19. Sewell (1971).

20. For example, the Complete College Tennessee Act of 2010 includes a provision for allocation of funding to the state's colleges and universities based on a set of "outcomes-based" measures rather than on enrollments. Tennessee Higher Education Commission (2010); also see Holzer (2010).
21. Christensen et al. (2011).
22. United States Department of Education (2004b).
23. Darling-Hammond (2010), pp. 88-90; Klima (2007).
24. See Knowles (1984) and StateUniversity.com (n.d.)
25. Howell et al. (2003).
26. Toffler and Toffler (2006), p.7.
27. Collins and Halverson (2009), p. 41.
28. Anup Shah's "Children as Consumers" web page is an excellent resource for related data through 2008 (Shah 2008).
29. Jaschik (2007).
30. For example, see Bejou (2005).
31. Vedder (2010).
32. Bejou (2010).
33. Lytle (2010).
34. For example, see Kohn (2002).
35. United States Department of Labor (2009).

Chapter 4. From Zero to Mainstream in 16 Years: How Online Learning Cyberized Education

1. In the corporate/organizational world, blended learning typically refers to the use of two or more distinct training or learning methods (Masie 2000, p.59; Harding et al. 2005). This definition expands the number of possible online and face-to-face combinations, for example blending online instruction with access to a mentor or coach, blending simulations with structured courses, etc. It can also include combinations with more than two modalities or delivery technologies (for instance, video simulations + online exercises + in-person training sessions; teleconferences + print materials + online discussions, etc.).
2. For example, the annual Sloan Survey of Online Learning (Allen and Seaman 2010a) defines a blended course as one in which 30-79 percent of the instruction is delivered online, while the Southern Association of Colleges and Universities (2010) sets the threshold for online and distance education courses at 50 percent, and the Commission for Higher Education (1998) used the same 50 percent threshold for online education programs.
3. Jeffries (n.d.); Willis (1993).
4. California Distance Learning Project (2005); Williamson (2009).
5. Miller, G. (2010a, 2010b).
6. Wiener (1948).
7. Fuller (1962), p.85.
8. Illich (1971).
9. Skinner (1958).
10. PLATO Learning Corporation (n.d.).

11. North Central Regional Educational Laboratory (n.d.).
12. Turoff (1980).
13. Online learning has evolved differently in the corporate training sector, most notably in its lack of emphasis on instructor facilitation and greater emphasis on content delivery. Instructor-led or facilitated online learning is still relatively rare in the corporate sector, where learner-content interaction typically prevails rather than instructor-learner interaction. Also see Sener (2004c); Cross and Hamilton (2002).
14. Harasim et al. (1995).
15. Harasim (2006); Hiltz (1994).
16. Turoff (1980).
17. Turoff and Hiltz (2011); NJIT's Robert W. Van Houten Library n.d. has a complete online list of reports which document the research conducted during this period.
18. University of Phoenix (2009).
19. Jones International University (n.d.).
20. Hiltz and Goldman (2005), p.7.
21. Hiltz and Goldman (2005), p.3.
22. Mayadas (1997).
23. Hiltz and Goldman (2005), p.8.
24. Griffiths (2002).
25. National Center for Supercomputing Applications (n.d.).
26. Washburn (2006), p.221; Matkin (2002).
27. Shea, C. (2001).
28. Zemsky and Massy (2004).
29. Sanders (2002).
30. Almeda and Rose (1999).
31. SchWeber (2005).
32. Shea, C. (2001).
33. University of Maryland University College (2010).
34. University of California, San Diego (2011).
35. Allen and Seaman (2010b); Allen and Seaman (2007).
36. The Ambient Insight report includes students from all postsecondary institutions which participated in Title IV federal student aid programs, including non-degree-granting institutions, while the Sloan-C reports include only degree-granting higher education institutions. Seaman (2011); Adkins (2011); Nagel (2011); Knapp et al. (2010).
37. The Sloan Consortium (Sloan-C) is a professional leadership organization focused on online education. Related report: Allen et al. (2007).
38. Hartman (2010a).
39. Swan (2010).
40. University of Illinois Springfield (2010); University of Wisconsin (2006).
41. Allen and Seaman (2010a).
42. Bennett et al. (2010), p.10; United States Senate (2010).
43. Kamenetz (2010), pp. 54-72.
44. Glenn (2008).

45. Ron Bonig, research director for higher education at Gartner, states that "It is pretty axiomatic that higher education institutions adapt technology with a lag of several years, in general...classroom adoption of technology can be very instructor-specific, and some teachers adopt and adapt the latest technology rapidly, but that is for their classes. Institutions as a whole usually adapt a bit later, and even then it is rarely ubiquitous." in Bacheldor (2010).
46. Moran et al. (2011), p.12, Table 13.
47. Miller, G. (2011a).
48. Turoff (1997).
49. Russell (1999).
50. San Millan Maurino (2006); Swan (2003).
51. Oliver and Raubenheimer (2006); Shortridge (2001); Cicognani (2000).
52. Keeton et al (2002); Poole (2000).
53. Kumari (2001).
54. Fairleigh Dickinson University (2010).
55. Turoff and Hiltz (2001).
56. For instance, see Hughes (2006).
57. Sener (2005).
58. Sener (2005); Burke (2005); Kassop (2003).
59. The reported proportion of skeptical faculty has remained more or less unchanged for many years (Allen & Seaman 2010a).
60. Sener (2004a).
61. The report called for randomized controlled experiments, production of predictive outcomes for individual learners, and tests with content or construct validity, none of which are commonly applied to classroom instruction; Phipps and Merisotis (1999).
62. Russell (1999).
63. Moore (1989).
64. For example, a large meta-analysis of studies conducted between 1990 and 2007 published in the Journal of the American Medical Association involving learners in the health professions (Cook et al. 2008) found that Internet-based instruction has a consistently large positive effect compared with no intervention and was equivalent to traditional instruction. The synthesized evidence associated Internet-based instruction with favorable learning outcomes across a wide variety of learners, learning contexts, and clinical topics.
65. Kassop (2003).
66. Hiltz et al. (2002), p.15-41.
67. Swan (2003), pp. 13-45.
68. WCET (n.d.).
69. National Survey of Student Engagement (2009; 2008).
70. United States Department of Education (2009a).
71. For example, see Vien (2010); Kamenetz (2010); Christian Science Monitor (2009).
72. For example, see Harding et al. (2005).
73. Sener (2004b).
74. Allen and Seaman (2007).

75. Seaman (2009a).
76. Hartman (2010b).
77. Picciano and Seaman (2009), p.3.
78. Homeschoolers may also be an unserved audience which drives greater adoption of K-12 online education, but they are still a relatively small in number compared to the non-traditional/lifelong learner audience which higher education reaches.
79. Picciano and Seaman (2009), p.4.
80. Patrick and Powell (2009), p.3.
81. Watson (2008), p.3.
82. 2005-06 estimates are from Picciano and Seaman (2007); 2007-08 estimates are from Picciano and Seaman (2009); 2009-2010 estimates are from Wicks (2010). The Picciano and Seaman reports only surveyed public schools; private schools and homeschoolers were not included in the survey.
83. Credit recovery most commonly refers to a process which enables students to pass and receive academic credit towards graduation for courses which were previously attempted unsuccessfully. Credit recovery programs generally focus of helping students stay in school and graduate on time (Watson and Gemin 2008). Credit recovery also refers to recovering lost credits as the result of transferring schools or moving from another state or country (Ombudsman.com n.d.).
84. Wicks (2010), p. 46.

Chapter 5. Six Scenarios for Thinking about the Future of Cyberizing Education

1. Flat: Friedman (2007); Spiky: Florida (2007); Open: Bonk (2009); Curved: Smick (2009).
2. Gleick (1999), p.6, 83-93.
3. Consider how dual-income parents scramble to make alternative arrangements during snow days or unexpected emergencies. Then imagine the ensuing chaos if all dual-income parents suddenly had to take care of their children during the workday, every day.
4. Dede (2008b).
5. Mitchell (2009), pp.12-13; Johnson (2007), pp.13-16.
6. The number of students who apply to six or more colleges doubled from 16 percent to 33 percent between 1989 and 2009 (Hoover 2010).
7. Institute for Alternative Futures (n.d.).
8. eLearninternational (2004).
9. Institute for Alternative Futures (n.d.), p.4.
10. Sener (2008a).
11. For example, see Caldwell (2010); Rasmus (2008).
12. Star and Cross (2004).
13. For another more detailed diagram of the Edinburgh Scenarios, see: http://www.jiscinfonet.ac.uk/infokits/learning-space-design/imagination/techniques/scenario-planning
14. Centre for Educational Research and Innovation (n.d.).

Chapter 6. To Market, To Market? The Driven Scenarios

1. Lenzenr and Johnson (1997).
2. Carey (2009).
3. CBS New York (2011)
4. Teachout (2009): "The real force for change is the market: Online classes are just cheaper to produce." For a rebuttal to this article, see Sener (2009a).
5. Ravitch (2010), pp.10-11.
6. Christensen et al. (2008).
7. Rasmus (2008).
8. Sener (2009b).
9. For example, see Gates (2010); Teachout (2009).
10. Also see Chapter 8 for a more complete list and discussion of the many roles which teachers fulfill.
11. Sener (2009b).
12. Teachout, in Parry (2009a).
13. Sener (2010a).
14. Duderstadt (2007).
15. Ravitch (2010), p.222: "The current obsession with making our schools work like a business...threatens to destroy public education." Also see Kohn (2002).
16. Although it's not the only force that animates business practice – the "triple bottom line" concept has made some limited headway, for example). Also see Sener (2009b).
17. Teachout (2009).
18. Ravitch (2010), pp. 167, 227, 230; Christensen et al. (2008), p.1.
19. For example, one market forecast reported that "about one-third of schools have some kind of online program in 2009-2010, and another 20% expect a program will be started by 2011-2012" (Simba Information 2010).
20. Lewin (2010); Lauerman and Deprez (2010).
21. Klor de Alva (2010).
22. Klor de Alva (2010); Lytle (2010).
23. Lynch et al. (2010).
24. U.S. Department of Education (1997).
25. Moe and Chubb (2009), p.x.; Ravitch (2010), pp. 21, 32.
26. Ede (2006).
27. Felch et al. (2010a).
28. Amrein-Beardsley (2008); Stewart (2006); Bracey (2004).
29. Buddin (2010).
30. Filch et al. (2010a).
31. Filch et al. (2010b).
32. For example: "There are scores of great teachers in LAUSD – and we can finally identify the elementary school ones by name..." Comment by Anthony Krinsky, in Mathews (2011).
33. Ravitch (2010), p.226.
34. Packer (2010).
35. Saltman (2010).

36. United States Department of Education (2009a).
37. Sener (2004a).
38. Dede (2008a).
39. Darling-Hammond (2010), p. 281.
40. Dede (2008a).
41. Gates (2010).
42. Ravitch (2010), pp.107-110; Darling-Hammond (2010), p. 97; Deniston and Gerrity (2010); Center for Education Policy (2009).
43. Darling-Hammond (2010), p. 72.
44. Strauss (2010).
45. Alliance for Children (2010).
46. McMahon, K. (2010).
47. For example, see Fehlen (2011); Sjoberg (2007).
48. Sener (2011).
49. Fromm (1971), p. 17.
50. Fromm (1971), p.18.
51. Fromm (1971), p. 123.
52. Fromm (1971), p. xiv: The drive for freedom inherent in human nature, while it can be corrupted and suppressed, tends to assert itself again and again."
53. Farber (1969).
54. Thomas (2007).
55. See Sener (2007a) for a more extended discussion of Judge Thomas's opinion as it relates to authoritarian education.
56. Katz (1971), pp.10-11.
57. Wikipedia (2011b).
58. Evergreen Freedom Foundation (2001).
59. Kohn (2010).
60. Darling-Hammond (2010), p. 167.

Chapter 7. Dream or Nightmare? The Dramatic Scenarios

1. Jarvik (2009); Wiley (2008).
2. Wiley 2008.
3. Carnegie-Mellon University (n.d.).
4. Johnstone (2005).
5. Shuttleworth Foundation and Open Society Institute (2007).
6. OER Commons web site: http://www.oercommons.org/
7. Bonk (2009), p.15.
8. MERLOT web site: http://www.merlot.org.
9. Bonk (2009), p.51, 203-248.
10. Overdrive Interactive (2011).
11. University of the People How It Works web page: http://www.uopeople.org/groups/how_it_works. About E-Learning web page: http://www.uopeople.org/groups/about_e-learning.
12. Parry (2009b).

13. P2PU Advisors web page: http://p2pu.org/advisors
14. P2PU Values web page: http://p2pu.org/values
15. Free Learning Rules advocates for dissolving formal education tend to focus more on higher education. Advocates who are focused on primary and secondary education – the homeschooling and "unschooling" movements in the US which have grown steadily for some time and now include millions of followers – are more focused on an in-person (more specifically, family-centered) approach to education, and they are more likely to focus on simply leaving the existing system than on dissolving it.
16. in Kamenetz (2010), p.87.
17. Bonk (2009), p. 169.
18. Bonk (2009), p. 367.
19. Bonk (2009), p. 7.
20. Siemens (2008).
21. Muegge et al. (2008).
22. Bonk (2009); Rawson and Thomes (2008); Siemens (2008).
23. Although LMS vendors have long promised that their systems are "interoperable", i.e., content produced in one LMS can be seamlessly ported to another LMS, this has not been the case in practice. Horror stories are common about difficulties in porting content from one version of an LMS to another, let alone from one LMS to another.
24. Brooks (2007).
25. Almansi (2010).
26. Carnegie-Mellon University (n.d.).
27. Carter (2009).
28. Horn (2009).
29. Albright (2006).
30. Digital Library Foundation (2005).
31. Rimer (2007).
32. MIT iCampus (2004).
33. Sener (2007b).
34. Guess (2007).
35. Enrollment was 179 students in two fields (computer science and business administration) in November 2009, and 380 students for its Winter 2009-2010 term; enrollments remained relatively small in 2010 and 2011. Carter (2009); Kolowich (2010); Wikipedia (2011c).
36. University of the People (2010).
37. OER leader David Porter's August 2010 posting in his blog *Conviviality*: "Regrettably, it *feels* like we are no closer to critical mass and sustainability on the OER front than we were this time last year" (Porter 2010). Commenters to his posting tended to agree with him.
38. This is the main limitation of the "DIYU" solution proposed by Kamenetz (2010): just as most people won't or can't be 'do-it-yourselfers' when it comes to home improvements, auto repair, etc., they won't be DIYers when it comes to education either. This works for learning because we are all learning creatures, but it does not work well for education.

39. Thanks to Lanny Arvan, retired economics professor at the University of Illinois, Urbana-Champaign, for these examples.
40. Thomas and Brown (2011), pp.50ff.
41. Open Yale Courses web site: http://oyc.yale.edu/
42. Vollmer (2010).
43. Carter (2011).
44. Green (2011).
45. Carey (2011).
46. Stoll (1995).
47. Cockroft (2009).
48. Derbyshire (2009).
49. Fendrich (2009).
50. Uniform rows of seats, broadcast transmission of information, rote learning, and assessment by regurgitation, were themselves designed in part by efficiency experts inspired by Frederick Taylor who wanted a more efficient, productive delivery method.
51. Turkle (2011), p.242.
52. See http://americanfolklore.net/folklore/2010/07/john_henry.html
53. This was a common strategy in the early days of online education and thankfully less so now. Code words such as "replicate," "copy", "transfer", or "convert" often indicate that this process is going on. Courses, like videotapes, lose some of their fidelity when copied, resulting in an inferior product relative to the original.
54. Gabriel (2011).
55. Also called "link rot"; Wikipedia (2011d) contains several references to scholarly and other articles on the problem.
56. Junco et al. (2011).
57. Turkle (2011), p. 243, 294.
58. Turkle (2011), pp.284-285.

Chapter 8. Change or Not? The Decisive Scenarios

1. Altbach (1998), p.14.
2. Balfanz (2009).
3. Wright (2009).
4. Prensky (2008).
5. Kelly (1971), in McNamee (2008).
6. Bratton and Toffler (2009).
7. Fagan (2007); Bielick et al. (2001).
8. Reimer (1971).
9. Christensen et al. (2009), pp.51-64.
10. Kamenetz (2010), p.5; Hamilton (2004).
11. Christensen et al. (2008), p.54
12. Kamenetz (2010), p. 12.
13. National Center on Education Statistics (n.d.), College Enrollment.
14. Cullinane (2008).

15. After rising spectacularly between 1900 (6.4 percent) and 1960 (69.5 percent), rates tapered off in the 1960s, and the ratio of high school graduates among American 17-year-olds has remained more or less flat for the past forty years, hovering between 68 and 77 percent during that entire period (National Center for Education Statistics 2009, 2005).

16. FinAid (2011).

17. McPherson and Shulenburger (2008).

18. McPherson and Shulenburger (2008), p.10.

19. Wire (2010).

20. Husser and Bailey (2008), Figures L, M, and Table 34.

21. Schroeder (2011a). Formerly named "New Realities in Higher Education", Schroeder changed the name in early 2010, reflecting the fact that recession *is* the new present reality in higher education.

22. Johnson et al. (2011).

23. Lataif (2011).

24. Chivvis (2010).

25. Associated Press (2010).

26. Johnson et al. (2011).

27. Wiley (2008), slide 32.

28. "…skills required to live better lives": More specifically, empowers individuals to reflect, make choices, and improve their lives; helps construct democratic societies; builds a sense of local, national, and global citizenship; builds a sense of shared global values to address global problems; improves human health; and supports improved productivity in the new knowledge economy. From Rischard (2002), pp. 66, 101-102.

29. Holt (1974).

30. Farenga (n.d.)

31. Sener (2009c); World Future Society (2008).

32. For example, Darling-Hammond and Bransford (2005), p.397; Lave and Wenger (1991).

33. The term "ambassador" is chosen deliberately; the world of academic subjects is an alien culture to most middle and high schoolers, even many of those who have had years of prior academic preparation.

34. Downes (2010).

35. Darling-Hammond (2010), p. 172, 182.

36. Vignare and Sener (2005).

37. Rourke et al. (2001); Richardson and Swan (2001); Gunawardena and Zittle (1997).

38. Diaz (2002).

39. Kuh (2006).

40. Metros (2003).

41. Sener (2007c).

42. Teaching and Learning Centre (2007); Garrison, Anderson, and Archer (2000).

Chapter 9. The Strategic Role of Online Education

1. Miller, G. (2011b).

2. The sections in this book on full scale online education are adapted from Sener (2010b).

3. United States Bureau of the Census (1990); also see Sener (2010b).

4. UCF's online enrollment: Hartman (2010b).

5. Seaman (2009b).

6. Allen and Seaman (2010a).

7. Moloney and Oakley (2006).

8. Schroeder (2011b).

9. Wise and Rothman (2010); Cavanaugh (2009); Christensen et al. (2008), pp. 100-102.

10. Lederman (2005).

11. Sloan Consortium (n.d.); Lorenzo (2006).

12. Sener (2008b).

13. Sloan Consortium (2008).

14. Kelderman (2009).

15. American Society of Mechanical Engineers Innovative Technologies Institute (2010).

16. Sener (2009d).

17. Institute for the Future (2006).

18. wtop.com (2009).

19. Maryland State Department of Education (2010).

20. United States Department of Education (2009b).

21. For example, see University of Maryland University College (2008); University of Washington (n.d.).

22. University of Illinois Online (2011).

23. Quality Matters web site: www.qmprogram.org

24. Davis and Rose (2007).

25. Dawley et al. (2010).

26. Southern Regional Education Board (2008).

27. Sener (2010b).

28. Sener (2010b).

29. Kidd et al. (2009); Havenstein (2007); Gehringer et al. (2007).

30. Miller, D. (2006).

31. California State University Monterey Bay (n.d.).

32. Cooper (2010).

33. Jarmon (ed.) 2002.

34. Math Emporium web site: http://www.emporium.vt.edu/.

35. Beatty (2008).

Chapter 10. Strategies for Re-Empowering Learning and Teaching

1. National Survey of Student Engagement (2010).

2. Bridgeland et al. (2006).

3. Knowles (1984), p.191.

4. Kidd et al. (2009); Ravid et al. (2008); O'Shea et al. (2007).

5. Miller, D. (2008), (2007).

6. Gehringer and Miller (2009).

7. Theroux (2009); Theroux and Kilbane (2004); Theroux (2004).

8. Also see Boettcher (2006).

9. For example, see McLeod (2011).

10. The anecdotal quotations from the focus group conversation are anonymous to maintain confidentiality.

11. cjencyclopedia.com. However, the cjencyclopedia web site also illustrates some of the downsides of maintaining open learning resources. The site was active between March 2005 and early 2010, but it was shut down in part because of relentless spamming which made site maintenance dauntingly difficult.

12. Jensen and Chamberlin (2009).

13. See the Mid-Atlantic Regional Collegiate Cyber Defense Competition website at http://www.midatlanticccdc.org/CCDC/ for additional information.

14. CyberWatch web site: http://www.cyberwatchcenter.org

15. Food Safety Knowledge Network web site: http://foodsafetyknowledgenetwork.org; training materials located at http://fskntraining.com.

16. Geith et al. (2010); Cwikowski (2010).

17. Sener (2007d).

18. Institute of Transpersonal Psychology (n.d.).

19. Riach (2011).

20. For example, Swan (2003); Shea, P. et al. (2002).

21. Swan (2003).

22. Anderson et al. (2001).

23. Staples (2011).

24. Minaei-Bidgoli (2004); Bloom (1984); Bloom (1956).

25. Betrus (1995); Clark (1995).

26. Minaei-Bidgoli (2004).

27. Kortemeyer (2010).

28. Carnegie-Mellon University (n.d.).

29. Szerdahelyi (2010).

30. Davis (1999).

31. Also from the aforementioned focus group; see note #10 above.

32. Khan Academy web site: http://www.khanacademy.org

33. The educational solution proposed by the book *Disrupting Class* suffers from this shortcoming, as it calls for the use of computer-based instructional systems to create individualized inputs, but then settles for standardized outputs such as better performance on standardized tests. This is also a common criticism of current standards-based initiatives such as the Common Core Standards.

34. Shupe (2007).

35. Shupe (2007).

36. Brown, G. (2011).

37. If instructors prespecify learning objectives, this short-circuits the inquiry process by focusing learners on achieving the prespecified objectives instead of on the inquiry itself (Gunawardena, in Duffy and Kirkley (2004), pp. 148).

38. Harasim (1990).

39. For example, Duffy and del Valle (2005); Malopinsky et al. (2002).

40. EDUCAUSE (2009).

41. Tobin (1998).

42. Waters (2011); Klingensmith (2009).

43. Attwell (2007).

44. EDUCAUSE (2009).

45. Kashdan (2010).

46. IBM Institute for Business Value (2010).

47. Johnson et al. (2009).

48. For example, see Cumming (2011); Brewster and Fager (2000).

49. Robbins and Kegley (2009).

50. For more info about WebQuests, see: www.webquest.org

51. Mintu-Wimsatt et al. (2007).

52. See http://www.slideshare.net/lyrlobo/presentations

53. Geo-Everything's Augmented Reality for Education web page (http://eder77901l60-geoeverything.wetpaint.com/page/Augmented+Reality+for+Education) contains numerous references, videos, and other explanatory information about augmented reality.

54. See http://www.360ed.com/Products/#ccir for more details.

55. See http://calculationnation.nctm.org/ for more details.

56. For example, see Brown et al. (2009); Wiggins (1993).

57. Darling-Hammond (2010), p.293.

58. Brown et al. (2009).

59. McMahon, J. (2011).

60. In practice, e-portfolios are defined in variety of different ways; for instance, see Wang (2009), Barrett (2007), and Batson (2002).

61. Fitch et al. (2008).

62. Goldsmith (2007).

63. Archer (2007); Baker (1989).

64. Barrett (2007).

65. Nichols (1997); Wiggins (1993).

66. Pink (2001).

67. Zuboff and Maxmin (2002).

68. Knowles (1984); Wedemeyer (1981).

69. City Colleges of Chicago (2008).

Chapter 11. Strategies for Revitalizing the Educational Enterprise

1. Smith (2010), p.52-53, 106-07.

2. Council for Adult and Experential Learning (2010); Thomas Edison State College (n.d.)

3. Council for Adult and Experential Learning (2010).

4. See the ACE College Credit Recommendation Service web page, http://www.acenet.edu/Content/NavigationMenu/ProgramsServices/CCRS/index.htm, for more details.

5. See, for example, UMUC's Course Challenge program, http://www.umuc.edu/students/support/exams/coursechallenge.cfm, and Thomas Edison State College's TECEP program: http://www.tesc.edu/701.php

6. Council for Adult and Experiential Learning (2010).
7. Servicemembers Opportunity Colleges (2009).
8. Lederman (2010).
9. Kannel (2010).
10. Learning Counts web site: www.learningcounts.org
11. Marquardt (2010).
12. Barr and Tagg (1995).
13. Rhodes and Brasington (2010).
14. Morgenthaler (2007).
15. UMUC School of Undergraduate Studies (2010).
16. See the *Journal of Asynchronous Learning Networks* 13(3), October 2009, an entire issue devoted to exploring factors which contributed to institutions with high completion rates in their courses.
17. Fasse et al. (2009).
18. Boston et al. (2009).
19. Swanson (2008).
20. Watson and Gemin (2008).
21. Stevens et al. (2008).
22. Smith (2010), pp.85-86.
23. Smith Bailey (2003).
24. Peter and Forrest Cataldi (2005).
25. One could argue that online education has decreased swirling because it is now easier for students to take online courses at the same institution instead of changing colleges. (Thanks to Lisa Cheney-Steen of Colorado Mountain College for making this point.) At the same time, it is also much easier for students to take online courses at other institutions while at home during the summer or simply to take an online course at another institution during the school year. The proliferation of online courses also makes it easier for the growing population of nontraditional students to 'mix and match' courses from multiple institutions. Until better statistics become available, it is a reasonable assumption that swirling has remained steady or increased.
26. Kesselman (1976).
27. Mullane (2009).
28. Council for Adult and Experiential Learning (2007).
29. Cheney-Steen (2010).
30. The works of John Bear catered to this type of student. as did the book *This Way Out* by John Coyne and Tom Hebert written in the 1970s.
31. Kamenetz (2010).
32. Frost (2009), pp. 220-227.
33. The value of serving these students is also undermined by legacy systems such as national educational statistics which are still geared toward traditional "first-time, full-time" students, so that none of these types of students count as "successes" for institutions, which also creates a lot of misleading information about the value of serving them.
34. Smith (2010), pp 85-86.
35. Center for Energy Workforce Development (n.d.).

36. National Association of Manufacturers (2009a).
37. Manufacturing Institute (2011).
38. National Association of Manufacturers (2009b).
39. United States Department of Labor (2010a).
40. United States Department of Labor (2010b).
41. Manufacturing Institute (2011).
42. Pruitt-Mentle et al. (2010).
43. National Science Foundation (2010).
44. For example, see Benderly (2010); Teitelbaum (2003).
45. Lipka (2010).
46. Lipka and Coddington (2010).
47. "Seat time" is the actual amount of time a learner is expected to have a physical presence in a course, usually sitting in a classroom.
48. Twigg, in Blumenstyk (2010).
49. Shupe (2011).
50. Lipka (2010).
51. Council for Higher Education Accreditation (2010).
52. American Speech-Hearing-Language Association (2010).
53. Patrick and Sturgis (2011).
54. Bloomberg Businessweek (2006).
55. Pink (2009).
56. Turoff (2010).
57. Cross (2007), p.3.
58. Mead (2010).
59. Fernandez (2009).
60. McCurdy and Schroeder (2006a).
61. Great Plains Interactive Distance Education Alliance (n.d.).
62. Lorenzo (2006).
63. See GoArmyEd website for more info: https://www.goarmyed.com/public/public_earmyu-about_earmyu.aspx
64. WISE Consortium (2011).
65. Institute of Museum and Library Services (2008).
66. McCurdy and Schroeder (2006b).
67. Kurth-Schai and Green (2006), p.21.
68. Sloan Consortium (2011); Shelton (2010); Sener (2004a); Moore (2002).
69. Compare Darling-Hammond (2010), p.238: "efforts to invent 21st century organizations tend to...build strong relationships and norms rather than relying solely on rules for governing behavior...[and] aim to stimulate greater thoughtfulness and creativity rather than focusing largely on enforcing compliance with predetermined procedures."
70. iNACOL (2010a; 2010b).
71. Champagne, in Duffy and Kirkley (2004), p.285.
72. Sachs (2007).
73. Shavelson et al. (2009).

74. National Survey of Student Engagement (n.d.).
75. EDUCAUSE (2010).
76. Capella University (2011).
77. New Leadership Alliance (2010).
78. Norris and Baer (2009).
79. Noel-Levitz (2010).
80. Lederman (2008).
81. Middlesex Community College (2010).
82. Wang et al. (2003).
83. For a more complete discussion, see Sener and Hawkins (2007).
84. Brown (2011).
85. Christensen et al. (2011), pp.47-50.
86. The Trustees of Indiana University (2011).
87. Ice (2010); Boston et al. (2009).

Chapter 12. The Distant Scenario: Education Rules?

1. Christensen et al. (2008), pp.51-64.
2. McNamee and Miller (2009).
3. Davies and Hammack (2005).
4. Karabel (1972).
5. FairTest.org (n.d.); Rampell (2009); Elert (1992).
6. Jorgensen (2009).
7. Benderly (2010).
8. Darling-Hammond (2010), p.26.
9. From Supreme Court Justice Oliver Wendell Holmes, Jr. ("taxes are what we pay for civilized society") during a speech made in 1904.
10. The Democratic party hasn't been much better, with its uncritical support of the destructively narrow definition of educational attainment which No Child Left Behind embodies.
11. Darling-Hammond (2010), p.119.

INDEX: